VOLUME 638   NOVEMBER 2011

THE ANNALS

of The American Academy of Political
and Social Science

Work, Family, and Workplace Flexibility

Special Editors:

KATHLEEN CHRISTENSEN
Alfred P. Sloan Foundation

BARBARA SCHNEIDER
Michigan State University

Los Angeles | London | New Delhi
Singapore | Washington DC

The American Academy of Political and Social Science

202 S. 36th Street, Annenberg School for Communication, University of Pennsylvania,
Philadelphia, PA 19104-3806; (215) 746-6500; (215) 573-2667 (fax); www.aapss.org

Origin and Purpose. The Academy was organized December 14, 1889, to promote the progress of political and social science, especially through publications and meetings. The Academy does not take sides in controverted questions, but seeks to gather and present reliable information to assist the public in forming an intelligent and accurate judgment.

Meetings. The Academy occasionally holds a meeting in the spring extending over two days.

Publications. THE ANNALS of The American Academy of Political and Social Science is the bimonthly publication of the Academy. Each issue contains articles on some prominent social or political problem, written at the invitation of the editors. These volumes constitute important reference works on the topics with which they deal, and they are extensively cited by authorities throughout the United States and abroad.

Membership. Each member of the Academy receives THE ANNALS and may attend the meetings of the Academy. Membership is open only to individuals. Annual dues: $94.00 for the regular paperbound edition (clothbound, $134.00). Members may also purchase single issues of THE ANNALS for $35 each (clothbound, $48). Student memberships are available for $52.00.

Subscriptions. THE ANNALS of The American Academy of Political and Social Science (ISSN 0002-7162) (J295) is published bimonthly—in January, March, May, July, September, and November—by SAGE Publications, 2455 Teller Road, Thousand Oaks, CA 91320. Periodicals postage paid at Thousand Oaks, California, and at additional mailing offices. POSTMASTER: Send address changes to The Annals of The American Academy of Political and Social Science, c/o SAGE Publications, 2455 Teller Road, Thousand Oaks, CA 91320. Institutions may subscribe to THE ANNALS at the annual rate: $827 (clothbound, $933). Single issues of THE ANNALS may be obtained by individuals who are not members of the Academy for $106 each (clothbound, $155). Single issues of THE ANNALS have proven to be excellent supplementary texts for classroom use. Direct inquiries regarding adoptions to THE ANNALS c/o SAGE Publications (address below).

All correspondence concerning membership in the Academy, dues renewals, inquiries about membership status, and/or purchase of single issues of THE ANNALS should be sent to THE ANNALS c/o SAGE Publications, 2455 Teller Road, Thousand Oaks, CA 91320. Telephone: (800) 818-SAGE (7243) and (805) 499-0721; Fax/Order line: (805) 375-1700; e-mail: journals@sagepub.com. *Please note that orders under $30 must be prepaid.* For all customers outside the Americas, please visit http://www.sagepub.co.uk/customerCare.nav for information.

Printed on acid-free paper

THE ANNALS

© 2011 by The American Academy of Political and Social Science

Editorial Office: 202 S. 36th Street, Philadelphia, PA 19104-3806
For information about membership* (individuals only) and subscriptions (institutions), address:
SAGE Publications
2455 Teller Road
Thousand Oaks, CA 91320

For SAGE Publications: Allison Leung (Production) and Lori Hart (Marketing)

From India and South Asia,
write to:
SAGE PUBLICATIONS INDIA Pvt Ltd
B-42 Panchsheel Enclave, P.O. Box 4109
New Delhi 110 017
INDIA

From Europe, the Middle East,
and Africa, write to:
SAGE PUBLICATIONS LTD
1 Oliver's Yard, 55 City Road
London EC1Y 1SP
UNITED KINGDOM

*Please note that members of the Academy receive THE ANNALS with their membership.
International Standard Serial Number ISSN 0002-7162
International Standard Book Number ISBN 978-1-45222-5340 (Vol. 638, 2011) paper
International Standard Book Number ISBN 978-1-45222-5333 (Vol. 638, 2011) cloth
Manufactured in the United States of America. First printing, November 2011.

Please visit http://ann.sagepub.com and under the "More about this journal" menu on the right-hand side, click on the Abstracting/Indexing link to view a full list of databases in which this journal is indexed.

Information about membership rates, institutional subscriptions, and back issue prices may be found on the facing page.

THE ANNALS

OF THE AMERICAN ACADEMY OF POLITICAL AND SOCIAL SCIENCE

Volume 638   November 2011

IN THIS ISSUE:

Work, Family, and Workplace Flexibility

Special Editors: KATHLEEN CHRISTENSEN
BARBARA SCHNEIDER

FORTHCOMING

Gender and Race Inequality in Management: Critical Issues, New Evidence
Special Editor: MATTHEW HUFFMAN

Advancing Reasoned Action Theory
Special Editor: MICHAEL HENNESSY

INTRODUCTION

Making a Case for Workplace Flexibility

By
KATHLEEN CHRISTENSEN
and
BARBARA SCHNEIDER

Fifteen years ago, the Alfred P. Sloan Foundation charted a dramatically new direction by developing a program of research, practice, and action to explore the disconnect between the needs of today's families and the demands of U.S. workplaces. Allocating more than a hundred million dollars to this initiative, the Alfred P. Sloan Foundation's Workplace, Work Force and Working Families Program was established to "enhance scholarly, business, and public understanding of the challenges facing today's working families and to identify how the workplace can be restructured to meet employees' work-family needs, as well as employers' performance needs" (Alfred P. Sloan Foundation 2010b). This volume of

Kathleen Christensen, previously a professor of psychology at the Graduate Center, City University of New York, founded and directs the Workplace, Work Force and Working Families Program, as well as the Working Longer Program, at the Alfred P. Sloan Foundation in New York City. Under her leadership, the foundation in 2002 launched the National Workplace Flexibility Initiative, a collaborative effort designed to make workplace flexibility a compelling national issue and a standard of the American workplace. The initiative grew out of a decade of Sloan-supported scholarly research on work-family issues.

Barbara Schneider is the John A. Hannah Distinguished Professor in the College of Education and Department of Sociology at Michigan State University. Her research focuses primarily on the social context of families and schools and their relationship to adolescent development. She codirected the Center on Parents, Children and Work at the University of Chicago, which resulted in the book Being Together, Working Apart: Dual-Career Families and the Work-Life Balance (Cambridge University Press 2005).

NOTE: We gratefully acknowledge the work of the Focus on Workplace Flexibility conference committee, Lois Backon, Ellen Galinsky, Chai Feldblum, and Katie Corrigan; and the support of the Alfred P. Sloan Foundation, especially the president, Paul Joskow. We thank Leigh Ann Halas for her help in editing and formatting all of the articles and Sarah-Kay McDonald for her excellent critique.

DOI: 10.1177/0002716211417245

The Annals of the American Academy of Political and Social Science makes a case for workplace flexibility. The articles are based on a series of research papers that were presented at a 2010 national conference, hosted by the Sloan Foundation and the Georgetown Law Center's Workplace Flexibility 2010 program, which examined the changing U.S. workforce and its implications for how, when, and where people work.

The Sloan investment in workplace flexibility began with an unusual strategic design that integrated empirical research with effective business practices and practical public policy solutions. Sloan was one of the first to recognize the changing face of today's U.S. labor force and how profoundly different it is from that of the late twentieth century. More than 60 percent of families with children under the age of 18 have two employed parents or an employed single parent (Bureau of Labor Statistics 2010)—almost a complete switch from the 1960s' family structure of the male breadwinner and female homemaker. As paid work has shifted from only men's work to men's and women's work, the arithmetic of the family has changed, with more jobs and the same or fewer adults in the household. In the traditional two-parent home, the demands of one paid and one unpaid job were sufficiently met by the resources of the family. In today's three-job, two-parent home (two paid outside, one unpaid inside), the demands of work in and out of the family increasingly outstrip the resources of the household. Even if there is complete equity, when three jobs are shared by two adults, each ends up with 1.5 jobs (Christensen and Gomory 1999). Paid and unpaid job demands are even greater for single-parent, single-earner households.

In addition to the challenges faced by working parents, other demographic and economic concerns are characteristic of today's U.S. workforce, including an aging baby boomer generation—many of whom are working beyond conventional retirement—stagnating incomes, job loss or instability, and increased responsibilities for eldercare. It is projected that half of workers will have eldercare responsibilities over the next five years (Galinsky and Bond 1998, 48; U.S. Department of Labor 1999). These situations are exerting new demands on workers and their families.

While few scholars in the 1980s and 1990s were examining how the organization of work was impacting family relationships, the media began covering the story during this time. Increasingly, concerns were voiced about the significant loss of human capital to the U.S. economy when working mothers "dropped out" of the workforce. However, little attention was paid to what happened to these women after they exited their full-time careers. Sloan's earliest steps in the mid-1990s were to fund studies on the extent to which career opportunities existed for women, and men, seeking part-time or short-term positions as a way to manage work and family responsibilities. It was evident that educated women frequently exited the labor force when part-time careers were not available. They then faced significant difficulties when trying to reenter the labor force (Hewlett and Luce 2005; Hewlett 2007).

These early findings highlighted a "mismatch" between the structure of traditional career paths and the life course patterns of women and men (Christensen

2005a). The one-size-fits-all, full-time, full-year, sequential jobs with rigid, linear career paths continued to reflect late-twentieth-century workplace norms. While the face of the U.S. workforce was changing, the organization of paid work remained, for many employees, the same.

Solving the Mismatch Problem

Recognizing the mismatch between the needs of twenty-first-century workers and the norms of twentieth-century workplaces—and some of the likely negative psychological, social, and economic consequences on U.S. society—Sloan decided to undertake a bold new initiative to address these problems. To accomplish this, the Sloan program on Workplace, Work Force, and Working Families was developed. Organized around five major goals, this program has been committed to improving lives, supporting business objectives, and strengthening the economy (Christensen 2005b). Specifically, the program has focused on (1) targeting and supporting research on working families, the workplace, and changes in the organization of work; (2) providing human capital to scholars, postdoctoral fellows, and graduate and undergraduate students pursuing research on the program's thematic strands; (3) building an infrastructure to sustain a community of scholars and disseminate findings to researchers, businesses, and federal, state, and local policy-makers; (4) encouraging voluntary employer adoption of workplace flexibility as a standard of practice through partnerships with businesses, local and state governments, and not-for-profit entities; and (5) promoting public understanding, as well as federal bipartisan consensus building, that advances workplace flexibility as a compelling national issue.

Developing a research base

Beginning in the mid-1990s and continuing through the next decade, more than 275 research grants were awarded that eventuated in a thriving group of investigators, many of whom were novices to this area of research. Since the program's inception, these research grants provided support for more than 180 PhDs and seventy postdoctoral scholars. Researchers from different fields—including anthropology, economics, law, linguistics, social psychology, and sociology— brought new and different methodological approaches to the examination of the intersection of work and family life. Multidisciplinary teams collected biological markers and extant materials, such as legal briefs and human resource records, interviews, observations, time diaries, surveys, and videos of family life. Some of the studies followed individuals over time, some compared results with larger national representative samples, and others conducted quasi-experiments that examined changes in employee satisfaction on the basis of workplace flexibility options. This extensive body of research identified numerous ways in which the workplace was misaligned with the needs of U.S. workers across the life course.

The results of these multiple studies of working families converged on an essential point: the lives of U.S. workers were becoming increasingly complicated, with unintended consequences for themselves and their children. For example, among middle-class dual-career couples, many parents work long hours—as much as 10 hours a week over the average number of paid work hours a week (Schneider and Waite 2005). Although many of them report experiencing a cognitive challenge and feeling productive when engaged in paid work, they also reveal high levels of stress from the combination of overwork and family responsibilities (Sexton 2005). Work appears to have the strongest influence on the social interactions mothers and fathers have with each other and with their children (Marchena 2005). These relationships can be particularly negative if the parents spend long hours at jobs that do not have flexible work arrangements. These long hours of work are related to disruptions in traditional family rituals and limited time together. One clear example is the family dinner hour, which is disappearing, with mothers, fathers, and children eating by themselves at different places and times (for the social import of family dinner, see Ochs and Shohet 2006; for information on the times, places, and spaces where dual-earner families are having dinner, see Ochs et al. 2010).

Nearly a third of U.S. workers consider work-life balance and flexibility to be the most important factor in considering job offers (A Better Balance 2008). However, the norms of most workplaces override the desire to take advantage of flexible work benefits such as parental/family leave with pay, personal days, flextime, or telecommuting when offered (Chesley and Moen 2006). Both mothers and fathers are concerned that careers will be damaged by partaking in family friendly workplace flexibility options (Bond et al. 2002).

Taking a life course perspective, some Sloan scholars have been studying the extent and take-up of workplace flexibility options for older workers. Retirement-eligible workers increasingly want to continue working but at reduced hours and with more flexible schedules (Haider and Loughran 2010). But much like mothers who leave the labor market because of the lack of opportunities for part-time work, when older workers leave the labor market, the desire to return is also constrained (Hewlett and Luce 2005; Haider and Loughran 2010). Furthermore, older workers who want to stay with their employers and phase into retirement find that formal phased retirement policies are practically nonexistent (Hutchens and Grace-Martin 2006). As the community of work and family scholars grew, the Foundation funded the development of the Sloan Work and Family Research Network, which evolved into the premier online destination for information on work and family[1] and provided a hub for disseminating research findings as well as for educating researchers, journalists, business practitioners, and policy-makers about work-family issues. The network is now transitioning into a professional society, the Work and Family Researchers Network.[2] At the same time, grants were made to public radio and television to increase public understanding of the issues faced by American working families and to highlight results of the research activities.

After nearly a decade of scholarly research, it became apparent that flexibility was essential for realigning the demands of the workplace to match the needs of workers. While this solution to the structural mismatch between the workforce and workplace resonated with academic and business communities, their efforts to address them, while positive, lacked coherence, momentum, and institutional infrastructure. To further the Sloan vision for workplace flexibility, a collaborative entity needed to be created that would synthesize the work of academics and practitioners to build a coordinated response among government, the private sector, organized labor, and diverse stakeholder groups to realign the workplace with the needs of workers.

Workplace Flexibility: A National Issue

In 2002, Sloan launched the National Workplace Flexibility Initiative (Alfred P. Sloan Foundation 2010a), a collaborative entity to make workplace flexibility a compelling national issue and the standard of the American workplace. Not only was this initiative in many ways a first of its type, the very words, "workplace flexibility," were not in use at the time. Two strategies were developed to achieve that goal: increasing voluntary employer adoption of workplace flexibility and forging a bipartisan conversation in Washington and beyond. Researchers, employer groups, labor leaders, lawyers, and public policy analysts began working together to devise and support both private and public solutions to the pressing social and economic challenges posed by twenty-first-century work-life conditions.

To achieve the voluntary employer adoption of workplace flexibility, several activities were undertaken. One of the key research projects supported by Sloan was the Family and Work Institute's National Study of the Changing Workforce (focusing on employees in 2002) and the National Study of Employers (focusing on employers in 2005 and 2008) to identify promising employer practices (Bond et al. 2002, 2005; Galinsky, Bond, and Sakai 2008).[3] Additionally, Sloan funded Corporate Voices for Working Families[4] to analyze previously proprietary data of twenty-one major U.S. corporations; these analyses resulted in a strong business case for workplace flexibility.

While research was necessary, it was not sufficient to induce employers to increase their implementation of flexibility practices. To that end, the Sloan Foundation challenged the Families and Work Institute (FWI) to create and evaluate a change experiment to increase the voluntary employer adoption of workplace flexibility. The resulting project, established in 2003 with Sloan Foundation funding, is called When Work Works. It has been directed since then by the FWI and its partners: the Institute for a Competitive Workforce, an affiliate of the U.S. Chamber of Commerce, and the Twiga Foundation. In 2011, the FWI partnered with the Society for Human Resource Management to scale up the program to its nearly six hundred affiliate chapters. At the core of When Work Works[5] is a competitive award program. This program has resulted in more than one thousand organizations receiving the Sloan Awards for Business Excellence in Workplace Flexibility (see When Work Works 2011). It has also resulted in coalitions of community leaders, who serve as champions of workplace flexibility, community-based educational events on effective and flexible workplaces, and media outreach that reframes flexibility from being viewed as an employee benefit to a business strategy of effective workplaces that can achieve the goals of employers, employees, and communities.

At the same time, Sloan also supported the establishment in 2003 of Georgetown Law Center's Workplace Flexibility 2010 (WF 2010 [Georgetown University Law Center 2010]) as a time-limited endeavor to broaden the policy discussion on flexibility, incorporate the voices of diverse stakeholder groups, and identify ways that Congress and the administration could advance workplace flexibility.[6] WF 2010 sponsored a variety of bipartisan activities to create a public dialogue on the value of workplace flexibility for society and economic progress. Some of these events included a series of U.S. bipartisan congressional briefings and hearings on workplace flexibility; the establishment of a high-level National Advisory Commission on Workplace Flexibility (NAC [see National Advisory Commission on Workplace Flexibility n.d.]), representing employers, organized labor, public sector officials, and other key stakeholders; and the articulation of a public policy platform identifying the roles the federal government could play in advancing workplace flexibility. Most recently, it has engaged in a number of activities to keep workplace flexibility at the center of public dialogue.

Genesis for This Volume

The momentum and reach of workplace flexibility exceeded expectations by 2010. Both the 2008 Democratic and Republican Party platforms, as well as candidate statements for the midterm elections, included agendas for increasing workplace flexibility. Building on the collective efforts of the FWI, Corporate Voices for Working Families, and WF 2010, the First Lady and President Obama convened a White House Forum on Workplace Flexibility in March 2010 that brought diverse stakeholders and political parties together to find common ground and craft consensus-based solutions. At the forum, the Council of Economic Advisers released a report, also significant for drawing national attention to the issues, titled *Work-Life Balance and the Economics of Workplace Flexibility* (see White House Office of the Press Secretary 2010; Council of Economic Advisers 2010). President Obama opened the forum reaffirming the problems of work-life balance:

> It wasn't that long ago that both of us were working full-time outside the home while raising two young daughters. I was away for days on end for my job and Michelle was working hard at hers, so a lot of times we felt like we were just barely keeping everything together. When we were at work, we were worrying about what was happening at home.

When we were at home, we were worrying about work. We both felt our overloaded schedules were taking a toll on our marriage.

The White House Forum spurred a number of meetings and events; the one most pertinent to this volume of *The Annals* was the national Sloan-supported conference, Focus on Workplace Flexibility, held in late November 2010 in Washington, D.C.[7] This conference brought together scholars, business leaders, and policy-makers to further the common purpose, dialogue, and dedication to workplace flexibility. Unique to this meeting was explicit consideration of the importance of workplace flexibility to national security, an issue addressed there and subsequently (see Pellerin 2011) by Admiral and Chairman of the Joint Chiefs of Staff Mike Mullen.

The purpose of the conference was to present the evidence-based case for workplace flexibility. To accomplish this, the conference began by highlighting significant research findings from Sloan-supported work and examining private and public sector workplace flexibility practices. The research findings focused on three major ideas: the demographic changes in the U.S. workforce; the consequences of these changes for diverse populations, including working families, the military, the academy, and low-wage workers; and the resulting pressing needs for workplace flexibility. The articles contained in this volume represent the research papers presented at this conference.

While they represent major strands of scholarship on workplace flexibility, it is important to recognize that these articles constitute only a limited portion of the depth of the Sloan program of research. To give some sense of the scope and depth of Sloan's research, from 1994 through 2010, Sloan researchers published more than one thousand scholarly journal articles, books, and book chapters.[8] An independent evaluation of the program conducted by NORC (National Opinion Research Center) at the University of Chicago revealed that Sloan research is frequently cited in standard academic citation indices and the impact of this research is significantly above the average standard for most social science publications (McDonald et al. 2011). Important findings generated from Sloan research that laid the groundwork for this volume are briefly described below.

Describing the Problem and Identifying the Consequences: The Articles in This Volume

The first set of articles in this volume explore demographic changes across generations and throughout the life course. They address such trends as the increase of job demands and the emergence of new pressures on dual-earner families, single parents, and older workers alike. The second set of articles discuss the consequences of the structural mismatch between workplaces and workers for families and children as well as the impacts on health and well-being of people working in specific occupations for which these problems are particularly acute.

Demographic and economic changes

The first article, by Suzanne Bianchi, presents an overview of the broad demographic changes in working families. Drawing on 40 years of time diary evidence, Bianchi identifies how families juggle paid work and unpaid caregiving for their children and elder relatives. Recognized as one of the leading demographers studying time use within the American family, Bianchi considers how family life has dramatically changed over the past 60 years. Women's employment has grown substantially, while marriage and childbearing are being delayed. The consequences of these changes have been that just as women are beginning to ascend the career ladder, they often face substantial family demands from children born late in life and eldercare family obligations. One of her most significant insights concerns the competing desire to engage in intensive child-rearing while at the same time devoting more time to paid work. Time-stretched working couples have too little time for themselves and each other. Mothers are giving up leisure time and increasingly multitasking to meet the demands of work and family. All of these findings suggest that mothers and fathers are unable to shoulder work and family demands without assistance. This is particularly the case for women in the United States, who continue to have primary care responsibilities and less public support for combining paid work with family caregiving compared to those in other countries. Work-family conflict is not a personal issue; it is a societal one, and Bianchi underscores the need for a mix of policy incentives and private initiatives to solve this problem.

The article by Claudia Goldin and Lawrence Katz, two leading U.S. economists, digs deeper into the costs of workplace flexibility for occupations at the upper education and income levels. The good news is that workplace flexibility has increased in many professions where women have entered in greater numbers—for example, medicine, veterinary medicine, and pharmacy, as well as in occupations in the technology sector—which Goldin and Katz suggest may be because these are newer organizations and thus more responsive to the needs of a changing workforce. Furthermore, the take-up of workplace flexibility options (such as job interruptions, short hours, part-time work, and flexibility during the workday) in these fields appears to be resulting in lower financial penalties than in other occupations. However, in some fields, such as business and finance, flexibility continues to lag and the costs are high. As more women enter educationally intensive fields, firms would do well to undertake efforts to decrease the penalties to women of exercising flexibility options.

An economic expert on income and health security, Richard Johnson argues in his article that older adults are an untapped labor source, which is often highly experienced, knowledgeable, and skilled. Many of these workers wish to remain working but at fewer hours; however, few organizations have phased retirement plans or options for flexible work arrangements for older adults. The limited number of phased retirement plans is primarily driven by complicated existing benefit plans that could potentially violate antidiscrimination rules, such as the Age Discrimination in Employment Act. If older adults were able to work longer,

Johnson maintains that there could be positive consequences for the U.S. economy, a rise in the standard of living for workers and nonworkers, and a generation of additional tax revenues that would increase other health and social benefits. Delaying retirement is also likely to promote physical and emotional health by keeping older workers active and engaged with their environments. To overcome some of the barriers to phased retirement and flexible work arrangements for older workers, Johnson discusses some of the legal changes and preemptive challenges that could be made and their likely costs, especially for low-wage and younger workers. He concludes by suggesting that the assumptions underlying current changes in policy need to be closely scrutinized and additional evidence be obtained before employers can effectively tap an older labor pool.

What happens when workers do not have flexibility options? Applying an ethnographic lens, Lawrence Root and Alford A. Young Jr. conducted an in-depth study of workers in a midwestern factory. Based on year-long observations and interviews, they show how the culture of the workplace interfaces and conflicts with the needs and family responsibilities of workers, particularly those who have low status in the plant. The reality of the workplace, especially for workers with long hours and shift work, is such that most employees—both women and men—express deep concerns about childcare and being able to participate in their children's in- and out-of-school events. When the organization is unresponsive to demands for flexibility, especially involving families, workers may take independent actions to meet their obligations, which can have negative consequences for the plant production cycle. Whether employees undertake these independent actions depends in part on the presence (or absence) of coworkers with cooperative attitudes who support each other and sympathetic supervisors who overlook such activities. As research shows, the culture of the workplace can sometimes deter workers from taking advantage of formal workplace flexibility practices. Root and Young argue that the key players for helping workers use formal and informal flexibility practices are the middle managers or supervisors. These individuals are those most likely to create a cultural change in the organization that enhances productivity and employee commitment. Government policies and top-down mandates for workplace flexibility will likely prove ineffective without middle managers' endorsement, their incorporation of flexibility practices into the daily lives of workers, and their support of flexibility as a criterion for their own career advancement.

Consequences of the structural mismatch

Barbara Schneider, a leading sociologist with a specialization in children's development, synthesizes results from multiple studies that the Alfred P. Sloan Foundation funded to show the consequences that long hours of work have on the lives of dual-career couples and their children. As President Obama remarked and multiple empirical Sloan studies indicate, working parents trying to meet work and family commitments report feeling stressed, emotionally and psychologically drained, and in danger of burn-out (Offer and Schneider 2010)—feelings that have negative implications for individuals' health and productivity. Trying to find ways to stretch the hours in their days, working parents are turning to buying essential services and engaging in multitasking. Empirical research shows that multitasking parents often feel very productive, but this sense of productivity comes with other emotional costs, such as feeling frustrated, irritated, and stressed. The lives of most working parents are harried; they worry about whether they are "good parents" and report concerns about their relationships with their spouse. Even though they know that long hours of work are creating an untenable situation for them at home, they are reluctant to stop, fearing negative repercussions at their workplaces. In this economy, fewer dual-earner couples can choose to give up one of their paid jobs, as the costs of running a household and meeting basic family needs increasingly require two incomes. Parents are going to continue working, and the stresses and pressures of work-family conflict are only likely to increase unless more flexibility options are implemented to meet their needs.

David Almeida and Kelly Davis, developmental psychologists with expertise in work and family stress, report the findings of a major new study on hourly hotel employees with children. Recognizing the benefits of workplace flexibility for managing the responsibilities of employment, caregiving, and personal needs, they examine the consequences of the lack of flexibility on the daily emotional and physical well-being of forty-seven female hourly hotel employees and their adolescent children. Using a series of multivariate statistics, they find that when comparing workers with high and low flexibility, those with low flexibility were more likely to report having more arguments, more work tensions, and more physical health symptoms. For low-flexibility employees, more work tensions on a given day were associated with greater negative affect and health symptoms, suggesting that work tensions have interactive effects on mood and physical health. Perhaps most disconcerting is that for low-flexibility workers, work tensions appear to be transmitted to their children; the higher the work tensions, the more likely their children were to report negative emotions. Almeida and Davis's findings suggest that it is imperative to help employees manage their day-to-day lives, and one mechanism for doing this is through promoting workplace flexibility, especially as it relates to scheduling options. They conclude, similarly to Root and Young, that changing work attitudes and the workplace culture helps employees to better manage their daily lives. Almeida and Davis also cite the work of Kossek and Hammer (2008), who find that supportive supervisors can change the work culture to become more accommodating to employees' family needs.

Experts on higher education policy and the law, Marc Goulden, Mary Ann Mason, and Karie Frasch have been investigating when and why female and male scientists leave the profession and what can be done to change the "leaky pipeline." In their article, using data from studies including the Survey of Doctorate Recipients, they find that for female scientists, family formation—specifically marriage and childbirth—account for the largest leaks in the pipeline between PhD and tenure. Female scientists who are married and have children are 35 percent less likely than males to enter tenure-track positions and 27 percent less likely to receive tenure. Currently, universities and federal agencies have inadequate policies providing supplements to support family responsive needs, which is the situation especially for junior faculty. The authors contend that the solution to this problem is for federal agencies, professional associations, such as The American Association for the Advancement of Science (AAAS), and universities to adopt more responsive family policies for faculty and researchers such as graduate students and postdoctoral fellows. They argue that ethical concerns and economic costs should drive more directive and active responses for patching the leaky pipeline.

Shelley MacDermid Wadsworth, a specialist in military family research, and coauthor Kenona Southwell, show how the U.S. military has been responding to issues of workplace flexibility during the armed conflicts in Iraq and Afghanistan. The authors show why there are strong incentives for the military to address work-family concerns, including prolonged family separations, psychological and physical injuries, and the challenges of reentry into civilian life. Although the military has in the past developed programs to support families, it is currently experimenting with innovative models that involve partnerships with civilian employers to offer more benefits to employees who serve and their family members. Much like other specialized populations, even with these programs, the response for workplace flexibility practices needs more extensive attention. However, Wadsworth and Southwell argue that in the instance of military service, which involves extreme work, we should be formulating extreme work-family support in return.

Summary

The emphasis of the articles in this volume is on how the lack of workplace flexibility is impacting different groups of people. The other side to this story focuses on the businesses that have embraced workplace flexibility practices and how their actions have contributed to corporate profits and production efficiency. Evidence of the benefits of workplace flexibility for commercial organizations has been steadily increasing. Business pages and case materials in college classes describe how flexibility, despite having fixed costs, can be an effective tool for attracting and retaining employees and increasing productivity (Council of Economic Advisers 2010). This volume of *The Annals* cannot cover the entire workplace flexibility landscape, but we would be remiss if we failed to mention the work of the FWI, which has constructed profiles of hundreds of companies with survey data and other information. Results from this work have identified new alternatives for structuring workplaces that not only engage workers to feel more satisfied and committed to their jobs, but also maximize the productivity of the companies in which they are employed (Galinsky, Bond, and Sakai 2008).

FWI conducts the National Study of Employers, which provides national baseline data for scoring the Sloan Awards for Business Excellence in Workplace Flexibility, discussed earlier. As a result of employers' interest in this award program, the Society for Human Resource Management (SHRM, the world's largest association devoted to human resource management) has chosen to partner with FWI and fund this business award program starting in 2012. SHRM has more than 250,000 members and more than 575 affiliated chapters within the United States; with this membership base, SHRM will be able to significantly expand the reach and scope of the award program and thereby move the private sector closer to making workplace flexibility the standard way of working in the United States.

In conjunction with the award program, Corporate Voices for Working Families is leading a coalition of organizations, including SHRM and FWI, on a national "Business Champions" campaign that encourages businesses and non-profits to sign a pledge of support for expanding workplace flexibility (see Corporate Voices for Working Families n.d.; SHRM 2010). The pledge is not tied to any legislation but is rather a commitment by employers to meet the needs of their businesses as well as their employees. The pledge has several components, including communicating the business imperative for workplace flexibility, expanding flexibility as a mechanism for advancing business results, supporting managers to develop skills for implementing flexibility practices, and ensuring that workplace flexibility is an integral and equitable part of the way work is organized and is available to all employees regardless of their level (SHRM 2010). The work of FWI, Corporate Voices for Working Families, and SHRM, along with the efforts of Georgetown Law Center's WF 2010, highlights the importance of building collaborative partnerships for moving workplace flexibility solutions from personal to societal ones.

As the articles in this volume underscore, current workplaces are not meeting the needs of today's workers. The lack of workplace flexibility is having huge human capital costs that are affecting not only our economy but every sector of our society. The solution to this problem lies outside the family. What needs to change is the culture of those workplaces that continue to demand a commitment to work at the expense of commitments to families, children, grandparents, and others who need time, attention, and care. For those in low-wage jobs, the workplace is unduly regulatory, offering few opportunities to meet personal needs. The call is not to lower standards of high performance but rather to make the workplace flexible in ways that are profitable for employers and also meet the needs of their employees.

Notes

1. See http://wfnetwork.bc.edu/.

2. Within the past four years, the Sloan Work and Family Research Network Web site has received more than 459,000 visits and was recognized as one of the top hundred Web sites for women by *Forbes*. In October 2010, the director, Judi Casey, announced that the new Work and Family Researchers Network, "a social and virtual connector for interdisciplinary work-family researchers," building on the work of the earlier network, was being established with Sloan support "to transition from a Foundation-funded project to a sustainable organization enhancing future work-family scholarship" (see Work and Family Research Network 2010).

3. Altogether, these studies provide one of the most comprehensive and detailed sources of firm-level data on programs and policies related to work-life balance (Council of Economic Advisers 2010). Combining profiles of hundreds of companies with survey data, results identified new alternatives for structuring workplaces that not only engaged workers to feel more satisfied and committed to their jobs but also maximized the productivity of the companies in which they were employed. The research that resulted from these studies reveals a pressing need for flexibility and the positive consequences it can have on business productivity; for example, employees with access to flexible workplace arrangements exhibit significantly better mental health than other employees, and low-income workers experience this positive effect even more strongly than higher earners. Workplace flexibility is one of the most effective means of reducing unplanned absences from work. As reported in Schneider's article in this volume, the accounting firm of Deloitte & Touche calculated savings of approximately $41.5 million in turnover-related costs in 2003 due to their flexibility programs.

4. See http://cvworkingfamilies.org/.

5. See http://www.familiesandwork.org/.

6. See http://www.workplaceflexibility2010.org/.

7. See http://www.workplaceflexibility.org.

8. Much of this research was conducted through seven research centers that Sloan established. With multiyear funding, these centers, each taking a distinctive approach, became regional and national laboratories for the study of the American working family. The Employment and Family Careers Institute at Cornell University, primarily sociological in focus, undertook a major study of working families across the life course, with an emphasis on the challenges of retirement. The Center on Working Families at the University of California, Berkeley, also sociological in its orientation, undertook mainly qualitative work, assembling a group of seasoned and young scholars to examine cultural norms affecting caregiving and receiving in the United States and the resulting demands on workers in diverse institutional settings. The Center on Parents, Children and Work at the University of Chicago was multidisciplinary, involving sociologists, economists, and social psychologists; it conducted a major study, the 500 Family Study, designed to examine the impact of work on parents and their children using a variety of diverse methods. The Center for the Ethnography of Everyday Life at the University of Michigan was anthropological in its approach and delved deeply into how union and farm families were coping with changes in the economy and consequences on their families and work conditions. The Center for Myth and Ritual in American Life at Emory University, also anthropological, examined how traditional aspects of American life were being impacted by dual-career couples. The Center on the Ethnography of Everyday Life of Families at the University of California, Los Angeles, anthropological with respect to its major disciplinary frame, conducted an intensive in-depth study of thirty-two working families in the Los Angeles area. Finally, the Workplace Center at the Massachusetts Institute of Technology examined how the conditions of work in specific industries (such as law and health care) resulted in significant demands for workplace flexibility.

References

A Better Balance. 2008. *The business case for workplace flexibility*. Available from www.abetterbalance.org/ (accessed 31 August 2010).

Alfred P. Sloan Foundation. 2010a. *Workplace, work force and working families: National Workplace Flexibility Initiative*. Available from http://www.sloan.org/program/32/page/81 (accessed 22 April 2011).

Alfred P. Sloan Foundation. 2010b. *Workplace, work force and working families: Sloan centers on working families*. Available from www.sloan.org/program/32/page/79 (accessed 22 April 2011).

Bond, James T., Ellen Galinsky, Stacy S. Kim, and Erin Brownfield. 2005. *2005 National Study of Employers*. Washington, DC: Families and Work Institute.

Bond, James T., Cindy Thompson, Ellen Galinsky, and David Prottas. 2002. *Highlights of the 2002 National Study of the Changing Workforce*. New York, NY: Families and Work Institute.

Bureau of Labor Statistics. 2010. Table 4: Families with own children: Employment status of parents by age of youngest child and family type, 2009–10 annual averages. Available from www.bls.gov/news.release/ famee.t04.htm (accessed 20 August 2010).

Chesley, Noelle, and Phyllis Moen. 2006. When workers care: Dual-earner couples' care-giving strategies, benefit use, and psychological well-being. *American Behavioral Scientist* 49 (9): 1248–69.

Christensen, Kathleen. 2005a. Foreword. In *Work, family, health and well-being*, eds. Suzanne M. Bianchi, Lynne M. Casper, and Rosalind Berkowitz King, ix–xi. Mahwah, NJ: Lawrence Erlbaum.

Christensen, Kathleen. 2005b. Leadership in action: A work and family agenda for the future. In *The work and family handbook: Multi-disciplinary perspectives and approaches*, eds. Marcie Pitt-Catsouphes, Ellen Kossek, and Stephen Sweet, 705–33. Mahwah, NJ: Lawrence Erlbaum.

Christensen, Kathleen, and Ralph Gomory. 2 June 1999. Three jobs, two people. *The Washington Post*.

Corporate Voices for Working Families. n.d. Business champions. Available from www.corporatevoices.org/our-work/flexcampaign/champions.

Council of Economic Advisers. 2010. *Work-life balance and the economics of workplace flexibility*. Available from www.whitehouse.gov/files/documents/100331-cea-economics-workplace-flexibility.pdf (accessed 20 August 2010).

Galinsky, Ellen, and James T. Bond. 1998. *The 1998 Business Worklife Study*. New York, NY: Families and Work Institute.

Galinsky, Ellen, James T. Bond, and Kelly Sakai. 2008. *2008 National Study of Employers*. New York, NY: Families and Work Institute.

Georgetown University Law Center. 2010. *Flexible work arrangements: Selected case studies*. Workplace Flexibility 2010. Available from http://workplaceflexibility2010.org/images/uploads/FWA_CaseStudies.pdf.

Haider, Steven J., and David Loughran. 2010. Elderly labor supply: Work or play? In *Workplace flexibility: Realigning 20th-century jobs for a 21st-century workforce*, eds. Kathleen Christensen and Barbara Schneider, 110–30. Ithaca, NY: Cornell University Press.

Hewlett, Sylvia A. 2007. *Off-ramps and on-ramps: Keeping talented women on the road to success*. Boston, MA: Harvard Business School Press.

Hewlett, Sylvia A., and Carolyn B. Luce. 2005. Off-ramps and on-ramps: Keeping talented women on the road to success. *Harvard Business Review* 83 (3): 43–54.

Hutchens, Robert, and Karen Grace-Martin. 2006. Employer willingness to permit phased retirement: Why are some more willing than others? *Industrial & Labor Relations Review* 59:525–46.

Kossek, Ellen E., and Leslie B. Hammer. 2008. Forethought frontline workers: Supervisor work/life training gets results. *Harvard Business Review* 86:36.

Marchena, Elaine. 2005. Adolescents' assessment of parental role management in dual-earner families. In *Being together, working apart: Dual-career families and the work-life balance*, eds. Barbara Schneider and Linda J. Waite, 333–60. New York, NY: Cambridge University Press.

McDonald, Sarah-Kathryn, Kevin L. Brown, Jen Hanis-Martin, Jacob Sachs, and Elizabeth Keating. 2011. *Impact and influence of the Alfred P. Sloan Foundation's Program on Workplace, Workforce, and Working Families*. Technical Report to the Alfred P. Sloan Foundation. Chicago, IL: NORC, University of Chicago.

National Advisory Commission on Workplace Flexibility. n.d. *About us*. Available from http://workplace-flexibility2010.org/index.php/about_us/our_work/NAC (accessed 22 April 2011).

Ochs, Elinor, and Merav Shohet. 2006. The cultural structuring of mealtime socialization. *New Directions for Child and Adolescent Development* 111:35–49.

Ochs, Elinor, Merav Shohet, Belinda Campos, and Margaret Beck. 2010. Coming together at dinner: A study of working families. In *Workplace flexibility: Realigning 20th-century jobs for a 21st-century workforce*, eds. Kathleen Christensen and Barbara Schneider, 57–70. Ithaca, NY: Cornell University Press.

Offer, Shira, and Barbara Schneider. 2010. Multitasking among working families: A strategy for dealing with the time squeeze. In *Workplace flexibility: Realigning 20th-century jobs for a 21st-century workforce*, eds. Kathleen Christensen and Barbara Schneider, 43–56. Ithaca, NY: Cornell University Press.

Pellerin, Cheryl. 2011. *Mullen: Workplace flexibility focuses on families, children*. Available from www.jcs.mil/newsarticle.aspx?ID=513.

Schneider, Barbara, and Linda J. Waite, eds. 2005. *Being together, working apart: Dual-career families and the work-life balance*. New York, NY: Cambridge University Press.

Sexton, Holly R. 2005. Spending time at work and at home: What workers do, how they feel about it, and how these emotions affect family life. In *Being together, working apart: Dual-career families and the work-life balance*, eds. Barbara Schneider and Linda J. Waite, 49–71. New York, NY: Cambridge University Press.

Society for Human Resource Management (SHRM). 14 October 2010. Got flexibility? Become a "business champion." Available from www.shrm.org/ (accessed 27 April 2011).

U.S. Department of Labor. 1999. *Futurework: Trends and challenges for work in the 21st century.* Washington, DC: U.S. Department of Labor.

When Work Works. 2011. *About the Sloan awards.* Available from www.whenworkworks.org/ (accessed 22 April 2011).

White House Office of the Press Secretary. 31 March 2010. President and First Lady host White House Forum on Workplace Flexibility. Available from www.whitehouse.gov/the-press-office/ (accessed 22 April 2011).

Work and Family Research Network. 2010. A message from the director. Available from http://workfamily .sas.upenn.edu/transition.html (accessed 19 April 2011).

Family Change and Time Allocation in American Families

By
SUZANNE M. BIANCHI

Delayed marriage and childbearing, more births outside marriage, the increase in women's labor force participation, and the aging of the population have altered family life and created new challenges for those with caregiving demands. U.S. mothers have shed hours of housework but not the hours they devote to childrearing. Fathers have increased the time they spend on childcare. Intensive childrearing practices combine with more dual-earning and single parenting to increase the time demands on parents. Mothers continue to scale back paid work to meet childrearing demands. They also give up leisure time and report that they "are always rushed" and are "multitasking most of the time." Time-stretched working couples reduce the time they spend with each other. A large percentage of both husbands and wives also report they have "too little time" for themselves. Delayed childbearing and the aging population also increase the likelihood that both (adult) children and elderly parents need support and care from workers later in life.

Keywords: time use; parenting; maternal employment; family demography; intergenerational caregiving

A question one might ask about U.S. families at the close of the first decade of the twenty-first century is, What happens after a revolution? For nothing short of a revolution has occurred in family life. In 1950, women provided the bulk of unpaid care in families but were supported in this effort by the "good" job and "family wage" of the men they married. Women married at young ages, had all their children with the same man, and stayed married to him throughout life. However, life was not perfect: Betty Friedan's book *The Feminine*

Suzanne M. Bianchi is distinguished professor of sociology and holds the Dorothy Meier Chair in Social Equities at the University of California, Los Angeles. Her research focuses on the changing American family, time use and gender equality, and intergenerational caregiving.

NOTE: The Alfred P. Sloan Foundation and a 2010–2011 visiting scholar appointment at the Russell Sage Foundation supported the research for this article.

DOI: 10.1177/0002716211413731

Mystique (1963) described the frustrations of a generation of educated, middle-class mothers who felt unfulfilled in lives centered on chores and children, where all the rushing about felt like it was unappreciated and amounted to little.

Today, American mothers are still rushing about but in families that are far more complex. Their labor force participation is arguably as important as men's participation to the economic well-being of their families. A new problem has arisen for many parents—mothers and fathers—the overload of a "second" shift of caregiving that must increasingly be tacked onto the "first" shift of paid work. The tension between paid work and family caregiving has become more apparent because the nation's unpaid caregivers—women—have joined the paid work-force in great numbers. This is one reason "work-family flexibility" has become such an important policy focus in Europe and the United States.

In this article, I chart what we know about the juggling of paid work and unpaid caregiving and the costs for those who do both. First, I discuss some of the broad demographic changes in the family. Then I review what we have learned from 40 years of time diary evidence about mothers' and fathers' care of (young) children. I also discuss the seeming intensification of investment in children among the middle class and the "slow" transition into adulthood among young adult children today. I describe the things parents "give up," at least temporarily, to afford time for paid work and childrearing. Finally, I discuss caregiving for adults and close kin who usually live outside the immediate family household—elderly parents, adult children, and grandchildren.

How Has the Demography of Families Changed?

Several key changes in the family set the stage for more diverse family forms in the twenty-first century. These changes include delayed marriage and child-bearing and more births outside marriage; the increase in women's labor force participation, particularly among mothers; and the aging of the population.

Marriage, divorce, and cohabitation

There has been a dramatic delay in entering into (legal) marriage and a rise in unmarried (heterosexual and same-sex) cohabitation. The median age at first marriage has risen to 28 years for men and 26 years for women in the United States (U.S. Census Bureau 2010)—and it is even higher in a number of European countries. Most Americans eventually marry, but those marriages fre-quently end in divorce or separation. Andrew Cherlin, in his book *The Marriage-Go-Round* (2009), argues that the United States is exceptional among developed countries for its high rates of marrying and divorcing and its pattern of cohabita-tion. In Europe, cohabitation is often "marriage-like," lasting for years; in the United States, cohabitation tends to be short-lived. Ten percent of U.S. women have had three or more partners (either husbands or cohabiting partners) by the time they reach age 35, more than twice the percentage for women in European countries with the highest rates of union dissolution (Cherlin 2009, 19). These high rates of partnering and repartnering make for a much more turbulent family system in the United States: children frequently do not live with both biological parents throughout childhood, and women spend more time as lone mothers than in most European countries (Cherlin 2009, 18).

Delayed childbearing and childlessness

Fertility is also distinctive in the United States because it remains high (at replacement level) compared with many European countries where levels have dropped to a little over one child per woman. However, this tends to mask important variation by social class in the United States. Among the highly educated, children are postponed, but most are born to two married parents. A sizable proportion of highly educated women in recent cohorts have remained childless, and highly educated women, as a group, tend to have fewer children than they say they want earlier in life. In the 1979 National Longitudinal Survey of Youth (NLSY79), the family size of college-educated women was lower (by about 0.5 births per woman, averaged over the group) than their stated intentions at the beginning of their childrearing years (Morgan forthcoming). This suggests that either these women had difficulty realizing their preferences for motherhood or their preferences changed as they grew older.

The rapid decline in fertility to very low levels in Southern and Eastern Europe and some countries in Asia, most notably Japan, may be due in part to a lack of change in the family role expectations for women in these countries (McDonald 2000). In countries where women's labor market opportunities expand but women are still expected to do most of the housework and childcare with little assistance from men, many women exercise the only choice available: they remain childless when work and family roles are too difficult to reconcile. Perhaps even in the United States, motherhood may be forgone as women devote time to careers and face the difficulty of "fitting it all in" when jobs are fulfilling but also demanding of time and energy. Currently in the United States, among women age 40 to 44, 20 percent have never had a child, double the percentage 30 years ago, and this percentage rises to 27 percent for those with graduate or professional degrees (Dye 2008).

Nonmarital childbearing

Among those with a high school education or less in the United States, marriage is delayed or forgone but children are not, resulting in a large proportion of births to unmarried women. Partly due to the fertility of this group, Americans have children at an earlier average age than mothers in many other developed countries. Less educated women end up with family sizes that exceed (by about 0.5 births per woman, on average) what they say they want earlier in life (Morgan forthcoming).

Currently, 40 percent of U.S. births are to women who are not married (Hamilton, Martin, and Ventura 2009). The father often lives with the mother at the time of birth, but these families are quite fragile; only a little over half are still together by the time the child is five years old (Carlson and McLanahan 2010). Many of the children born to unmarried mothers will have weak ties to their fathers and paternal grandparents, a situation that is partially offset by stronger ties to maternal kin, particularly their maternal grandmothers (Bianchi 2006).

Maternal employment

Changes in marriage and fertility have gone hand-in-hand with the increase in women's, especially mothers', employment outside the home. Labor force rates for mothers with children under age 18 increased from 45 to 78 percent between 1965 and 2000, with the increase in full-year employment (50+ weeks) rising from 19 to 57 percent during the same period (Bianchi and Raley 2005, Table 2.2). Mothers' employment rates plateaued after 2000, fueling a debate about whether mothers were increasingly "opting out" of the paid workforce (Belkin 2003; Boushey 2005; Hoffman 2009; Stone 2007). Some argued that a slowdown or even retrenchment in the trend toward gender equality might be under way in the United States (Cotter, Hermsen, and Vanneman 2004).

Many mothers curtail employment to rear young children full time, whereas fathers seldom do so. In 2007, 24 percent of couples with children under age 15 had a mother who was out of the labor force for an entire year, presumably to care for children. "Stay-at-home" fathers accounted for only 3 percent of families with children under age 15 in 2007 (Kreider and Elliott 2009). Mothers (and daughters) are still on the front lines of caregiving to children and older parents, but the time they allocate to paid and unpaid pursuits has shifted dramatically in recent decades. More children have employed mothers, and more families have all adults in the workforce. When older parents require assistance, it is increasingly common that their adult daughters and daughters-in-law, as well as their sons and sons-in-law, are employed outside the home. This intensifies the juggling that has to take place between hours of paid work and unpaid family caregiving throughout the life course.

Population aging

A final trend altering family life in the United States and other developed countries is population aging—a result of both the decline in fertility and the increase in life expectancy. In the United States, the fraction of the population age 65 and older is projected to increase from the current 12 percent to 20 percent in 2030 (He et al. 2005). Future generations of elderly are likely to have fewer biological children on whom they can rely for care: in the United States the baby boom generation, now reaching retirement age, had much smaller families than the ones they were born into—averaging two children per family rather than the three or four children of their parents' generation (Uhlenberg 2005). The number of stepchildren an older parent has is expanding due to high levels of union disruption and repartnering. However, it is not clear that norms of obligation to assist family members are as strong among step-kin as among biological kin (Coleman and Ganong 2008).

Older people are healthier than in the past, with declining rates of disability. Partially because they are healthier, older adults are also working longer. During the past 15 years, the labor force rates for those in their 60s and 70s have risen (Gendell 2008).

Summary

Women's employment has grown substantially, reducing the number of hours that they—the primary caregivers in the past—have available to provide unpaid care to family members. Delayed marriage and childbearing heighten the likelihood that the greatest childrearing demands come at the same time that job and career demands are great—particularly among the well educated. Delayed childbearing increases the likelihood that one's parents may begin to suffer ill health and need assistance before one's children are fully launched. Difficulty with balancing work and family demands may also be contributing to the increase in childlessness. More single parents are trying to both support and provide time to children without the help of a partner. Work-family balance may be particularly elusive for this group, a group that may rely heavily on support from their own parents. Those parents are increasingly likely to be employed, at least part time, as older adults remain in the labor force longer than in the past. Given this complex picture, many Americans will experience multiple periods during their working lives when caregiving demands compete with work demands. The most intense period will likely remain the years of rearing young children. However, the later years of the life course also may entail a complex mix of obligations to elderly parents, a spouse who experiences a health crisis, or the needs of adult children and grandchildren.

Time (Re)Allocation in American Families with Children

Time diary evidence can be used to track changes in unpaid and paid work of mothers and fathers since the 1960s in the United States. The evidence suggests three important conclusions.

1. *Mothers.* As U.S. mothers increase their labor force participation, they shed hours of housework but not the hours they devote to childrearing.
2. *Fathers.* Fathers have increased the time they spend on childcare over the past two or three decades. For fathers, more childcare hours were added to

long work hours, especially for married fathers who average more than 40 hours of paid work per week (regardless of the age of their children).
3. *Children.* At the very time that families increasingly had all adults in the paid workforce as a result of more dual-earning and single parenting, rearing children seemingly took on an intensive form. Also, launching children into financial independence takes longer than in the past.

Time allocation of mothers

Currently, the time mothers report spending in direct or primary childrearing activities is higher than that during the 1960s when a far higher proportion of mothers were in the home full time. In *Changing Rhythms of American Family Life* (Bianchi, Robinson, and Milkie 2006), I, together with colleagues John Robinson and Melissa Milkie, use the historical time use data collections in the United States as well as two collections we undertook at the University of Maryland in 1998–1999 and 2000 to document changes in maternal employment, housework, and childcare in families with children under age 18. Table 1 extends this time series using the American Time Use Survey (ATUS) data collected between 2003 and 2008. As mothers increased market work, they reduced their time on housework but not childcare. The average hours of market work reported by mothers more than doubled (from 8 to 19 hours per week) between 1965 and 1985, continued to rise (to an average of 23 hours in 1995), and then leveled off and fluctuated between 21 and 23 hours over the 2003 to 2008 period. Housework hours for mothers declined from an average of 32 hours per week (reported in 1965 time diaries) to an average of 17 to 18 hours per week in the 2003 to 2008 period, a decline of 14 hours (from 1965) that "matches" the increase in market work.

As market work increased, mothers' time in childcare activities declined from 10 to 8.5 hours per week between 1965 and 1975, but then increased. After 1985, primary childcare time of mothers rose to almost 12.6 hours per week by 2000 and has fluctuated around 14 hours per week during the 2003 to 2008 period. Note that this is not the total time mothers spend with their children; that is much higher. It is the time they devote to meeting the child's needs and are directly engaged in taking care of the child or interacting with the child in activities such as play or reading to/with the child.

The average of 14 hours per week over the 2003 to 2008 period is the highest estimate of primary childcare time for mothers of any time point. Routine caregiving, or the bulk of childcare (e.g., feeding, clothing, and bathing children and taking them to the doctor), generally remained steady: it dipped between 1965 and 1985 and returned to (and slightly exceeded) 1965 levels by 2000. Time spent in interactive childcare activities, such as playing with children, reading to them, or helping with homework, almost tripled from 1.5 hours per week in 1965 to 4.0 hours per week reported in the ATUS (Bianchi, Wight, and Raley 2005).

TABLE 1
Time Use Trends of Mothers (Hours per Week), 1965–2008

Activity	1965	1975	1985	1995	2000	2003	2004	2005	2006	2007	2008	2003–2008
Total paid work	9.3	16.1	20.9	25.7	25.3	22.0	24.1	22.4	22.6	23.7	24.2	23.2
Work	8.4	14.9	18.8	23.4	22.8	20.6	22.5	20.8	21.2	22.2	22.6	21.6
Commute	0.9	1.2	2.1	2.3	2.5	1.3	1.6	1.6	1.5	1.5	1.6	1.5
Family care	49.5	37.9	36.2	36.0	39.8	39.4	39.3	39.4	39.3	38.4	37.8	38.9
Housework	31.9	23.6	20.4	18.9	18.6	18.2	18.0	18.1	18.2	17.5	17.4	17.9
Childcare	10.2	8.6	8.4	9.6	12.6	14.1	13.8	13.9	13.5	14.1	13.9	13.9
Shopping/services	7.4	5.6	7.3	7.5	8.6	7.1	7.5	7.4	7.5	6.8	6.5	7.1
Personal care	74.4	76.3	74.9	71.8	71.3	75.0	73.9	75.0	75.6	75.2	74.6	74.9
Sleep	55.4	58.4	56.3	57.8	54.7	59.6	58.9	59.8	60.5	59.8	59.1	59.6
Meal	8.9	8.7	6.4	4.9	7.3	7.0	6.8	7.0	7.1	7.2	7.1	7.0
Grooming	10.1	9.2	12.2	9.0	9.3	8.4	8.2	8.1	8.0	8.2	8.4	8.2
Total free time	34.8	37.7	36.0	34.4	31.8	31.5	30.7	31.2	30.5	30.7	31.4	31.0
Education	0.7	1.2	1.5	2.8	2.3	1.8	2.2	2.1	1.9	1.8	2.0	2.0
Religion	1.1	2.3	1.7	0.7	1.3	1.1	0.7	0.9	0.9	1.1	1.1	1.0
Organizations	1.4	1.9	1.0	0.7	0.6	1.7	1.6	1.7	1.5	1.4	1.4	1.5
Event	1.2	0.5	0.4	1.2	1.0	0.8	0.8	1.0	0.8	0.9	0.7	0.9
Visiting	9.0	7.1	6.6	7.5	7.3	4.3	3.9	4.1	4.1	4.2	4.2	4.1
Fitness	0.6	0.8	1.4	1.6	1.4	1.2	1.2	1.2	1.1	1.3	1.1	1.2
Hobby	2.8	2.9	2.4	1.2	1.6	0.7	0.8	0.8	0.7	0.9	0.8	0.8
TV	10.3	14.1	13.7	12.5	11.5	13.4	13.4	13.4	13.2	13.4	14.2	13.5
Reading	3.4	2.6	2.3	2.1	1.4	1.5	1.6	1.5	1.5	1.5	1.3	1.5
Stereo	0.3	0.4	0.3	0.0	0.2	0.1	0.1	0.1	0.2	0.1	0.1	0.1
Communication	4.0	3.9	4.6	4.1	3.2	4.8	4.5	4.4	4.6	4.2	4.4	4.5
Total time	168.0	168.0	168.0	168.0	168.2	168.0	168.0	168.0	168.0	168.0	168.0	168.0
N	(417)	(369)	(903)	(307)	(999)	(4,542)	(2,925)	(3,088)	(3,104)	(2,786)	(2,825)	(19,270)

SOURCE: Author's calculations from the 1965–66, 1975–76, 1985, 1994–95, 1998–99, 2000 time use studies (Bianchi, Robinson, and Milkie 2006) and the 2003–08 ATUS.

NOTE: Age of selected sample ranges from 18 to 64 years.

Time use data from European countries show similar patterns of increases in maternal time in primary childcare across a number of developed countries (Gauthier, Smeeding, and Furstenberg 2004). Despite rapid increases in women's labor force participation in virtually all European economies, there has not been a decline in mothers' average time in primary childcare (Joshi 1998). Sharon Hays (1996) labels this the cultural contradiction of modern motherhood: mothers assume the coprovider role but still feel compelled to be "all-giving" and "ever-available" to their children. A schema of "devotion to family" competes with "devotion to work" even among high-income, professional mothers who are most heavily invested in their jobs (Blair-Loy 2003).

Although trends seem to suggest that the increase in market work of mothers was largely "financed" by a decrease in housework—and not childcare—employment still takes a toll on mothers' provision of childcare. Employed mothers do not spend as much time in childcare as nonemployed mothers. For one thing, mothers who take time out of the labor force in any given year have younger children than those who are employed, and young children require more hours of care. What has happened over time is that the allocation of time to children has ratcheted upward for both employed and nonemployed mothers; employed mothers today record as much childcare in their diaries as the nonemployed mothers of the past (Bianchi, Robinson, and Milkie 2006). At the very time when mothers in some sense could least afford to increase their time tending to children's needs, because they were working more hours outside the home, that is exactly what they did do.

Time allocation of (married) fathers

As mothers increased their market work and shed housework, how did fathers respond? Fathers more than doubled their housework hours between 1965 and 1985, from 4 to 10 hours per week, and then housework time for fathers leveled out. Fathers' time doing primary childcare was stable at about 2.5 hours per week in the 1965 though 1985 diaries but then increased substantially. By 2000, fathers had nearly tripled their time on childcare, reporting almost 7 hours per week of childcare in their diaries. In the 2008 ATUS, fathers were averaging almost 8 hours per week in childcare (see Table 2).

The overall time fathers report doing primary childcare—an average of over an hour a day—is only about one-quarter of the amount of time a father spends with his children on the diary day (about five hours a day for those with a child under age 13). The same is true for mothers—the majority of the time they are with their children, their primary activity is not a caregiving activity. Rather, children are "with them" as they do the myriad of daily activities, and parents are "on call" in case children need them.

Mothers' longer work hours are associated with increased father involvement in children's lives. Husbands who are part of an intact, dual-earner family and who are married to women with longer work hours have more "parental knowledge"

TABLE 2
Time Use Trends of Fathers (Hours per Week), 1965–2008

Activity	1965	1975	1985	1995	2000	2003	2004	2005	2006	2007	2008	2003–2008
Total paid work	46.4	45.4	39.8	39.5	41.8	42.7	41.5	42.1	42.9	43.5	42.8	42.6
Work	42.0	41.4	35.7	35.1	37.0	39.5	38.2	38.4	39.1	40.1	39.5	39.1
Commute	4.3	4.0	4.1	4.4	4.8	3.3	3.3	3.7	3.8	3.4	3.3	3.4
Family care	11.9	12.3	17.8	18.7	21.9	21.6	21.2	20.8	21.3	21.1	21.5	21.2
Housework	4.4	6.0	10.2	10.2	10.0	9.6	9.5	9.2	9.7	9.5	9.5	9.5
Childcare	2.5	2.6	2.6	4.2	6.8	6.9	6.9	6.8	6.6	6.9	7.8	7.0
Shopping/services	5.1	3.7	5.0	4.3	5.1	5.1	4.8	4.9	5.0	4.7	4.2	4.8
Personal care	74.7	74.7	73.5	67.0	69.3	71.2	72.0	73.1	72.0	71.1	71.8	71.9
Sleep	55.7	56.7	55.1	53.0	53.8	56.9	56.8	57.7	57.3	56.6	57.0	57.1
Meal	10.5	10.5	6.9	6.5	7.8	7.5	7.9	8.2	7.8	7.9	7.8	7.8
Grooming	8.5	7.6	11.4	7.5	7.6	6.8	7.3	7.2	6.9	6.6	7.0	7.0
Total free time	35.0	35.7	36.9	42.9	35.2	32.5	33.3	32.0	31.9	32.3	32.0	32.3
Education	1.2	1.2	1.6	2.2	3.1	1.2	1.5	1.5	1.4	1.5	1.2	1.4
Religion	1.2	1.3	0.8	0.5	1.5	1.0	0.9	0.5	0.7	0.9	1.0	0.8
Organizations	1.0	1.0	1.0	0.5	0.9	1.4	1.6	1.5	1.4	1.5	1.3	1.4
Event	0.6	0.6	0.6	0.7	0.9	0.9	0.8	0.8	0.8	0.9	1.0	0.9
Visiting	8.4	6.8	6.5	8.0	5.6	3.6	3.7	3.5	3.5	3.2	3.0	3.4
Fitness	1.3	2.0	2.9	7.1	2.4	1.9	2.4	1.9	2.1	2.3	2.0	2.1
Hobby	1.2	2.4	2.3	3.9	1.7	1.1	1.2	1.1	1.4	1.2	1.3	1.2
TV	13.4	14.7	15.0	15.0	14.5	14.7	15.6	15.1	15.1	15.5	16.3	15.4
Reading	4.2	2.7	2.2	1.8	1.1	1.3	1.3	1.2	1.2	1.0	1.0	1.2
Stereo	0.6	0.4	0.5	0.1	0.2	0.3	0.3	0.2	0.2	0.2	0.1	0.2
Communication	2.0	2.5	3.5	2.9	3.4	5.1	4.1	4.6	4.1	4.2	3.7	4.3
Total time	168.0	168.0	168.0	168.0	168.1	168.0	168.0	168.0	168.0	168.0	168.0	168.0
N	(343)	(251)	(693)	(180)	(632)	(3,082)	(2,071)	(2,072)	(2,052)	(1,938)	(1,980)	(13,195)

SOURCE: See Table 1.
NOTE: Age of selected sample ranges from 18 to 64 years.

than husbands whose wives work fewer hours (Crouter et al. 1999). Fathers in dual-earner couples in which the wife works a nonstandard shift are more likely to participate in childcare, compared with other dual-earner couples (Casper and O'Connell 1998). Fathers appear to be "picking up some of the slack" induced by increasing paid work of mothers. Yet fathers continue to work longer hours than mothers, and their long hours of paid work may be part of the reason why mothers in many two-parent families curtail their hours of employment. Someone must focus on family caregiving—and that someone remains, more often than not, the mother.

A note on single parenting

With the high rates of divorce and increase in nonmarital childbearing, children are increasingly likely to reside in households headed by a single parent, usually their mother. Excluding cohabiting parents from the count of single-parent households, current estimates are that single parents account for about one-quarter of U.S. households with children under the age of 18 (Kreider and Elliott 2009). Although the number of coresident single fathers has increased since the 1970s, accounting for about 15 percent of all single parents in 2007, single mothers are still overrepresented among single parents at 85 percent (Kreider and Elliott 2009).

Parents who do not coreside with children spend far less time caring for their children than coresident parents—and the great majority of parents who do not coreside with their children are fathers. This is somewhat compensated for by the fact that men often are the "step" or "social" fathers to other men's children, when the men remarry. However, the quantity—and perhaps also the quality—of time spent parenting is lower for step- than biological coresident fathers (Hofferth et al. 2002).

Researchers and policy-makers have focused on the economic constraints that single parents face in rearing their children, but they also experience severe time shortages (Vickery 1977). They may have as many demands on their time as married parents but half as many adults to meet those demands. Without a partner, it is difficult for single parents to provide the time and attention that children receive in two-parent homes—especially as involvement with children increases for both mothers and fathers in two-parent families.

Both married and single mothers' childcare time has increased over the past several decades, perhaps allaying fears about time shortages in single-mother households (Bianchi, Robinson, and Milkie 2006). Yet single mothers spend less time in childcare than married mothers—less total childcare, less routine care, less time playing with and interacting with their children, and less total time with children (Kendig and Bianchi 2008). Single mothers spend almost three fewer hours per week in direct care of their children and five fewer hours per week with their children than married mothers. Still, single mothers average 83 to 90 percent (depending on the measure and subgroup of single mothers) as much time with their children as married mothers. Single mothers have higher rates of employment and tend to be less educated, both of which are associated with reduced childcare time. Cohabiting "single" mothers do not differ from married mothers in the time they spend with their children: cohabiting mothers are less educated and have lower incomes than married mothers (factors associated with less time with children), but they also have younger children who increase time demands.

One thing that limits the quantity and perhaps also the quality of the time single mothers have for their children is their much greater need for employment to support their children than among married mothers. Most single mothers do not have the flexibility to drop out of the labor force or reduce their hours in response to the needs of very young children—unless their extended families or the government steps in. Since the mid-1990s in the United States, the effort has been to encourage employment of poor single mothers rather than long-term reliance on welfare support.

Never-married single mothers are disadvantaged relative to divorced single mothers and married mothers, who tend to be older and better-educated. Never-married single mothers have less than one-fourth the family income of two-parent families; the average income of families headed by divorced mothers is about half that of two-parent families. Part of the economic inequality between never-married single mothers and divorced single mothers is due to the father's propensity to contribute child support. Mothers who never marry the father of their children are less likely to receive child support (20 percent report receiving it regularly) than are divorced or separated mothers (60 percent report receiving some support [Casper and Bianchi 2002]).

Intensive parenting of children

A number of studies suggest that American parents, at least middle-class parents, are engaged in an ever more intensive form of child-rearing. Middle-class children participate in a large number of extracurricular activities that often require parental involvement and require parents to transport children to and from activities (Lareau and Wieninger 2008). A number of factors may have increased the time parents spend (or feel they must spend) engaged with children in their activities (Sayer, Bianchi, and Robinson 2004). First, as couples have fewer children and have them later in life, they may time parenthood for a period in their lives when they want to devote their energies to childrearing. Second, parents fear for children's safety when they are not supervised. More children live in urban areas where they cannot walk unaccompanied to school or activities and where parents supervise children on playgrounds or in public spaces. More working parents also means that neighborhoods are not full of adults who might look after children who are unaccompanied by an adult. Third, an increased amount of time is required merely to transport children to daily activities in suburban spaces with traffic congestion. Fourth, parents may be increasingly concerned with giving their children a wide range of opportunities with the hope that this will ensure children's later educational success (Ramey and Ramey 2010). Annette Lareau (2003) labels this type of parenting "concerted cultivation." Parents feel this type of investment in young children is required to achieve their children's later educational and career success.

Despite parents' heavy involvement in childrearing, the majority of mothers and fathers still say they have "too little time" with their children (Bianchi, Robinson, and Milkie 2006). This may reflect the hurried nature of modern family life—when time together is often spent rushing to the next activity or commitment. The feeling that one has too little time with one's children is much more prevalent among employed than nonemployed mothers. Approximately 18 percent of nonemployed mothers report they have too little time with their children, while this sentiment is shared by nearly one-third of part-time employed mothers and over half of full-time employed mothers (Bianchi and Wight 2010). Fathers are even more likely than mothers to feel they have too little time with their children, largely because they work so many hours. Gender differences in a perceived time shortage with children disappear once the longer paid work weeks of fathers are controlled, suggesting that this measure may be picking up something about the "subjective cost" of spending more time away from home and family among the employed (Milkie et al. 2004).

Raising children in the contemporary United States also takes a long time and requires substantial financial investment by parents, as young adults delay the transition to adulthood and as parents often financially "backstop" children who are having trouble securing a foothold in the job market. Using multiple data sets, Schoeni and Ross (2004) show that there was a 10 percent rise in the likelihood of young adults 18 to 34 years old living with parents between 1970 and 1990. They estimate that this resulted in a 13 percent increase in the assistance young adults received from parents. Indeed, the vast majority of those in their early 20s—regardless of whether they are enrolled in school—receive some sort of economic assistance from their parents. Furstenberg (2010) argues that as the transition to adulthood lengthens in the United States, parents bear a greater burden of supporting adult children relative to their European counterparts, where governmental programs invest more heavily in the education, health care, and job prospects of their young people. The lack of government investment in the United States also makes for greater diversity and more inequality in young adult outcomes, reflecting inequality in the economic resources parents have to assist adult children.

What Do Parents Give Up to Devote Time to Work and Family?

According to the 1997 National Study of the Changing Workforce, about one-quarter to one-third of workers report feeling that they do not have enough time for themselves or their family because of their jobs (Jacobs and Gerson

2004). In addition, many parents say that they would prefer to work fewer hours per week and fewer weeks during the year (Christensen 2005; Reynolds 2005). The trend toward desiring fewer hours has been increasing among mothers over the past decade. According to a report by the Pew Research Center, the proportion of mothers who reported that full-time work was the ideal situation for them declined from 32 percent in 1997 to 21 percent in 2007. Conversely, 60 percent of mothers today prefer part-time work (up from 48 percent in 1997 [Taylor, Funk, and Clark 2007]). The desire to reduce work hours stems from a number of factors reflecting both job demands and personal and family life considerations (Reynolds 2005). The tension between work and family life may be especially pronounced in the United States because American workers dedicate more hours to paid work and vacation less than do their European counterparts. American parents also work the longest annual hours and have the highest percentage of dual-earner couples who work long workweeks (Gornick and Meyers 2003).

Time tends to be a "zero-sum game," with time devoted to any one activity increasing only if another activity suffers an equal loss, unless individuals engage in large-scale multitasking, a stressful proposition. As more and more families have all members employed—but also strive to keep time with children high— "what gives"? The accumulated evidence suggests a number of things:

1. Mothers continue to scale back work hours when childrearing demands are highest and when they are able to do so financially. This has long-term negative consequences for women's income security later in life, especially in the event that their marriage dissolves, and it tends to retard progress toward gender equality in occupational attainment and earnings.
2. Time diary evidence suggests that time-stretched working parents reduce the time they spend with each other—both the total amount of time and time alone as a couple. In addition, large percentages of both husbands and wives report they have "too little time" for themselves.
3. Working mothers in particular give up leisure time and sleep (compared with mothers not in the labor force) to meet demands of children and jobs. Large percentages of mothers, no matter their labor force status, report they "are always rushed" and are "multitasking most of the time."

Reduced employment and pay penalties for women

Time diary studies suggest that total workloads of mothers and fathers are similar but remain gender-specialized. Mothers average about half the paid work hours that fathers do (23 hours per week versus 43, averaged over all couples with children under age 18 and over the 2003–2008 ATUS data collections). Conversely, fathers contribute about half as much unpaid work in the home, or family care, as do their wives. (That is, mothers average 39 hours a week compared with 21 hours for fathers.)

Ample evidence suggests that women incur a wage penalty for the time they devote to childrearing (Budig and England 2001; Joshi 2002; Waldfogel 1997), yet mothers continue to curtail market work despite the economic disadvantages of discontinuous labor market participation. Mothers' employment hours are highly responsive to the age of the youngest child: only 46 percent of married mothers with a child under age one report any paid work hours, compared with 73 percent of those whose children are all over the age of six (Bianchi and Raley 2005, Table 4). Some mothers exit the labor force for the first year or few years of their children's lives, while others reduce their labor force status to part-time (Klerman and Leibowitz 1999). When mothers return to (full-time) employment, they may structure their employment hours so as to overlap as much as possible with children's school schedules (Crouter and McHale 2005). These strategies tend to narrow the gap in childcare time between employed and nonemployed mothers, particularly when children are young.

Obviously there are benefits to women's families and children of curtailing market work. Many women may consider more time with children or a less harried lifestyle worth the economic risk of time out of the labor force. Cross-sectional time use data do not allow us to sort out causality on this issue, but they do allow us to describe hours forgone in other activities when more hours are spent in market work. The picture of "nonmarket costs" when mothers work outside the home (discussed below) is that some childcare time and sleep are forgone but also a great many hours of free time and housework go by the wayside.

Relatively few mothers work extremely long hours, particularly when their children are young, a sizable percentage of married mothers (more than one-third) are employed no hours, and an additional 20 percent of mothers work part-time hours (Bianchi and Wight 2010). Without knowledge of parents' preferences, it is not entirely clear how to interpret these facts. On one hand, mothers who are *not* putting in long hours may be doing so because they feel they must preserve sufficient time for the family. Full-time hours may be difficult to reconcile with family caregiving. At the same time, these mothers may be forgoing the best jobs in the economy.

Mothers who are working no hours may or may not be doing so out of choice. A sizable fraction of these mothers have only a high school education or less, and the costs of employment (e.g., childcare) may outweigh the economic benefit. Another issue for all mothers (and fathers) is whether they can afford to "outsource" tasks such as housework and whether they are able and comfortable with "outsourcing" the care of their children and the other tasks of family caregiving. The percentage of nonemployed mothers who say they would prefer not to work outside the home has increased over the past 10 years from 39 to 48 percent (Taylor, Funk, and Clark 2007).

A note on nonstandard work hours

Both long work hours in jobs with standard schedules as well as jobs with irregular or nonstandard schedules can spill over into parts of the day often reserved for family time (e.g., evenings) and restrict parents' traditional "downtime" activities that provide rest and relaxation. Evidence from the ATUS about those who, on their diary day, worked most of their hours outside the 8:00 a.m. to 4:00 p.m. standard daytime schedule shows that, regardless of whether they worked most of their hours in the evening or night, those with nonstandard hours spent significantly less time than their standard daytime counterparts with a spouse, and less time watching television and sleeping (Wight, Raley, and Bianchi 2008). Mothers who worked most of their hours in the evening spent less time in routine childcare activities and were less likely to read to their children than were mothers who worked most of their hours during the day. Fathers who worked evenings or nights actually spent more time in routine childcare than their counterparts who worked daytime hours. Evening work schedules reduced the likelihood of parents being present at the dinner table (Wight, Raley, and Bianchi 2008). When paid work hours intersect with culturally sanctioned "nonwork" periods of the day, whether as a result of nonstandard work schedules or long standard daytime schedules, the ability to engage in nonwork activities with other family members is limited.

Spouses' time together and marital quality

Analysis of time diary data on "with whom" time is spent suggests that time with a spouse is lower in households where both parents are employed than in those where someone, almost always the wife, has stopped working for pay. Increases in both individual work hours and the combined work hours of a couple are associated with declines in marital quality (Barnett 2004). Similarly, feelings of role overload or not having enough time for oneself are associated with lower levels of marital quality (Crouter et al. 2001). Among a sample of white, married, middle-class professionals, an increase in work hours was associated with higher reports of family-role difficulty and higher levels of marital tension (Hughes, Galinsky, and Morris 1992). In a sample of 190 dual-earning families, the more hours a husband worked, the less time he spent with his wife (Crouter et al. 2001).

The effect of employment on a couple's marital relationship may be patterned along gender stereotypic lines, with women's hours of employment more highly correlated with divorce than the work hours of men. Among parents, an additional hour of employment by a father is linked to a lower probability of divorce, whereas an additional hour worked by a mother is associated with a higher risk of divorce (Johnson 2004). Lower marital quality and a heightened likelihood of divorce are also found to be associated with certain nonstandard work schedules (e.g., working nights [Presser 2000, 2003]).

Sleep, leisure, the family dinner, and a sense of well-being

Bianchi and Wight (2010) use the ATUS to compare the time allocations of mothers by employment status (and husbands by the wife's employment status). Employed mothers do less childcare (8 hours less), less housework (10 hours less), and a little less shopping (1 hour less) per week than nonemployed mothers; they also get a little less sleep (3 hours less) and have substantially less free time (9 hours less). Compared with part-time employed mothers, full-time employed mothers do less childcare (5 hours less), do less housework (5 hours less), do slightly less shopping (1 hour less), get a little less sleep (almost 1 hour less), and have less free time (about 6 hours less). The free time of employed mothers is also less likely to be the most relaxing type of free time—free time that is not spent in charge of children or combined with some unpaid domestic activity like folding laundry. Feelings of "time pressure" may also be heightened when long work hours curtail time for rest and relaxation (Bianchi, Robinson, and Milkie 2006; Nomaguchi, Milkie, and Bianchi 2005).

The difference in fathers' paid work hours across families is much less pronounced. Fathers in couples where both spouses work 35 or more hours per week average about 2 hours less paid work than their counterparts in couples with a part-time employed wife. Otherwise, fathers' time allocations are quite similar in households where wives work full or part time.

The number of nights the family has dinner together also differs between couples with a nonemployed versus an employed mother/wife, which suggests that this family activity is also a little more difficult for dual-earner couples than for families where the mother/wife is not employed. Couples with a nonemployed wife eat together approximately 5.1 nights a week. Among part- and full-time employed mothers, this number drops to about 4.4 nights per week (Bianchi 2009).

The evidence suggests that parents have been managing to do both "work and family"—and with a somewhat more egalitarian division of labor than in the past. However, women still do far more of the unpaid, caregiving hours in the home and men do more of the paid hours in the labor market. And the total hours (paid plus unpaid) add up to high average workloads per week for both mothers and fathers when there are young children in the home and high levels of expressed stress over time pressures. Activities that "give" to meet family demands include mothers' paid work hours, spouses' time together, the family dinner, and mothers' rest and relaxation.

Beyond the couple and the family: Socializing and civic engagement

Parents' connections to extended kin and a wider circle of friends and organizations may also be curtailed when lives are overwhelmed with work and child-rearing demands. Most recent accounts indicate that employment reduces a woman's time available for volunteering, although trends over time are unclear (see Bianchi [2000] for a review). Civic engagement in organizational activities, such as PTA meetings, differs by maternal employment: employed mothers do about 1.3 hours of this type of activity per week compared with 2.8 hours for nonemployed mothers. There are no differences for fathers in the two types of households (Bianchi 2009).

Other activities form the "glue" of relationships—socializing, attending events with others, and doing hobbies with others (Bianchi, Robinson, and Milkie 2006). Overall, all groups report a significant number of hours in such activities—as many as 20 hours per week for nonemployed mothers. Employed mothers engage in four fewer hours of social leisure than nonemployed mothers. There is a parallel difference among fathers, with those married to employed wives spending about four hours less per week in social pursuits than those married to a mother at home full time (Bianchi 2009).

An alternative estimate of the social fabric of family life is the time people spend with friends and relatives. Here there is no significant difference between mothers or fathers depending on a mother's employment status. However, single mothers participate less in this type of socializing now than in the past, suggesting that their lives have become busier with less time for the adult company and interactions that may sustain them in their role as a lone parent (Bianchi 2009; Bianchi, Robinson, and Milkie 2006).

Obligations to extended kin

One of the major changes affecting the demography of family life is the aging of the population. The good news is that given the lengthening of healthy life expectancy, most adults do not face serious caregiving demands from their parents until their own children are older and less demanding of day-to-day care. Thus, a relatively small proportion (around 9 percent of women in late middle age) are "sandwiched" between intensive care of a parent and young children (Pierret 2006), though these individuals face a substantial burden. When eldercare needs do arise, they often result from an unexpected health crisis such as a fall and hence are difficult to anticipate.

A number of data sets provide estimates of care and help given to older and disabled adults. The ATUS asks specifically about care for adults who do not live in the same household. Table 3 shows that between 12 and 17 percent of those over the age of 35 report providing some adult care on their diary day. When adult care is provided, individuals spend close to an hour and a half providing this care on their diary day. Gender differences in reports of providing care to adults are small, especially in comparison to care of children where women do much more of the day-to-day childrearing than do men. There may be a number of reasons for this. Help for adults may involve the types of things men typically do—help with yard work or household repairs, for example. One important activity is helping with transportation, and men and women do this about equally (data not shown).

Based on reports from the Wisconsin Longitudinal Study (WLS) on help that older adults (in their 50s and 60s) report giving to adult children, elderly parents, and friends and neighbors, women still dominate in providing emotional support to these groups (see Table 4). Women are more likely than men to assist elderly parents, usually an older, widowed mother. But men are very much involved in

TABLE 3
Percentage of Women and Men Who Provide Care for Other Adults

	Percentage Reporting		Minutes of Care Conditional on Report	
	Women	Men	Women	Men
Age 35 to 54	14.4	12.5	81.2	89.1
Age 55 to 59	16.8	13.0	98.3	88.6
Age 60 to 64	16.3	14.0	109.0	99.8
Age 65 to 69	15.7	14.4	87.2	98.8
Age 70 plus	11.7	14.0	99.7	98.8

SOURCE: Author's calculations from the 2003–07 ATUS.

providing help around the house to adult children and parents, again, in part, because the help that is needed is probably yard work and household repairs. As men transition from their 50s to their 60s, and as many of them retire from the labor force, they also become increasingly involved in the care of their grandchildren, and the gender gap in providing childcare assistance to adult children narrows significantly (Kahn, McGill, and Bianchi 2011). This suggests an active network of exchanges among family members and across generations that extends across the life course.

Discussion and Conclusion

The United States, like Australia, Canada, Great Britain and many countries in Europe, has witnessed monumental economic, social, cultural, and demographic changes since the 1960s that have altered family forms in the twenty-first century. Similar to these other countries, the United States has experienced a postponing of marriage; declines in marriage among some subgroups; increases in divorce, nonmarital childbearing, and cohabitation; a decline in fertility; the aging of the population; and increases in women's labor force participation, resulting in a shift in the household division of labor. American families and children experience much more instability in family forms than families in other countries, with Americans churning in and out of marriage and cohabitation.

Increasing economic inequality, diversity in family forms, and family instability raise questions about the family's ability to shoulder work and family demands without greater public assistance. However, in the United States, compared with Europe, government is much less often viewed as having the responsibility to fill the void when families are not strong, stable, or economically secure enough to ensure children's well-being. In the first decade of the twenty-first century, U.S. policy was to encourage and support the formation and maintenance of healthy marriages. The widespread recession at the end of the decade made clear that

TABLE 4

Provision of Help (%) by Gender and Year, Married WLS Graduates

| | 1993 | | 2004 | | Gender Gap (Women − Men) | |
	Women	Men	Women	Men	1993	2004
Sample: All married respondents (n = 4,044)						
Any help to anyone	98.0	94.6	95.2	92.3	3.4	2.9
Any transportation/errands	71.1	65.0	64.0	59.5	6.1	4.5
Any housework/repairs	42.8	53.4	33.9	50.6	−10.6	−16.7
Any emotional support	93.6	85.3	88.4	78.2	8.3	10.2
Any childcare/babysitting	52.8	32.3	55.3	49.6	20.5	5.7
Has a parent alive?	63.0	64.3	24.8	25.0	−1.3	−0.2
Has an adult child?	95.7	93.5	97.1	96.6	2.2	0.5
Help to parents						
Sample: Those with a living parent in both 1993 and 2004 (n = 1,007)						
Any help to parents	62.3	51.7	64.5	55.3	10.6	9.2
Transportation/errands for parent	40.8	31.4	48.8	38.0	9.4	10.8
Housework/repairs for parent	22.2	29.5	28.2	23.1	−7.3	5.1
Emotional support to parent	43.9	29.4	44.3	35.0	14.5	9.3

(continued)

TABLE 4 (continued)

	1993		2004		Gender Gap (Women – Men)	
	Women	Men	Women	Men	1993	2004
Help to adult children						
Sample: Those with an adult child in each year	(n = 3,826)		(n = 3,917)			
Any help to adult child	82.7	73.8	80.7	77.0	8.9	3.7
Transportation/errands for adult child	35.0	34.9	28.0	30.6	0.1	-2.6
Housework/repairs for adult child	19.6	19.4	19.0	26.3	0.2	-7.3
Emotional support to adult child	67.9	58.5	62.4	54.4	9.4	8.0
Childcare/babysitting for adult child	46.4	28.3	54.6	49.8	18.1	4.8
Help to nonkin						
Sample: All married respondents (n = 4,044)						
Any help to nonkin	68.0	67.9	57.2	54.4	0.1	2.8
Transportation/errands for nonkin	28.3	29.6	24.5	24.7	-1.3	-0.2
Housework/repairs for nonkin	10.3	23.4	8.8	23.2	-13.1	-14.4
Emotional support to nonkin	60.8	52.8	49.0	37.1	8.0	11.9

SOURCE: Author's calculations from the Wisconsin Longitudinal Study.

many families, even stable two-parent families, can become vulnerable to economic loss and unforeseen circumstances. Merely promoting family stability is probably not sufficient to sustain the healthy and happy families we all desire.

Analyses over the past decade based on time diary data and other sources shed light on why—some 40 years after the gender revolution and despite increased educational, occupational, and early career opportunities for women—once children arrive, mothers reduce market employment in favor of more time in the home. Although attitudes toward maternal employment have become more accepting and many couples espouse an ideal of gender egalitarianism in work and family life (Casper and Bianchi 2002), this ideal has proven quite difficult to realize. The continued high rate of temporary labor force exits by mothers when children are young and the reduction in women's labor market hours throughout the childrearing years partially explain why it has been difficult for women, even highly educated women, to achieve labor market parity with men. Despite rapid increases in maternal employment, mothers' investment in childrearing remains high, and meeting children's needs remains paramount for mothers (and fathers).

There are costs to increased maternal employment, especially in the U.S. context, where public policy support for combining paid work with family caregiving remains weak in comparison to Europe. For children, the cost of their mothers working outside the home may come in the form of somewhat less time with their mothers than children of nonemployed mothers, dirtier homes, fewer family dinners, and perhaps more strain between their parents. For employed parents, especially mothers, the costs are less rest and relaxation and heavy workloads.

Good jobs in the U.S. economy come with long work hours. Husbands in jobs with long hours induce mothers to shorten their hours, presumably because they decide this is best for the family. The current recession, with the increased attention to women's breadwinning roles, suggests that shortening fathers' hours or curbing long hours in good jobs may pressure mothers to increase their paid work hours. This may be good for gender equality in the family, but it may not do much to ensure adequate time for family caregiving or the other activities of daily life that contribute to balance, health, and well-being. Finding the right mix of policy incentives and private initiatives to support workers when caregiving demands are overwhelming is the challenge we face in the United States if we want productive workers but also strong families to support those workers.

References

Barnett, Rosalind C. 2004. Work hours as a predictor of stress outcomes. Paper presented at the Conference on Long Working Hours, Safety, and Health: Toward a National Research Agenda, 29–30 April, Baltimore, MD.

Belkin, Lisa. 26 October 2003. The opt-out revolution. *New York Times Magazine*.

Bianchi, Suzanne M. 2000. Maternal employment and time with children: Dramatic change or surprising continuity? *Demography* 37 (4): 139–54.

Bianchi, Suzanne M. 2006. Mothers and daughters "do," fathers "don't do" family: Gender and generational bonds. *Journal of Marriage and Family* 68 (4): 812–16.

Bianchi, Suzanne M. 2009. "What gives" when mothers are employed? Parental time allocation in dual- and single-earner two-parent families. In *Handbook of families and work*, eds. D. Russell Crane and E. Jeffrey Hill, 305–30. Lanham, MD: University Press of America.

Bianchi, Suzanne M., and Sara Raley. 2005. Time allocation in working families. In *Work, family, health, and well-being*, eds. Suzanne M. Bianchi, Lynne M. Casper, and Rosalind B. King, 21–42. Mahwah: NJ: Lawrence Erlbaum.

Bianchi, Suzanne M., John P. Robinson, and Melissa Milkie. 2006. *Changing rhythms of American family life*. New York, NY: Russell Sage Foundation.

Bianchi, Suzanne M. and Vanessa Wight. 2010. The long reach of the job: Employment and time for family life. In *Workplace flexibility: Realigning 20th century jobs to 21st century workers*, eds. Kathleen Christensen and Barbara Schneider. Ithaca, NY: Cornell University Press.

Bianchi, Suzanne M., Vanessa R. Wight, and Sara B. Raley. 2005. Maternal employment and family caregiving: Rethinking time with children in the ATUS. Paper presented at the ATUS Early Results Conference, 5–6 December, Bethesda, MD.

Blair-Loy, Mary. 2003. *Competing devotions: Career and family among women executives*. Cambridge, MA: Harvard University Press.

Boushey, Heather. 2005. Are women opting out? Debunking the myth. Center for Economic Policy Research Briefing Paper, Washington, DC.

Budig, Michelle J., and Paula England. 2001. The wage penalty for motherhood. *American Sociological Review* 66 (2): 204–25.

Carlson, Marcia J., and Sara S. McLanahan. 2010. Fathers in fragile families. In *The role of the father in child development*, 5th edition, ed. Michael E. Lamb, 241–69. Hoboken, NJ: Wiley.

Casper, Lynne M., and Suzanne M. Bianchi. 2002. *Continuity and change in the American family*. Thousand Oaks, CA: Sage.

Casper, Lynne, and Martin O'Connell. 1998. Work, income, the economy, and married fathers as child care providers. *Demography* 35 (2): 243–50.

Cherlin, Andrew. 2009. *The marriage-go-round*. New York, NY: Vintage Books.

Christensen, Kathleen. 2005. Achieving work-life balance: Strategies for dual-earner families. In *Being together, working apart: Dual-career families and the work-life balance*, eds. Barbara Schneider and Linda Waite, 449–57. New York, NY: Cambridge University Press.

Coleman, Marilyn, and Lawrence H. Ganong. 2008. Normative beliefs about sharing housing with an older family member. *International Journal of Aging and Human Development* 66 (1): 49–72.

Cotter, David A., Joan A. Hermsen, and Reeve Vanneman. 2004. *Gender inequality at work*. The American People Census 2000 Series. New York, NY: Russell Sage Foundation and Population Reference Bureau.

Crouter, Ann C., Matthew F. Bumpus, Melissa R. Head, and Susan M. McHale. 2001. Implications of overwork and overload for the quality of men's family relationships. *Journal of Marriage & Family* 63 (2): 404–16.

Crouter, Ann C., Heather Helms-Erikson, Kimberly Updegraff, and Susan M. McHale. 1999. Conditions underlying parents' knowledge about children's daily lives in middle childhood: Between- and within-family comparisons. *Child Development* 70 (1): 246–59.

Crouter, Ann C., and Susan McHale. 2005. Work, family, and children's time: Implications for youth. In *Work, family, health, and well-being*, eds. Suzanne M. Bianchi, Lynne M. Casper, and Rosalind B. King, 21–42. Mahwah: NJ: Lawrence Erlbaum.

Dye, Jane L. 2008. *Fertility of American women 2006*. Current Population Reports, P20-558. Washington, DC: U.S. Census Bureau.

Friedan, Betty. 1963. *The feminine mystique*. New York, NY: Norton.

Furstenberg, Frank F., Jr. 2010. On a new schedule: Transitions to adulthood and family change. *Future of Children* 20 (1): 67–87.

Gauthier, Anne H., Timothy M. Smeeding, and Frank F. Furstenberg, Jr., 2004. Are parents investing less time in children? Trends in selected industrialized countries. *Population and Development Review* 30 (4): 647–71.

Gendell, Maury. 2008. Older workers: Increasing their labor force participation and hours of work. *Monthly Labor Review* 131 (1): 41–54.

Gornick, Janet C., and Marcia K. Meyers. 2003. *Families that work: Policies for reconciling parenthood and employment.* New York, NY: Russell Sage Foundation.

Hamilton, Brady E., Joyce A. Martin, and Stephanie J. Ventura. 2009. Births: Preliminary data for 2007. *National Vital Statistics Reports* 57 (12): 1–23.

Hays, Sharon. 1996. *The cultural contradictions of motherhood.* New Haven, CT: Yale University Press.

He, Wan, Manisha Sengupta, Victoria Velkoff, and Kimberly DeBarros. 2005. *65+ in the United States: 2005.* U.S. Census Bureau, Current Population Reports Special Studies no. P23-209. Washington, DC: Government Printing Office.

Hofferth, Sandra L., Joseph Pleck, Jeffrey L. Stueve, Suzanne Bianchi, and Liana Sayer. 2002. The demography of fathers: What fathers do. In *Handbook of father involvement: Multidisciplinary perspectives,* eds. Catherine Tamis-LeMonda and Natasha Cabrera, 63–90. Mahwah, NJ: Lawrence Erlbaum.

Hoffman, Saul D. 2009. The changing impact of marriage and children on women's labor force participation. *Monthly Labor Review* 132 (2): 3–14.

Hughes, Diane, Ellen Galinsky, and Anne Morris. 1992. The effects of job characteristics on marital quality: Specifying linking mechanisms. *Journal of Marriage & Family* 54 (1): 31–42.

Jacobs, Jerry A., and Kathleen Gerson. 2004. *The time divide: Work, family and gender inequality.* Cambridge, MA: Harvard University Press.

Johnson, John H. 2004. Do long work hours contribute to divorce? *Topics in Economic Analysis and Policy* 4 (1): 9–23.

Joshi, Heather. 1998. The opportunity costs of childbearing: More than mothers' business. *Journal of Population Economics* 11 (2): 161–83.

Joshi, Heather. 2002. Production, reproduction, and education: Women, children, and work in British perspective. *Population and Development Review* 28 (3): 445–74.

Kahn, Joan R., Brittany McGill, and Suzanne M. Bianchi. 2011. Help to family and friends: Are there gender differences at older ages? *Journal of Marriage and Family* 73 (1): 77–92.

Kendig, Sarah, and Suzanne M. Bianchi. 2008. Single, cohabitating, and married mothers' time with children. *Journal of Marriage and Family* 70 (5): 1228–40.

Kreider, Rose M., and Diana R. Elliott. 2009. *America's families and living arrangements: 2007.* Current Population Reports, P20-561. Washington, DC: U.S. Census Bureau.

Klerman, Jacob A., and Arleen Leibowitz. 1999. Job continuity among new mothers. *Demography* 36 (2): 145–55.

Lareau, Annette. 2003. *Unequal childhoods: Class, race, and family life.* Berkeley and Los Angeles: University of California Press.

Lareau, Annette, and Elliot Wieninger. 2008. Time, work and family life: Reconceptualizing gendered time patterns through the case of children's organized activities. *Sociological Forum* 23 (3): 419–54.

McDonald, Peter. 2000. Gender equity in theories of fertility transition. *Population and Development Review* 26 (3): 427–39.

Milkie, Melissa A., Marybeth J. Mattingly, Kei Nomaguchi, Suzanne M. Bianchi, and John P. Robinson. 2004. The time squeeze: Parental statuses and feelings about time with children. *Journal of Marriage and Family* 66 (3): 739–61.

Morgan, S. Philip. Forthcoming. Thinking about demographic family differences. In *Social class and changing families in an unequal America,* eds. Marcia Carlson and Paula England. Palo Alto, CA: Stanford University Press.

Nomaguchi, Kei, Melissa Milkie, and Suzanne M. Bianchi. 2005. Time strains and psychological well-being: Do dual-earner mothers and fathers differ? *Journal of Family Issues* 26 (6): 756–92.

Pierret, Charles R. 2006. The "sandwich generation": Women caring for parents and children. *Monthly Labor Review* 129 (9): 3–9.

Presser, Harriet B. 2000. Nonstandard work schedules and marital instability. *Journal of Marriage and Family* 62 (1): 93–110.

Presser, Harriet B. 2003. *Working in a 24/7 economy: Challenges for American families.* New York, NY: Russell Sage Foundation.

Ramey, Garey, and Valerie A. Ramey. 2010. The rug rat race. *Brookings Papers on Economic Activity* (Spring): 129–76.

Reynolds, Jeremy. 2005. In the face of conflict: Work-life conflict and desired work hour adjustments. *Journal of Marriage and Family* 67 (5): 1313–31.

Sayer, Liana C., Suzanne M. Bianchi, and John P. Robinson. 2004. Are parents investing less in children? Trends in mothers' and fathers' time with children. *American Journal of Sociology* 110 (1): 1–43.

Schoeni, Robert F., and Karen E. Ross. 2004. Material assistance received from families during the transition to adulthood. In *On the frontier of adulthood: Theory, research, and public policy*, eds. Richard A. Settersten Jr., Frank F. Furstenberg Jr., and Ruben G. Rumbaut, 396–416. Chicago, IL: University of Chicago Press.

Stone, Pamela. 2007. *Opting out? Why women really quit careers and head home*. Berkeley and Los Angeles: University of California Press.

Taylor, Paul, Carolyn Funk, and Alison Clark. 2007. *From 1997 to 2007: Fewer mothers prefer full-time work*. Washington, DC: Pew Research Center.

Uhlenberg, Peter. 2005. Historical forces shaping grandparent-grandchild relationships: Demography and beyond. *Annual Review of Gerontology and Geriatrics* 24 (1): 77–97.

U.S. Census Bureau. 10 November 2010. Press release. Available from www.census.gov/newsroom/releases/archives/families_households/.

Vickery, Clair. 1977. The time-poor: A new look at poverty. *Journal of Human Resources* 12 (1): 27–48.

Waldfogel, Jane. 1997. The effect of children on women's wages. *American Sociological Review* 62 (2): 209–17.

Wight, Vanessa, Sara Raley, and Suzanne M. Bianchi. 2008. Time for children, spouse and self among parents who work nonstandard hours. *Social Forces* 87 (1): 243–74.

The Cost of Workplace Flexibility for High-Powered Professionals

The authors study the pecuniary penalties for family-related amenities in the workplace (e.g., job interruptions, short hours, part-time work, and flexibility during the workday), how women have responded to them, and how the penalties have changed over time. The pecuniary penalties to behaviors that are beneficial to family appear to have decreased in many professions. Self-employment has declined in many of the high-end professions (e.g., pharmacy, optometry, dentistry, law, medicine, and veterinary medicine) where it was costly in terms of workplace flexibility. The authors conclude that many professions have experienced an increase in workplace flexibility, driven often by exogenous factors (e.g., increased scale of operations and shifts to corporate ownership of business) but also endogenously because of an increased number of women. Workplace flexibility in some positions, notably in the business and financial sectors, has lagged.

Keywords: workplace flexibility; occupational choice; compensating differentials; careers; professions; gender; family

By
CLAUDIA GOLDIN
and
LAWRENCE F. KATZ

W e explore the cost of workplace flexibility for occupations at the upper end of the education and income spectra. We study the pecuniary penalties for various family-related amenities, how women have responded to them, and whether the

Claudia Goldin is Henry Lee Professor of Economics at Harvard University and director of the Development of the American Economy Program at the National Bureau of Economic Research (NBER). She is the coauthor (with Lawrence F. Katz) of The Race between Education and Technology *(Belknap Press 2008).*

Lawrence F. Katz is Elizabeth Allison Professor of Economics at Harvard University and a research associate at the NBER. He is the coauthor (with Claudia Goldin) of The Race between Education and Technology *(Belknap Press 2008).*

NOTE: This article summarizes part of the authors' ongoing project on career and family. A longer, more complete version of the article will be issued as "The Career Cost of Family." Goldin gratefully acknowledges sabbatical support from the Alfred P. Sloan Foundation and data from the American Veterinary Medical Association.

DOI: 10.1177/0002716211414398

penalties have changed over time. We find that the costs of workplace flexibility vary greatly across high-end careers. More important is that the cost appears to have decreased over time in many of them.

The costs of workplace flexibility include penalties to labor supply behavior that is more compatible with having a family. These behaviors include job interruptions, short hours, part-time work during some part of the working life, and work flexibility during the day. Self-employment in professions with office practices (e.g., dentists) or in retail sales (e.g., pharmacists) often requires more hours of work because of classic agency problems. Self-employment in these professions allows less workplace flexibility. In other professions, however, where self-employment does not involve considerable investment in capital and the management of other workers (e.g., management consulting), it gives women the ability to employ themselves for shorter hours and with greater flexibility than allowed in the corporate sector.

Individuals make career choices at various moments in their life cycles with imperfect knowledge about the workplace flexibility penalties and uncertainty about their family responsibilities. People sort across careers for various reasons, and career and family goals are two of them. As the penalties to family have decreased in various careers, women have flocked to them.

The choice that employees make is not between having some workplace flexibility and having no workplace flexibility. Their decision concerns how much they are willing to pay for flexibility. The cost of flexibility differs by industry and by occupation. Employees have different demands for workplace flexibility and are willing to pay different amounts. The equilibrium cost of workplace flexibility is the trade-off between earnings and the amenity. Such costs derive from the supply and demand for workplace flexibility.

Many occupations at the upper end of the income and education distributions have experienced large changes in the costs of providing flexibility as well as in the demand for workplace flexibility. The labor market equilibrates the two sides of the market (the demand for flexibility and the supply of it) and generates different amounts of workplace flexibility and different costs.

We develop a framework to understand the impact of demand-side changes by individuals who want a more family-friendly workplace and the impact of supply-side changes by firms with changing costs of providing these amenities. We then present vignettes for various high-end professions and subspecialties within professions. The implications of the framework are considered concerning changes in the cost of the amenity, the fraction female in the profession or subspecialty, the gender gap in earnings, the fraction working part time, and the fraction who are self-employed. We end with an analysis of about ninety of the highest-paying and most skilled occupations, showing that some impose greater penalties than others on women and men who would like workplace flexibility.

A Compensating Differentials Framework of Gender Differences in Earnings and Occupations

Certain occupations at the high end are more enabling of family than are other high-income jobs, and some firms are more family-friendly than are others. Many professions now have more workplace flexibility than they had a few decades ago. What these statements generally translate into is that occupations and professions differ in their pecuniary penalties for certain characteristics that are considered family-friendly amenities. What happens in the labor market when there is a shift in worker demand for greater flexibility? What happens when there is a technological change that reduces the costs of providing such flexibility? To explore these questions, we develop a model of an occupation having an amenity that is costly to offer.

We model the provision of the amenity, such as workplace flexibility, by borrowing from Sherwin Rosen's (1986) model of "compensating differentials," which in turn is a formalization of ideas dating back to Adam Smith.[1] The model reveals the differential impacts of an increase in the demand for the amenity (or a decreased willingness to work with the disamenity) and a decrease in the cost of providing the amenity (or reducing the disamenity).

We do not have the space here to explain the full model in detail. It is contained in our longer work (Goldin and Katz forthcoming). Various aspects of work are disamenities to some but are not overly bothersome to others. We focus on workplace flexibility, but these disamenities can include workplace hazards among others. The ability to shift hours during the day may be highly valued by some but not worth much to others. The fact that some professions heavily penalize job interruptions and disproportionately tax short hours may be important to some workers and not to others. The same is true with other aspects of workplace family-friendliness, including the provision of on-site daycare and paid family leave policy.

We model the amenity of job flexibility as a discrete variable. Jobs are either inflexible or flexible. The inflexible jobs come with a disamenity ($D = 1$). Alternatively, jobs can be flexible and not have the disamenity ($D = 0$).

On the demand side of the market for the amenity, workers value income and they are assumed to be heterogeneous in their tastes for the disamenity (D). Assume that the compensating differential in earnings between a job with the disamenity and one without is ΔW. Workers who have a high value for the amenity will opt for the job without the disamenity and will pay ΔW for it. Alternatively, those who have a low value for it will not.

On the supply side of the market, the firms' technologies that produce the amenity (or that ameliorate the disamenity) are assumed to be distributed continuously. Firms are assumed to be heterogeneous in the productivity benefit of the disamenity and thus in the costs of getting rid of it. For some firms or sectors, the provision of part-time work is not costly, whereas for others it is. If ΔW^* is the given wage differential firms are paying to employees who take the disamenity, the firms with lower costs of providing the amenity would do so, and firms with higher costs would not.

The equilibrium for the amenity occurs when its supply equals its demand. If the supply of the amenity is equal to the demand for the amenity at the going wage differential, then the market is in equilibrium. If the supply of the amenity were greater than its demand, the price of the amenity (the wage differential) would fall, and if the supply were less than the demand, the price of the amenity would rise.

The model can be made relevant to the issues explored here by considering two types of workers: males and females. If at every ΔW, women demand more of the amenity than men, men will walk away with a higher salary and incur the disamenity about which they care little.

Two main changes can alter the equilibrium. The first is a labor supply shift. An influx of women (who presumably are more willing than men to pay for the amenity) into an occupation will mean that, at the going wage differential, demand for the amenity will exceed its supply, and the price of the amenity will rise. A larger wage differential between jobs with and without the amenity will result, the fraction of jobs offering the amenity will increase, and a greater fraction of men who opt for the amenity will decrease since they are less willing to pay for it.

If, on the other hand, the cost of providing the amenity (or, alternatively, the productive benefit of the disamenity) decreases, more firms will want to offer the amenity at the current wage difference, and pressure will mount for ΔW to decrease to attract more workers to purchase the amenity. More men and more women will shift into flexible jobs, but it is likely that relatively more women than men will be enticed into these positions. Men, in fact, might shift into the more highly compensated inflexible jobs.

In sum, the framework shows that individuals with a greater willingness to pay for the amenity earn less than others and that a decrease in the cost of supplying the amenity increases their relative earnings. An increase in the supply of individuals who value the amenity will increase the equilibrium amount paid for the amenity and widen the gap in earnings between men and women. We present evidence for several professions suggesting that the provision of job flexibility changed exogenously and due to supply-side factors. But we also present evidence showing that the supply of the amenity, and probably its price, was responsive to increased demands for more flexibility within occupations and sectors.

The compensating differentials framework embeds two cases to understand the dynamics of workplace flexibility and gender earning differences in the workplace. One case is that the change in workplace flexibility comes about because of an increase in the group with the greater demand for the amenity or comes about because of a change in preferences for the amenity. That is the demand-side case. The implications are (1) an increase in the cost of the amenity and, by implication, an increase in the gender gap of earnings; and (2) an increase in the fraction of the total workforce with the amenity (but a decrease in the fraction of men with the amenity since its price rises). In the other case, the costs to firms of providing the amenity or of reducing the amount of the disamenity decreases.

That is the supply-side case. The implications are (1) a decrease in the cost of the amenity and, by implication, a decrease in the gender gap of earnings; and (2) an increase in the fraction of the total workforce with the amenity (and an increase in the fraction of men with the amenity since its price decreases).

In both cases, a higher fraction of workers will take the amenity after the change, although it will be greater in the second case. The major difference between the two cases concerns the equilibrium wage difference. In the first case the gender gap in earnings increases; in the second case it decreases.

Earnings Penalties for Job Interruptions

Earnings penalties for job interruptions differ greatly by type of advanced degree. The clearest evidence we have encountered of these penalties comes from our Harvard and Beyond (H&B) survey data. The H&B surveyed members of Harvard College's graduating classes from 1969 to 1992 (see Goldin and Katz 2008). A large fraction of the women (and men) in these classes—around 60 to 65 percent—pursued one of the four advanced degrees: MBA, JD, MD, and PhD.

The penalty incurred from taking time off is largest proportionately for MBAs. The MDs have the lowest penalty, and the PhDs and JDs are in the middle of the pack. These penalties are computed from the (log) earnings regressions given in Table 1. The log earnings penalty experienced by individuals from each of the four degree groups, had they a job interruption of one-tenth of their post-BA period, is 53 log points for the MBAs and 34 log points for the PhDs and JDs but just 17 log points for the MDs. Translated into the fraction of earnings forgone, MBAs give up 41 percent, PhDs and JDs 29 percent, and MDs just 16 percent for a job interruption equivalent to 18 months during the 15 years after receiving their BA.

Job interruptions are entered in the regressions as "any job interruption" (a dummy variable) and as the "share of post-BA years" in which the individual was not employed (a continuous variable).[2] The penalty for "any job interruption" is substantial for the MBAs and is larger than that for any of the other three degree groups. The MDs have almost no penalty for "any job interruption," and all of their loss comes from actual time off. The JDs and PhDs are penalized moderately for both.

Occupational Vignettes

Women at the top of the educational distribution have been heading in great numbers to various professions. As can be seen in the top part of Figure 1, women have increased their presence in many high-end professions, such as medicine, law, and business, less so in dentistry. The fraction female among first-year law students increased from around 5 percent in the late 1960s to more than 30

TABLE 1

Penalties from Job Interruptions by Highest Degree: Log Earnings Regressions for Four Career Tracks Using the Harvard and Beyond Data

Log (Annual Earnings) in 2005	(1) MBA	(2) JD	(3) MD	(4) PhD
Female	−0.441 (0.0979)	−0.370 (0.0667)	−0.332 (0.0466)	−0.310 (0.0509)
Job interruptions ≥ 6 months				
Any	−0.449 (0.103)	−0.299 (0.0743)	−0.0637 (0.0687)	−0.368 (0.0664)
Share of post-BA years	−0.819 (0.487)	−0.463 (0.351)	−1.09 (0.382)	0.297 (0.276)
GPA at Harvard	0.711 (0.127)	0.580 (0.0902)	0.114 (0.0690)	0.226 (0.0790)
SAT math × 10^{-2}	−0.0670 (0.0721)	0.0377 (0.0501)	0.0311 (0.0431)	0.0527 (0.0442)
SAT verbal × 10^{-2}	−0.149 (0.0689)	−0.0419 (0.0498)	−0.112 (0.0352)	−0.107 (0.0428)
Dummy variables				
Part-time, full-year	−0.452 (0.193)	−0.661 (0.145)	−0.464 (0.143)	−0.625 (0.129)
Full-time, part-year	−0.785 (0.162)	−0.786 (0.112)	−0.608 (0.0707)	−0.734 (0.0969)
Part-time, part-year	−1.67 (0.149)	−1.67 (0.123)	−1.88 (0.126)	−1.43 (0.103)
49 Harvard concentrations	Yes	Yes	Yes	Yes
Year of Harvard graduation	Yes	Yes	Yes	Yes
R^2	.433	.387	.442	.401
Number of observations	944	1,381	1,064	1,190
Penalty from job interruptions of 0.1 of post-BA years	53.1 log points	34.5 log points	17.3 log points	33.8 log points

SOURCE: Harvard and Beyond data. See Goldin and Katz (2008). The full sample is used here and consists of three "cohorts" of Harvard College graduates: graduating 1969–1972 (plus women from 1973), 1979–1982, 1989–1992.

NOTE: The dependent variable is annual earnings in 2005 dollars. Standard errors are in parentheses under the coefficients. The omitted dummy for work status is full-time, full-year. Dummy variables for missing GPA and missing SAT are included. The last line ("penalty from job interruptions of 0.1 of post-BA years") is computed from the coefficients under "job interruptions."

FIGURE 1
Fraction Female among Professional School Graduates, c. 1955 to c. 2010

A. Four Larger Professions

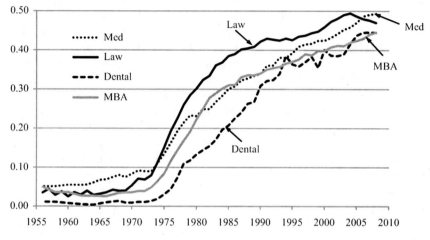

Year of Professional School Graduation

B. Four Smaller Professions

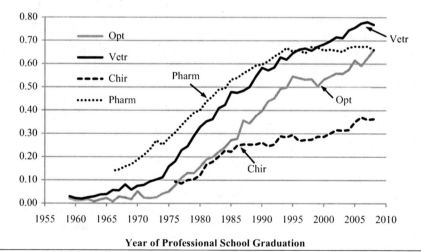

Year of Professional School Graduation

SOURCE: See data appendix in Goldin and Katz (forthcoming).

percent in the late 1970s and reached approximate parity with men in about 2000. The increase among MBAs was also rapid in the 1970s, although the levels were lower and continue to be below those achieved by women in law and medicine. In dentistry, which appears to have been eschewed by women, an increase is apparent in the late 1970s.

As can be seen in the bottom of Figure 1, women have also greatly increased their numbers in some of the smaller high-end professions, such as veterinary medicine, pharmacy, and optometry, less so in chiropractic medicine. In fact, some of the largest gains can be found in many of the smaller professions. Among these, veterinary medicine is the most striking. Whereas women were less than 10 percent of all graduating veterinarians in 1970, they are almost 80 percent in the most recent years. Optometry, once a male bastion, is about 60 percent female now. Pharmacy graduates are also around 60 percent female now but were 30 percent in the mid-1970s. Women were pharmacy graduates to a greater degree than these other professions in the earliest years in the figures, but they have clearly increased in number even as the requirements to be a practicing pharmacist have increased.[3]

But have women been heading in the direction of greater workplace flexibility and a lower price to this choice, or have they simply been going into professions that were previously male-dominated and were at the top of the salary and prestige hierarchy?

In general, women appear to be moving in the direction of choosing professions and specialties within professions that are consistent with their greater desire for workplace flexibility. Although some professions have changed exogenously, largely due to changes in the scale of operations, other professions and worksites have changed because of the influx of women. Both changes have altered the trade-offs between work amenities desired by women, such as workplace flexibility, and their earnings per unit time. It is more difficult to model and analyze the impact that women have had on professions as they have greatly increased their employment share in these professions.

For each of the four professions—medicine, veterinary medicine, business, and pharmacy—we discuss evidence that we have currently assembled on aspects of workplace flexibility; earnings trade-offs; and choice across specialties, practice settings, and worksites. These vignettes are suggestive and will form the basis of a larger study. Of the various professions that we have included here, the largest in terms of degrees awarded in 2008 is business, with more than 155,000 graduates. Medicine is a distant second with 15,646, and pharmacy is next with 10,932. Veterinary medicine is the smallest, with just 2,504 degrees awarded.

Medicine

Women have greatly increased in number in medicine. But they have increased in relative number in some specialties far more than in others, according to the most recent data from 2007. As can be seen in the top portion of Figure 2, younger female physicians (under 45 years old) are 42 percent of all physicians

FIGURE 2
Fraction Female by Physician Specialty and Age of Physician, 2007

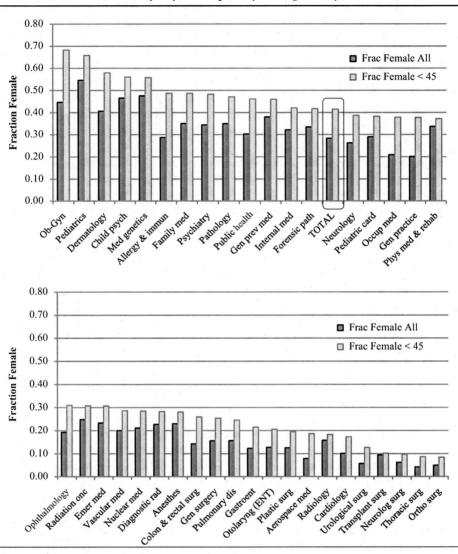

SOURCE: American Medical Association (2009).

(see the "total" group). But they dominate Ob-Gyn, pediatrics, dermatology, child psychiatry, and medical genetics, in which they are more than half of all specialists. They exceed their average of 42 percent, but are less than 50 percent, in allergy and immunology, family practice, psychiatry, pathology, public health, general preventive medicine, internal medicine, and forensic pathology.[4] The bottom portion of Figure 2, which continues the graph, reveals that the younger group of female physicians are rare in fields such as gastroenterology, otolaryngology, plastic surgery, aerospace medicine, radiology, cardiology, and various surgical specialties (urological, transplant, neurological, thoracic, and orthopedic).

Not only are the levels different across the specialties, ranging from almost 70 percent to less than 10 percent, but the rates of increase also differ in interesting ways. The ratio of the two bars (the lighter vs. the darker) shows the growth or slowdown of women in each of the specialties relative to men or to all in that specialty.[5] Women have increased their fraction in all of the specialties, and that is not surprising, given that women are 42 percent of the under-45-year-old group and 46 percent of the under-35-year-old group, but 28 percent of all included physicians.

Some specialties have had a large fraction of women for a long time (e.g., pediatrics), whereas others have a low fraction of women (e.g., surgical specialties). Some have had extremely large increases in the fraction female, as is the case for Ob-Gyn, dermatology, allergy and immunology, and occupational medicine. Others that were once popular among women (e.g., diagnostic radiology, radiology, and anesthesiology) have had relatively slow growth. On the other hand, some at the low end, such as colon and rectal surgery, gastroenterology, ophthalmology, and urology, have had large increases in women. What can account for the levels differences and changes in the fraction female among the various specialties?

We have used various printed guides (e.g., Iserson 2006; Freeman 2007) intended to assist medical students in making decisions about residency and fellowship programs and to obtain information on the requirements and work life for each of the specialties. Because requirements for each specialty can change, we first examine the relationship between fairly recent data on clinical and patient hours per week and the fraction female among those less than 45 years old.

Women appear to be attracted to specialties with lower weekly hours, although the causation could be that specialties with a higher fraction female have lower average hours because women work fewer hours by choice.[6] The surgical specialties tend to be in the higher end of the hours distribution, but there may be other reasons why women eschew many of the surgical fields, including their longer residency period. But even without the various surgical specialties, the relationship between hours and fraction female is still negative.

Weekly clinical and patient hours do not provide a complete picture of the time demands of physicians. A complementary indicator of workload, and one that is more exogenous than actual hours, is whether the specialty has on-call, emergency, or night hours on a regular basis. We created an indicator variable for this characteristic. The specialties that have relatively few younger female physicians are generally those with more excessive demands. Among the twenty-six specialties with information on workload characteristics, eight of the thirteen with the lowest fraction female had high demands, but just three of the thirteen with the highest fraction female had high demands (one of which is Ob-Gyn). Women, in addition, are less apt to be in specialties with the longest residency and fellowship training periods.

Some physician specialties have undergone large changes in the fraction female during the past several decades. The reason for the change often reveals much about the demand for workplace amenities. Gastroenterology provides one of the best examples. For years, this specialty was among those with the lowest fraction female. In 2007, just 5 percent of these specialists were women 55 to 64 years old, 11 percent were 45 to 54 years old, 18 percent were in the 35- to 44-year-old group, and 30 percent were less than 35 years old. One of the reasons for the large shift of women to this specialty is the expansion of routine and scheduled colonoscopies. That growth meant a large increase in the demand for those who perform colonoscopies, such as gastroenterologists and colon and rectal surgeons.[7]

Veterinary medicine

The fraction female among veterinarians from the 1970s to the present day is one of the largest among all the professions, rising from around 10 percent for those graduating more than three decades ago and currently 60 years old to almost 80 percent for the most recent graduates of veterinary colleges. What are the reasons for women's enormous inroads in this field? Female veterinarians like to emphasize their attraction to the caring nature of their profession, but that aspect of the job has not changed much. Compelling evidence suggests that the increasing ability of many veterinarians to schedule their hours and reduce or eliminate on-call, night, and weekend hours has been a contributory factor.

The organizational changes that transformed many veterinary practices involve the rise of regional veterinary hospitals and other emergency facilities. During nights and weekends, these hospitals care for the clients of smaller veterinary practices, allowing these practices to be closed during all but regular daytime hours. Another factor is that female veterinarians appear to shy away from being equity stakeholders in their practices, and there is a recent movement to larger, corporate ownership of veterinary practices. These two factors are not the only reasons for the relative increase of female veterinarians.

Because the total number of active veterinarians in the nation is small (probably around sixty thousand), the more usual sources, such as the Current Population Survey (CPS) and even the decennial census, do not yield adequate information with which to explore the preferences of female veterinarians relative to male veterinarians and to understand the time series changes.[8] We are fortunate to have a data set of almost four thousand veterinarians in 2007 from a biennial survey taken by the American Veterinary Medical Association (AVMA).[9]

The AVMA data show that female veterinarians decrease their hours of work a few years after joining a practice and then, if the cross-section data provide any guide, continue to work considerably shorter hours than male veterinarians. Their hours of work average around 44 per week, whereas male veterinarians average around 53.

Related to the data on hours of work is that, among the ever-married group, more than 20 percent of female veterinarians work part time from their late 30s to their early 50s (once again, if the cross-section is a reasonable guide). Among male veterinarians, less than 5 percent work part time. The interesting finding for female veterinarians is that part-time work is relatively the same from around the mid-30s to the early 50s. It would appear that ever-married women decide to work shorter hours or to have no on-call, night, and weekend hours when young and then continue with that routine.

About 40 percent of female veterinarians in private practice in 2007 (versus 27 percent of male veterinarians) stated that they put in no emergency hours. Rural veterinarians and those outside major urban areas put in more emergency hours than did those in large cities, and many worked on-call and had night duty. But hours in general for veterinarians are lower than are those for physicians, and a greater fraction work part time.

A far higher fraction of male than female veterinarians in private practice have an equity stake in their practices, and men have considerably more of their own funds invested given that more men have any equity stake. These relationships exist across all ages and are not just a product of the more recent surge in female veterinary students. The fraction of women with an equity stake is less than half that for men at all ages. Whereas about 75 percent of male veterinarians in private practice in their late 40s and 50s have some equity stake in their practices, about 35 percent of female veterinarians do. In addition, conditional on having any equity stake, male veterinarians have a far higher amount invested in their practices. On average, men have almost $100,000 more than women invested in their practices, given their age.[10]

An important factor to emphasize is the impact of taking any time off from veterinary practice. We showed earlier that the career penalty from job interruptions, using our H&B data, varied considerably by profession. MDs had the lowest penalties and MBAs the highest. The penalty for time off using our veterinary data is relatively small—just 9 log points for any time off. It is closer to the estimate for the MDs in the H&B data than it is to that for any of the other professions. When the specification is identical to the one we use for the H&B data (see Table 1), the impact of any time off is no different from zero, and the entire impact of job interruptions comes from the amount of time off rather than whether any time was taken.

In sum, women have greatly increased in number in veterinary medicine. There is no specialty in medicine that has a greater fraction female and none in which the fraction female has increased as much since 1970. Female veterinarians state that they find the field attractive because of their love of animals and because they do not have to interact as much with the public as in medicine. But the extraordinary relative growth among women is probably due to changes in the organization of the industry, which, in turn, may have been hastened by a critical mass of female veterinarians.

MBAs: The corporate and financial sectors

We noted earlier that among the most numerically important professions in our H&B sample, MBA women have the lowest labor force participation rates, the longest periods of job interruption when they have children, and forfeit the largest fraction of their income when they take time off. To understand why MBA women's career trajectories are more extreme than those of other female professionals and to comprehend how women have fared in this highly lucrative sector, Marianne Bertrand and the two of us surveyed the 1990 to 2006 MBA graduates from the Chicago Booth School (Bertrand, Goldin, and Katz 2010).

Our sample consisted of about twenty-five hundred MBA graduates, 25 percent of whom are female. Because the survey is retrospective, the resulting data set contains more than 18,000 person-years on earnings and hours, other employment information, and detailed information on marriage and family.

At the start of their careers, earnings by gender are almost identical. But five years out, a thirty-log-point difference in annual earnings develops, and 10 to 16 years out the gender gap in earnings grows to sixty log points (or that uncorrected, women earn 55 percent what men do). Three factors in our data set can explain 84 percent of the gap. Training prior to MBA receipt (for example, finance courses and GPA) accounts for 24 percent. Career interruptions and job experience account for 30 percent, and differences in weekly hours are the remaining 30 percent. All aspects of the gender labor supply gap expand with time since MBA including the fraction not working in a year, the part-time share, and hours worked among full-time workers.

The dynamics of gender differences in labor supply can be seen in changes in hours per week with time since MBA; share working full time, full year (FT-FY), which declines to about 0.60 for women; and the share not working, which rises to about 0.17 for women. Thus at 10 to 16 years out, 23 percent of Booth School MBA women who are in the labor force work part time. Cumulative time not working is about one year for all women 10 to 16 years after the MBA. At 10 to 16 years out, 60 percent work FT-FY; 51 percent do, for those with children; the rest is about equally divided between part-time work and opting out. Interestingly, more than half of those working part time employ themselves.

The gender gap in earnings, as we noted, is small directly following MBA receipt and then widens substantially. But even this gap can be largely "explained" by the three main factors: training prior to the MBA and MBA coursework, career interruptions, and job experience and hours worked. Importantly, there is a large penalty from taking *any* time out, which is about two-thirds of the total penalty from job interruptions.

Not surprisingly, children are the main contributors to labor supply differences, such as career interruptions and hours worked. Women with children have labor force rates that are 20 percentage points lower than are men's or women's without children. They work 24 percent fewer hours than men or women without children. The impact of children on female labor supply differs strongly by spousal education or income. MBA moms with high-earning spouses (>$200,000 in 2006 dollars) have labor force rates that are 18.5 percentage points lower than those with lesser earning spouses. They work 19 percent fewer hours (when working) than those with median or lower earning spouses. MBA moms with non-high-earning spouses show no effect on participation from kids, but they do work fewer hours than women without kids. The effect of husband's income, moreover, holds up in individual fixed-effects estimation.

Another important result is that the impact of a birth on labor supply grows over time in an individual, fixed-effects estimation. The effect after one year is about 60 percent to 70 percent the effect measured at five-plus years. A year after a first birth, women's hours are reduced by 17 percent and their participation by 13 percent. But three to four years later, hours decline by 24 percent and participation by 18 percent. It is as if some MBA moms try to stay in the fast lane but ultimately find it is unworkable. The increased impact years after the first birth, moreover, is not due to additional births.

One of the most revealing parts of the analysis, and one that hints at the mechanism, comes from dividing the sample by the income of the husbands. Women with richer husbands decrease their participation by 31.5 percentage points, work 20 percent fewer hours, and earn about $200,000 less at five years since the first birth than they otherwise would. The changes, moreover, increase significantly with time since the birth. Those with lower-income husbands do not decrease their participation and have a far lower "hit" to their income; although they do work fewer hours.

Women who marry high-earning spouses and who do not have children work more, not less, than those who marry the lower-earning spouses. The interaction of kids and high-earning husbands is what matters.

Part-time work in the corporate sector is uncommon, and part-timers are often self-employed (more than half are at 10 to 16 years out). Because of the use of self-employment, the opt-out group is actually smaller than the part-timers. Disparities in career interruptions and hours worked by gender are not large, but the corporate and financial sectors impose heavy penalties on deviation from the norm. Some female MBAs with children, especially those with high-earning husbands, find the trade-offs too steep and leave or engage in self-employment.

In sum, the MBA lure for women is large—incomes are substantial even though they are far lower than those of their male peers. But some women with children find the inflexibility of the work insurmountable. Some leave or become self-employed. Gender differences in labor supply are largely driven by the presence of children, and those with well-off spouses exit the labor force more often and work fewer hours. MBA moms with less well-off spouses employ more childcare services, whereas those with high-income spouses who drop out take care of their own kids. When MBA moms leave the labor force, they give "family" as the reason, not career, and therefore it does not appear that MBA moms are forced out.

Pharmacy

The pharmacy industry experienced large structural changes precisely when female pharmacists greatly increased in number. Women were about 8 percent of all pharmacists in 1966 and are almost 60 percent today. Similarly, the fraction female among pharmacy school graduates increased from 14 percent in the mid-1960s to almost 70 percent today (see Figure 3).

Pharmacists are found in several sectors. The most important numerically is retail sales, but pharmacists are also employed in hospitals, government, industry,

FIGURE 3

Pharmacists: Fraction Female and Fraction Working in Independent Pharmacies

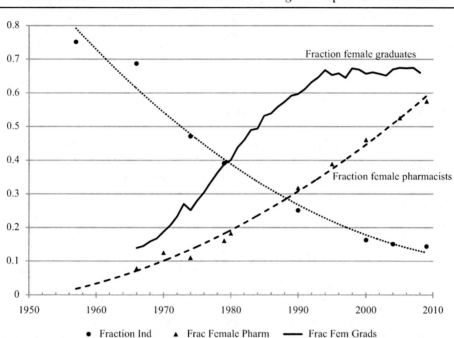

SOURCE: Fraction female: Reinhart (1969); U.S. Department of Health, Education and Welfare (1978); Mott et al. (2002); Pedersen et al. (2000). Fraction independent pharmacists: Reinhart (1969); Fulda (1974); U.S. Department of Health, Education and Welfare (1978); Kapantais (1982); U.S. Department of Health and Human Services (2000). Fraction female graduates of pharmacy programs: see Figure 1.

NOTE: A pharmacist in an independent practice can be an owner or employee. "Independent practice" means a unit or series of units for which one of the owners makes the majority of the decisions. Independent practices can have several stores but are not "chains" in the sense that they are not run by large corporations. Pharmacists can be employed by retail establishments, hospitals, industry, academia, and government. The fraction in independent practice is obtained by taking the number in independent retail practice relative to all active pharmacists.

and academia. About 55 percent of all full-time pharmacists are employed in retail today, 25 percent in hospitals, and the remaining 20 percent in the other sectors. In 1974 almost 75 percent of all pharmacists were in retail sales.

The vast majority of pharmacists are now employees, either staff members or managers. In the year 2000, just 7.6 percent of all pharmacists were owners or partners, and a mere 5.6 percent were self-employed in 2007. In both years, men were owners at four times the rate of women. In contrast, more than 35 percent of all pharmacists were self-employed in 1970, and 30 percent were owners or partners in 1974. Increased pharmaceutical employment in chain stores and supermarkets has been the largest single reason for these industry changes.[11]

The fraction of pharmacists who are owners or employees in independent practices also declined substantially—a fact that is related to the decline of ownership and the decreased fraction of pharmacists in retail. In the late 1950s, about 75 percent of all pharmacists were owners or were employed by an independent practice; in 1974, 45 percent were; and today just 14 percent are. All of these changes occurred just in the retail sector, even though the data given are for all pharmacists, and, therefore, their impact on retail establishments alone is much larger.[12]

Each of the changes just mentioned has had major implications for the pharmacy work environment and has decreased the cost to pharmacists of working part time, part year, and not being owners or equity stakeholders. The impact on female pharmacists has, in consequence, been large, and these changes are probably the single most important factors prompting the enormous increase in female pharmacists.

Interestingly, female pharmacists in the 1950s were employed part time to about the same extent they are today. They located part-time work in independent pharmacies as assistants to the owner. Their earnings were considerably less than those of the owners, who were the residual claimants and the main decision-makers. As chain stores expanded, however, more pharmacists became employees. Their earnings no longer included a premium to compensate for the added risk and responsibility, and their hours were reduced.

The large organizational and structural changes in the pharmacy industry decreased the costs of offering job amenities in retail sales. The changes in retail sales reduced the compensating differential to ownership, long hours, and being the residual claimant. Structural changes in pharmacy (and for similar reasons in optometry) were rooted in larger shifts in retailing in America, and elsewhere in the world, that increased the benefits of large-scale organizations. It would be hard to assign credit for the spread of Wal-Mart, Target, Costco, CVS, Rite Aid, Walgreens, and other chains that have pharmacies to women's increased numbers in the pharmacy profession.[13]

Integrating the Vignettes, the Data, and the Model

Data from the 1970 U.S. decennial census and the 2006–2008 American Community Surveys (ACS; termed 2007 for convenience) allow us to compile information on incomes, hours, and self-employment for most of the professions just discussed as well as for some others. We present the information in Table 2 for six professions—dentists, lawyers, optometrists, pharmacists, physicians, and veterinarians—for men and women separately and expressed as ratios for males and females. The main findings concern the relative fraction working part time and self-employed and the gender earnings gap in each profession. Although not shown in Table 2, the relative increase of women across all the professions was large, and these "stock" data reinforce the findings from the "flow" data in Figure 1.

TABLE 2

Income, Hours, and Self Employment by Gender for Selected Professions: 1970 and 2007

	Males		Females		M/F	M/F
	1970	2007	1970	2007	1970	2007
Dentists						
Mean hours/week	n.a.	39.9	n.a.	36.9	n.a.	1.081
Fraction part time	0.118	0.218	0.363	0.34	0.325	0.641
Fraction self employed	0.898	0.724	0.411	0.505	2.185	1.434
Median income	$22,950	$155,763	$8,250	$103,842	2.782	1.500
Lawyers						
Mean hours/week	n.a.	48.5	n.a.	43.7	n.a.	1.110
Fraction part time	0.053	0.047	0.18	0.139	0.294	0.338
Fraction self employed	0.575	0.37	0.345	0.2	1.667	1.850
Median income	$18,600	$122,000	$10,550	$90,000	1.763	1.356
Optometrists						
Mean hours/week	n.a.	41.8	n.a.	34.6	n.a.	1.208
Fraction part time	0.068	0.13	0.194	0.395	0.351	0.329
Fraction self employed	0.831	0.679	0.484	0.397	1.717	1.710
Median income	$18,050	$103,842	$9,250	$86,498	1.951	1.201
Pharmacists						
Mean hours/week	n.a.	42.9	n.a.	37	n.a.	1.159
Fraction part time	0.05	0.078	0.361	0.272	0.139	0.287
Fraction self employed	0.38	0.094	0.159	0.024	2.390	3.917
Median income	$12,950	$106,788	$8,550	$100,000	1.515	1.068
Physicians						
Mean hours/week	n.a.	54.7	n.a.	49.1	n.a.	1.114
Fraction part time	0.041	0.048	0.18	0.152	0.228	0.316
Fraction self employed	0.605	0.325	0.314	0.195	1.927	1.667
Median income	$27,150	$186,916	$12,050	$112,128	2.253	1.667
Veterinarians						
Mean hours/week	n.a.	50.5	n.a.	42.5	n.a.	1.188
Fraction part time	0.045	0.061	0.321	0.23	0.140	0.265
Fraction self employed	0.662	0.554	0.377	0.261	1.756	2.123
Median income	$17,050	$97,000	$9,050	$72,690	1.884	1.334

SOURCE: 1970 U.S. Census of Population; 2007 is 2006–2008 American Community Survey (ACS). The year 1970 aggregates six 1 percent samples and is a 6 percent sample. The ACS is a 1 percent sample and the three years are aggregated. The census data are produced and distributed by the IPUMS.

NOTE: The sample for each year consists of individuals who worked at least one week in the previous year. Professions are identified using the contemporaneous occupation codes in each respective census. Part time is less than a 35-hour work week. Median incomes are based on wage earnings plus business and farm earnings for those working full time and full year (more than 39 weeks per year and more than 34 hours per week) with implicit hourly earnings greater than one-half the minimum wage in that year. Top-coded incomes are multiplied by 1.4 in all years. Incomes are in current dollars. See also Goldin and Katz (forthcoming). n.a. = not available.

The fraction of male professionals working part time was considerably less than that for females in all years and all professions. That is not unexpected. What is surprising is that the ratio of males to females working part time increased from 1970 to 2007 in many cases and that in all of those cases, the reason is that a greater fraction of men were working part time. In fact, for most of these professions, the fraction of women working part time changed only slightly during the past 40 years. A large fraction of female professionals have always worked part time since 1970. Because women's share of total employment in these professions increased, the fraction working part time for the entire group increased.

In most of these professions, something changed that enabled women and some men to work part time. That change, it appears, was a decrease in the benefit of the disamenity to the firm. In some cases it is related to the decrease in self-employment. Women could always work part time, but the pecuniary penalty for working part time was large, and in consequence, it was less advantageous for them to enter these professions.

Self-employment fell for men but remained considerably higher than the rate for women for each of the professions. In some cases, such as medicine and pharmacy, the decrease in self-employment for males was considerable. In 1970, 60 percent of all male physicians were self-employed (75 percent were in 1940); today just over a third are self-employed. In 1970, 38 percent of male pharmacists were self-employed (40 percent were in 1940); but just 9 percent are today.

The decrease in self-employment is consistent with the theory outlined above, in which change in the cost of flexibility is caused by a decrease in the cost to firms for providing the amenity. The change from owners to employees meant that these professionals became better substitutes for each other. Whereas an owner of a pharmacy worked or was on call whenever the pharmacy was open, pharmacists working as employees under a manager can put in as many hours as they want at a constant hourly rate.

Median earnings of men compared to women decreased in all of the professions listed, somewhat less so in law than in the health-related professions (although without a microanalysis of the data it is not clear what factors account for the change in relative earnings). Using the compensating differentials framework developed above, the change suggests that technology changes reduced the costs of amenities preferred by women, or there were other supply-side reasons for the change.

Each of the vignettes presented concerns a profession with a rapidly rising female presence during the past four decades. Although some experienced little change in work flexibility during those decades, most underwent substantial change. These organizational changes greatly impacted the ability of these professionals to work fewer hours, engage in part-time work, have job interruptions, and partake in self-employment to suit their living styles.

We note that technological change greatly affected some professions and specialties. That was the case, for example, in gastroenterology and in colon and rectal surgery—specialties that had a large influx of female physicians in part because of the diffusion of a technology used in a scheduled procedure. Organizational and structural changes occurred in other professions, as in veterinary medicine and pharmacy. Some, however, experienced little or no change. We show that many of the occupations that employ MBAs impose large penalties for deviance from the norm of long hours and no job interruptions and that some medical specialties still require night, weekend, and on-call hours.

We have made a case for the exogeneity of change in the pharmacy and optometry sectors with the rise of chain and multigood stores with pharmacies and eyeglass dispensaries. Similarly, in veterinary medicine, scale advantages in the use of expensive medical equipment and the hiring of veterinary specialists prompted the rise of regional veterinary hospitals. These hospitals enable veterinarians in private practice to reduce night, weekend, and on-call hours. The appearance of emergency veterinary facilities preceded the increase of female veterinarians, but these facilities took off after the expansion in female veterinarians. Some of the growth of regional veterinary hospitals may, therefore, have been an endogenous response to an increased demand by veterinarians for shorter and more flexible hours.

Similarly, for some medical specialties, such as pediatrics, the high and increasing fraction female of the total group may have led to changes in practice settings and enabled greater amounts of part-time work. Surveys of the American Academy of Pediatrics show that the fraction of female pediatricians working part time increased from 28 percent in 2000 to 32 percent in 2003 and rose to 36 percent in 2006 (Cull, O'Connor, and Olson 2010). That for male pediatricians increased from 4 percent to 8 percent from 2000 to 2006. The increase, moreover, was found across all age groups but was greatest for younger and older pediatricians.

The changes noted in the previous section concerning the decrease in self-employment and the increase in part-time work would probably have decreased the earnings of those who placed only a small value on the amenity. That is, in some professions, the ratio of female to male earnings should have increased. The evidence in Table 2 supports this implication. Relative earnings of women increased in almost all professions and especially in those, like pharmacy, optometry, and veterinary medicine, in which self-employment declined and probably did so for exogenous reasons.

Regressions using the microdata for the 2007 ACS confirm that the decrease in self-employment could have increased the relative earnings of women in many professions. Across all high-education professions in which the self-employed are a relatively high fraction, men who are self-employed earn more than their employee counterparts, but self-employed women do not.[14] The detailed information on veterinarians from the AVMA data corroborates that ownership greatly increases earnings and that the amount of equity is important. Because women hold less equity, they gain less from ownership.

Another implication of the theory is that as the cost of providing the amenity decreases, the group that values it most (generally women) will increase relative to the group that values it least (generally men). As the premium to residual claimants and owners decreases, those who prefer ownership will leave for, or train in, another occupation. In professions such as pharmacy and veterinary medicine, the increase in the fraction female may have been fostered by both an increase in women, who wanted the amenity at a lower cost, and a decrease in men, who wanted the higher compensation awarded to those who were willing to accept the disamenity. In professions such as dentistry and chiropractic medicine, self-employment decreased far less, and the fraction female did not increase as much as in other professions.

A Bigger Picture and Conclusion

We have examined a small number of important, high-end occupations in detail. We have found that family friendliness differs in terms of the "cost" to the workers and to the firm and that exogenous and endogenous changes have altered these costs.

To understand earnings differences between men and women more generally and the implicit role of workplace amenities, we examined the relative incomes of men and women in the top eighty-seven occupations by male income.[15] After accounting for potential experience, hours worked, weeks worked, and other observable factors, the remaining difference between men and women by occupation is largely due to the penalties imposed on women for greater job interruptions and their need for more flexibility. The results for 2006 to 2008 given in Figure 4 are striking.

Each dot is one of the occupations listed in the census (465 in total). The horizontal axis gives (male) income in natural logs, and the vertical axis gives the earnings gap in log points (approximately the percentage penalty) between the average man and woman in an occupation, given potential job experience, hours of work, weeks of work, region, and race.[16] The occupations are divided into those that concern business, health, science, technology, and all others.

All eighty-seven occupations are situated just at or below the horizontal axis. That is, in all occupations, women make less than men given the somewhat rich group of covariates included in the regression. More interesting is the manner in which the occupations group together. The business occupations (squares) are generally the most negative, whereas the technology occupations (dark triangles) are the most positive. The health occupations (diamonds) are mixed, with those having the greatest fraction self-employed being the most negative and the ones that had decreases in self-employment being the least negative.

Business occupations, it was previously noted, place heavy penalties on employees who deviate from the norm. But why do the technology occupations appear to penalize women far less? One possibility is that the technology occupations are so recent that their work organizations are structured to deal better with a labor force that needs greater work flexibility.

We have estimated the same equation across all occupations in 1980. The results (not shown here) reveal the enormous change in the presence of women in high-end occupations and in their relative (corrected) remuneration during the four decades that separate the two periods. In 1980 the various health professions were

FIGURE 4
Female Earnings Differentials for the Eighty-seven Highest-Paid
Occupations, 2006 to 2008

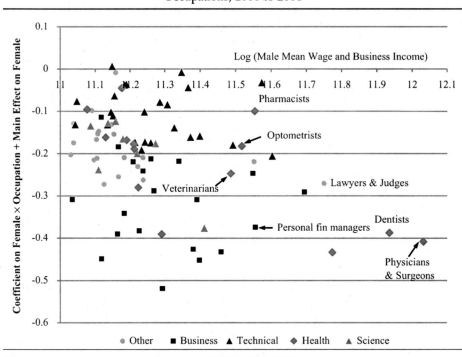

SOURCE: American Community Survey (2006, 2007, 2008).
NOTE: The vertical axis is the coefficient on female × occupation + the main coefficient
on female from a (log) annual earnings (wage plus business and farm income) estimation on
male and female full-time (>35 hours), full-year (>40 weeks) workers. The covariates included
are age, age-squared, ln (hours), ln (weeks), and race. The regressions were estimated using
3,176,730 individual observations including all occupations. The occupations in this figure
account for about 800,000 individuals. The main effect on the female dummy variable is
–0.2026. The entire sample contains 465 census occupations. The group shown in the figure
consists of the top 87 occupations ranked by male wage and business income.

at the very low end of the female coefficient distribution, meaning that they penalized women the most. The business professions were also low, but there were not
as many of them. The technology occupations penalized women the least but not
as low as in 2006 to 2008. And far fewer women were employed in upper-end
occupations.

In sum, we have examined the relationships among workplace conditions, the
costs and the benefits of various workplace amenities, and the fraction female in
professions requiring substantial educational investment. We have accomplished
this by studying several professions in detail and the implications of a model of

compensating differentials. Our main findings are that occupations differ in the degree to which workplace amenities related to flexibility are effectively taxed. Furthermore, these amenities have become less expensive in many health-related occupations as well as in the technology sector.

Notes

1. Our framework is, as well, a generalization of that in Mincer and Polachek (1974), which emphasizes the impact of career interruptions for the gender wage gap and occupational choice. Whereas Mincer and Polachek treat the mix of jobs as given, we endogenize it.

2. Job interruptions in the H&B are defined as spells of more than six months (post-BA) for which the individuals state they are not employed at all and are not in school.

3. The American Association of Colleges of Pharmacy, a long-standing arbiter of pharmacy credentials, makes recommendations concerning the requirements for first professional degrees in pharmacy. In 1907 a two-year curriculum was recommended; it was increased in 1925 to a three-year curriculum and then in 1932 to a four-year curriculum. In 1960 a five-year curriculum as part of a BS program was recommended, and most recently, in 1992, a six-year curriculum was recommended. The American Council on Pharmaceutical Education adopted accreditation standards requiring the "PharmD" program in 1997, and the pharmacy graduating class of 2005 was the last to have the five-year BS in pharmacy as the standard. See Smith, Wertheimer, and Fincham (2005).

4. Some of the specialties, it should be noted, are far smaller than others. Among those at the high end of the fraction female distribution, public health, occupational medicine, medical genetics, immunology, general preventive medicine, and forensic pathology each contain less than 1 percent of all physicians. Ob-Gyn, pediatrics, psychiatry, and family practice each have more than 5 percent of all physicians.

5. Let F = females, T = (females and males), y = the younger group (<45 years), and a = all physicians in each specialty, i. Then the bar for the younger group is (F_i^y/T_i^y) for each specialty and (F_i^a/T_i^a) for all ages. The ratio of these two ratios gives the growth of women in each specialty relative to the growth of all physicians in each specialty, if the younger group represents the increase in physicians during some time period.

6. The positive outliers are two fields (pediatrics and Ob-Gyn) that have a client base that is disproportionately female or child.

7. The increase in the fraction female with age for colon and rectal surgeons is similar to that for gastroenterologists. There are almost ten times as many gastroenterologists as there are colon and rectal surgeons. Although the former do many of the scheduled colonoscopies and endoscopies, colon and rectal surgeons also perform many colonoscopies. See American Medical Association (2009).

8. Data available from http://bhpr.hrsa.gov/healthworkforce/reports/factbook02/FB505.htm give 60,100 total active veterinarians for the year 2000 or 21.8 per 100,000 population in the United States.

9. The published version is American Veterinary Medical Association (2007).

10. The $100,000 figure comes from a regression of the amount of equity invested in the practice, conditional on being greater than zero, on age, age squared, and a dummy for male. The coefficient on the male dummy in a regression of log (equity) and the same covariates is about seventy log points.

11. The 2000 figure comes from Pedersen et al. (2000) and is nearly identical to the 2000 figure from the U.S. population census. The 2007 figure is from the American Community Surveys for 2006–2008 (see Table 2). The 1970 figure is from the data underlying Table 2 and that for 1974 is from Northrup, Garrison, and Rose (1979).

12. See sources in Figure 3; ownership data are from Northrup, Garrison, and Rose (1979, Table III-10).

13. See Bottero (1992) for a similar discussion of data from the United Kingdom.

14. Eleven occupations are considered for which the fraction self-employed exceeds around 25 percent and mean years of education exceeds 16. The regression of log income (including business and farm income) holds various factors constant, such as potential job experience; hours, weeks, and years of education; race; and region. The regression excludes lawyers for whom self-employment is more ambiguous.

15. The top eighty-seven by male income includes all of those above and includes postsecondary school teachers.

16. The sample includes 25- to 64-year-olds who work full time (>34 hours per week), full year (>39 weeks per year).

References

American Medical Association. 2009. *Physician characteristics and distribution in the US, 2009.* 41st ed. Chicago, IL: AMA Press.

American Veterinary Medical Association (AVMA). 2007. *AVMA report on veterinary compensation.* Schaumburg, IL: AVMA.

Bertrand, Marianne, Claudia Goldin, and Lawrence F. Katz. 2010. Dynamics of the gender gap for young professionals in the corporate and financial sectors. *American Economic Journal* 2 (3): 228–55.

Bottero, Wendy. 1992. The changing face of the professions? Gender and explanations of women's entry to pharmacy. *Work, Employment, and Society* 6 (3): 329–46.

Cull, William L., Karen G. O'Connor, and Lynn M. Olson. 2010. Part-time work among pediatricians expands. *Pediatrics* 125 (1): 152–57.

Freeman, Brian. 2007. *The ultimate guide to choosing a medical specialty.* 2nd ed. New York, NY: McGraw-Hill.

Fulda, Thomas. 1974. *Prescription drug data summary, 1974.* Baltimore, MD: Social Security Administration.

Goldin, Claudia, and Lawrence F. Katz. 2008. Transitions: Career and family life cycles of the educational elite. *American Economic Review* 98 (2): 363–69.

Goldin, Claudia, and Lawrence F. Katz. Forthcoming. The career cost of family. NBER Working Paper, Cambridge, MA.

Iserson, Kenneth V. 2006. *Iserson's getting into a residency: A guide for medical students.* 7th ed. Tucson, AZ: Galen Press.

Kapantais, Gloria. 1982. *Summary data from the national inventory of pharmacists: United States, 1978–79.* Atlanta, GA: National Center for Health Statistics.

Mincer, Jacob, and Solomon Polachek. 1974. Family investments in human capital: Earnings of women. *Journal of Political Economy* 82 (2): S76–S108.

Mott, David A., William R. Doucette, Caroline A. Gaither, Craig A. Pedersen, and Jon C. Schommer. 2002. A ten-year trend analysis of pharmacist participation in the workforce. *American Journal of Pharmaceutical Education* 66 (3): 223–33.

Northrup, Herbert R., Douglas F. Garrison, and Karen M. Rose. 1979. *Manpower in the retail pharmacy industry.* Philadelphia: University of Pennsylvania, Wharton School Industrial Research Unit.

Pedersen, Craig A., William R. Doucette, Caroline A. Gaither, David Mott, and Jon C. Schommer. 2000. *National pharmacists workforce survey, 2000: Final report.* Alexandria, VA: American Association of Colleges of Pharmacy.

Reinhart, George R. 1969. *Pharmacy manpower, United States 1966.* Washington, DC: U.S. Department of Health, Education and Welfare, Public Health Service, Health Services and Mental Health Administration.

Rosen, Sherwin. 1986. The theory of equalizing differences. In *The handbook of labor economics, vol. 1,* eds. Orley Ashenfelter and Richard Layard, 641–92. Amsterdam: Elsevier.

Smith, Michael Ira, Albert I. Wertheimer, and Jack E. Fincham, eds. 2005. *Pharmacy and the U.S. health care system.* 3rd ed. New York, NY: Pharmaceutical Products Press.

U.S. Department of Health and Human Services. 2000. The pharmacist workforce: A study of the supply and demand for pharmacists. *Report to Congress.*

U.S. Department of Health, Education and Welfare, Public Health Service, Health Resources Administration. 1978. *Pharmacy manpower resources.* Hyattsville, MD: U.S. Department of Health, Education and Welfare, Public Health Service, Health Resources Administration.

Phased Retirement and Workplace Flexibility for Older Adults: Opportunities and Challenges

By
RICHARD W. JOHNSON

Phased retirement programs that allow older workers to reduce their hours and responsibilities and pursue more flexible work schedules could satisfy both the employee's desire for flexibility and the employer's need to maintain an experienced workforce. However, few employers have established formal programs, because they often complicate the provision of other benefits and might violate antidiscrimination rules. For example, federal laws limit retirement plan distributions to employees who are still working for the plan sponsor, which discourages phased retirement because few older workers can afford to reduce their work hours unless they can receive at least some retirement benefits. Many employers do not provide fringe benefits to part-time employees, and making exceptions for older workers could violate antidiscrimination rules. Federal laws requiring that benefits provided through tax-qualified plans be evenly distributed between highly compensated and lower-paid employees also complicate formal phased retirement programs. Reforming these policies could promote phased retirement.

Keywords: older workers; phased retirement; pensions; age discrimination

Older adults are emerging as a major untapped labor source that could expand the pool of available workers and offset the slow growth in the number of adults ages 25 to 54 who have traditionally made up the bulk of the nation's workforce. As the U.S. population ages and the number of Americans reaching traditional retirement ages increases, employers may need to attract and retain more older workers, many of whom are highly experienced, knowledgeable, and skilled. Several indicators suggest that many older adults are willing and

Richard W. Johnson is a senior fellow at the Urban Institute, where he directs the Program on Retirement Policy. His research focuses on income security at older ages.

NOTE: The author is grateful to the Alfred P. Sloan Foundation for financial support. Opinions expressed are those of the author and do not necessarily reflect the views of the Urban Institute, its trustees, or its funders.

DOI: 10.1177/0002716211413542

able to work longer. Survey respondents often report that they wish to remain working after traditional retirement ages. Health status at older ages is generally better today than in the past, physically strenuous jobs are now less common than they once were, and the current generation of Americans age 50 and older is better educated than any previous generation. Indeed, labor force participation rates at age 62 and older have soared over the past decade and a half. Nevertheless, participation rates remain lower today than they were 40 years ago.

Employers may need to rethink traditional workplace practices to attract older workers. Because many older people who wish to remain employed do not want traditional full-time work schedules, some employers are experimenting with flexible work arrangements, including part-time employment, flexible schedules, telework, contract work, and job sharing. Some employers are formalizing these initiatives into phased retirement programs, which allow older, seasoned workers to move gradually from full-time employment to full retirement by reducing their hours and responsibilities.

This article describes the opportunities and challenges of phased retirement. By allowing older employees to move to part-time work with fewer responsibilities, phased retirement appeals to those who no longer wish to work traditional full-time schedules, because of additional personal obligations, worsening health, declining physical energy, or a growing preference for leisure. It also offers important benefits to employers, potentially enabling them to retain the skills, experience, and accumulated knowledge of veteran workers and managers who might otherwise leave the organization and be difficult to replace. Nevertheless, formal phased retirement programs are difficult to implement. They complicate the provision of fringe benefits, especially pensions, and could raise age discrimination concerns. Policy reforms could mitigate these problems, but they would necessarily reduce some protections for older workers.

Benefits and Challenges to Engaging Older Workers

The aging population threatens the nation's economic security. The growth of the older population will increase the number of Americans who qualify for publicly financed retirement and health benefits in coming years, relative to the number of younger adults who typically work and pay taxes. Between 2000 and 2020, the number of working adults for every nonworking adult age 65 or older will fall from 4.5 to 3.3, if current employment patterns continue (Johnson and Steuerle 2004). The shrinking labor pool threatens American economic growth, living standards, Social Security and Medicare financing, and funding for all other government programs. If current employment patterns and benefit levels persist, workers will have to pay higher taxes to support more retirees, employers will face tighter labor markets, retirement benefits will likely be cut, and the growth in per capita economic output will slow.

But demographic change tells only part of the story. Future outcomes depend largely on workers' and employers' individual employment decisions. Although labor force participation rates for older women have been rising over the past half-century as paid employment increased for women of all ages, participation rates for older men are lower now than they were decades ago, when health problems were more prevalent and jobs were generally more physically demanding. In 2010, for example, only 22 percent of men age 65 or older participated in the labor force, down from 47 percent in 1948 (Bureau of Labor Statistics [BLS] 2011). If people work longer, the economy can produce more goods and services, boosting living standards for both workers and nonworkers and generating additional tax revenue to fund all kinds of government services. For example, if men age 55 or older in 2020 worked at the same rate as they did in 1950, instead of the rate that prevailed in 2000, the ratio of working adults to nonworking older adults in 2020 would be 4.1 instead of 3.3 (Johnson and Steuerle 2004). Restoring the 1950 labor force participation behavior of older men would eliminate about two-thirds of the expected drop in the old-age dependency ratio between 2000 and 2020. Alternatively, if every worker delayed retirement by five years, relative to retirement plans based on current work patterns, the additional income and payroll taxes they would pay would more than cover the Social Security trust fund deficit for the foreseeable future (Butrica, Smith, and Steuerle 2007).

In addition to improving the economic outlook, working longer can enhance individual well-being. Those who delay retirement can raise their own retirement incomes by avoiding early retirement reductions to their Social Security and defined benefit (DB) pension benefits, accumulating more Social Security and pension credits and other savings, and reducing the number of retirement years that they must fund. By working until age 67, instead of retiring at age 62, for example, a typical worker could gain about $10,000 in annual income at age 75, net of federal income taxes and health insurance premiums (Butrica et al. 2004).[1] Delaying retirement may also promote physical and emotional health by keeping older adults active and engaged and imbuing their lives with meaning (Calvo 2006).

The Changing Retirement Landscape

The crucial question, then, is whether coming demographic changes will lead to higher employment rates and later retirements for older adults. A number of factors suggest that employment rates for older Americans will rise in the coming years. Improved health and declines in physical job demands leave older people better able to work today than in the past (National Center for Health Statistics 2010; Johnson, Mermin, and Resseger 2011; Steuerle, Spiro, and Johnson 1999).[2] Recent Social Security changes increase work incentives at older ages. The retirement age for full Social Security benefits recently increased from 65 to 66 and will reach 67 for those born after 1959. Delayed retirement credits have been raised to better compensate retirees who take up benefits after the full retirement age. And Congress repealed the earnings test—which reduces Social Security benefits for employed recipients who earn more than a limited amount—for beneficiaries past the full retirement age.

Changes in employer-provided pension and retiree health benefits also encourage older workers to remain at work. Traditional DB pensions, which provide workers with lifetime retirement annuities usually based on years of service and earnings near the end of the career, discourage work at older ages (Stock and Wise 1990). They often provide substantial subsidies for early retirement and penalize workers who remain on the job past the plan's normal retirement age, because workers who delay retirement by a month forfeit a month of benefits.

Over the past 30 years, however, employers have been shifting from traditional DB pensions to defined contribution (DC) plans (BLS 2010; Pension and Welfare Benefits Administration 2001–2002), which do not encourage early retirement.[3] Employers typically make specified contributions into individual DC accounts that workers access at retirement, generally as lump-sum payments. Because contributions continue as long as plan participants remain employed and workers with a given account balance can receive the same lifetime benefit regardless of when they choose to begin collecting, DC plans do not generally penalize work at older ages. As a result, people in DC plans tend to work about two years longer than DB participants (Friedberg and Webb 2005). The continued shift to DC plans, then, should increase older Americans' labor supply.

The erosion in employer-provided retiree health benefits is also likely to limit early retirement. Retiree health insurance, which pays health expenses for early retirees who have not reached the Medicare eligibility age of 65, discourages work by reducing retirement costs that arise from the loss of employer health benefits. Workers offered retiree health benefits by their employers retire earlier than workers who lose their health benefits (Johnson, Davidoff, and Perese 2003; Rogowski and Karoly 2000). Rising health care costs and the introduction of an accounting rule in 1993 that requires employers to recognize on their balance sheets the full liability of future retiree health costs have led many employers to terminate their retiree health plans. In 2010, only 28 percent of employers with more than 200 employees offered retiree health benefits, down from 66 percent in 1988 (Kaiser Family Foundation and Health Research and Educational Trust 2010). Additionally, the retiree health benefits that employers provide have generally become less generous over time and now shift more costs to retirees (Johnson 2007; Laschober 2004). However, the health reform bill (the Patient Protection and Affordable Care Act) signed by President Obama in 2010 will likely lower the impact of employer-provided health insurance on future retirement decisions. The creation of health insurance exchanges in 2014 is expected to reduce substantially the cost of nongroup health insurance, limiting the incentive for workers without access to retiree health benefits to remain with their employer until they qualify for Medicare.

It is not surprising, then, that older adults are now working longer than they did 20 years ago. The share of older men participating in the labor force declined steadily until about 1990, but then began increasing among those age 62 and older. Between 1994 and 2010, male labor force participation rates increased from 45 to 55 percent at age 62 to 64 and from 27 to 37 percent at age 65 to 69 (see Figure 1). The increase among men older than 65, when Medicare eligibility begins,

FIGURE 1
Older Men's Labor Force Participation Rates, by Age, 1963–2010 (%)

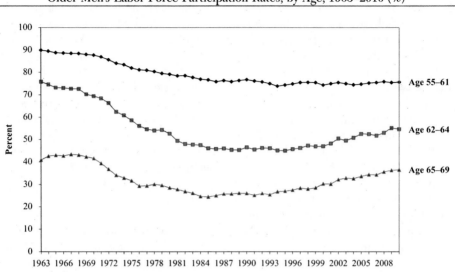

Source: Federal Interagency Forum on Aging-Related Statistics (2008) and author's calculations from BLS (2011).

suggests that the desire for health insurance coverage is not the sole factor boosting participation rates. Over the same period, female labor force participation rates rose from 33 to 45 percent at age 62 to 64 and from 18 to 27 percent at age 65 to 69 (see Figure 2), reflecting the aging of a cohort of women with higher participation rates at younger ages than earlier cohorts.

Several surveys also suggest that baby boomers intend to work into old age. For example, 70 percent of older workers in a 2007 poll said they intended to work in retirement (AARP 2007e). The mean self-reported probability of working full time past age 65 among workers age 51 to 56 participating in the Health and Retirement Study increased from 27 percent in 1992 to 33 percent in 2004 (Mermin, Johnson, and Murphy 2007). A MetLife survey found that boomers are increasingly concerned about their ability to afford an early retirement (MetLife Mature Market Institute 2005).

Challenges Confronting Older Workers and Employers

Despite these encouraging signs, a number of obstacles remain to lengthening work lives, discouraging both employees from working longer and employers from hiring and retaining older workers. On the labor supply side, Social Security payroll taxes create disincentives to work at older ages for people who have spent most of their adult lives in the labor force. Social Security benefits are based on average indexed monthly earnings, computed over the 35 years with the highest indexed

FIGURE 2
Older Women's Labor Force Participation Rates, by Age, 1963–2010 (%)

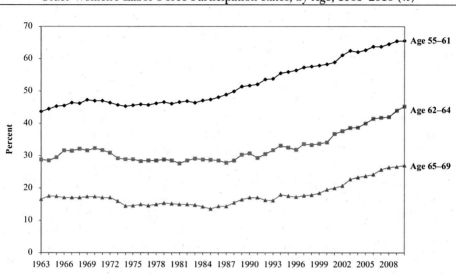

Source: Federal Interagency Forum on Aging-Related Statistics (2008) and author's calculations from BLS (2011).

earnings. For workers with fewer than 35 years of employment, an additional year of work and contributions eliminates a year of zero earnings from the benefit computation, often raising future benefits substantially. But for those with longer employment histories, an additional year of work will raise future Social Security benefits only if current earnings exceed adjusted earnings in the least remunerative of the top 35 years already used in the computation. This gain in benefits is not typically large enough to compensate for the additional payroll taxes that workers must pay (Butrica et al. 2004).

Even for older workers who have not completed 35 years of qualified work, the net increase in Social Security benefits is often small because the benefit formula favors people with low lifetime earnings over those with high lifetime earnings. In addition, workers married to higher-earning spouses often receive no additional Social Security benefits in return for the payroll taxes they pay, because many end up collecting benefits based on their spouse's earnings history.[4]

Social Security's retirement earnings test remains in effect for those who have not yet reached the full retirement age—currently 66. The earnings test reduces current benefits for this age group by $1 for every $2 of earnings above a specified annual threshold, set at $14,160 in 2011 (and adjusted each year by the average change in earnings). Many of those whose benefits are taxed away would eventually recover or more than recover them (depending on how long they live) through higher benefits in the future, but many people are unaware of (or do not respond to) this feature of the law. In addition, the earnings test may signal older people that they should not work, discouraging employment more than the financial incentives alone imply.

Certain fringe benefits also discourage work at older ages. As noted earlier, workers in DB pension plans often lose pension wealth if they work beyond the plan's normal retirement age. Although these plans are much less common now than they once were, they continue to cover about one in five workers in the private sector (particularly those in large, unionized firms) and nearly all workers in the public sector (BLS 2010). Retiree health benefits also encourage retirement before age 65 by providing affordable health insurance before Medicare eligibility for people who choose to stop working. Many people without retiree health benefits are forced to work until they qualify for Medicare at age 65 because private non-group insurance is expensive at older ages, especially for people with health problems. Although these benefits are also disappearing, nearly all public sector workers and about one in six private sector workers had access to retiree health benefits from their employers in 2003 (Buchmueller, Johnson, and Lo Sasso 2006).

On the demand side, the perceived high costs of older workers may deter employers from hiring and retaining them. For example, wages usually rise with age. If this relationship reflects only age-related productivity gains, then it should not pose employment barriers for older workers. But it may also reflect the workings of internal labor markets that tie pay to seniority regardless of individual productivity. Average health care costs also rise with age, raising the cost of employing older people and often making total compensation rise with age more quickly than productivity. Medicare secondary payer rules, which designate employer-sponsored health benefits as the primary payer of health care costs for Medicare-covered workers, further raise the costs for workers age 65 and older. DB pension plans increase the cost of hiring and retaining older workers because pension benefits in traditional plans that pay benefits based on highest earning years accrue rapidly in the years immediately before the plan's retirement age.

Older workers may also face age discrimination in the workplace. In a 2005 survey of 800 adults working or looking for work, 36 percent said that employers treated older workers less fairly than younger workers, and 71 percent said that older workers were more likely to be laid off (Reynolds, Ridley, and Van Horn 2005). Fully 60 percent of workers age 45 to 74 responding to a 2002 survey said they felt older workers were the first to go when employers reduced their workforces (AARP 2002). Two-thirds of the same group of respondents said they believed workers face age discrimination in the workplace, based on what they had experienced or seen.

Quasi-experimental evidence provides additional indication that some employers may favor younger workers over older workers. One study examining how managers reacted to hypothetical workplace situations found that managers generally perceived older workers as less flexible and more resistant to change than younger workers and that they were reluctant to promote older workers to jobs requiring flexibility, creativity, and high motivation (Rosen and Jerdee 1995). Another study found that employers were less likely to call back older job applicants than otherwise identical younger applicants (Lahey 2008). And it takes laid-off workers age 50 and older much longer than younger workers to become reemployed, even though older unemployed workers appear to search just as intensively as their younger counterparts (Johnson and Mommaerts 2011).

There is also evidence that some employers are reluctant to invest in training older workers (Frazis, Gittleman, and Joyce 1998). Without adequate training, older workers run the risk of having their skills become obsolete, particularly in industries undergoing rapid technological change. Employers may fear that they will be unable to recoup their training costs before older workers retire.

Using Phased Retirement to Promote Workplace Flexibility

Flexible work arrangements are a potential tool that employers can use to retain older workers. They generally appeal to older adults who no longer wish to work traditional full-time schedules, either because of additional personal obligations (such as the need to care for aging parents or spouses or help with grandchildren), worsening health, declining physical energy or stamina, or simply a preference to sacrifice some income for more control over their time without giving up paid employment entirely. Older workers may have accumulated enough savings or gained full or partial access to pension benefits and employer-sponsored health benefits so they can maintain their living standards with lower earnings, but they still need some labor income. An AARP poll found that 38 percent of older workers want to phase into retirement gradually instead of leave the labor force altogether (AARP 2005b). These arrangements typically include part-time employment and flexible schedules. They often require changes in work assignments to accommodate new work schedules.

Many younger workers also value flexible work arrangements, which can help maintain work-life balance throughout the life course. Some employers, however, offer these arrangements only to older workers who are transitioning into retirement. These opportunities for phased retirement, which combine flexible work schedules and reduced hours with reduced job responsibilities, can enable employees to extend their careers with the same employer (or at least the same occupation or industry) instead of moving to self-employment or to different occupations or sectors where part-time work schedules are more common (such as retailing). By enabling older workers to stay in the same firm or occupation, these arrangements benefit both workers and their employers. Employees can continue to use the human capital and experience that they have accumulated over a lifetime of work, allowing them to earn more with their existing employers than with different employers. Employers are able to retain the specialized skills and knowledge that their seasoned workers have developed and avoid the search, hiring, and training costs that result when employees leave.

Phased retirement programs are often difficult to administer, however. They complicate the provision of fringe benefits, especially for employees in DB pension plans. Most older workers cannot afford to reduce their work hours and earnings, particularly before they begin collecting Social Security, unless they can receive employer-sponsored pension benefits. As Sheaks, Pitt-Catsouphes, and Smyer (2006) point out, access to benefits depends on whether phased retirees move directly from full-time work to part-time work or return to the employer after a temporary absence, and whether they are classified as employees or independent contractors or consultants. Uncertainty surrounding legal, regulatory, and tax issues involving employee benefits plans and antidiscrimination protections creates additional challenges for employers.

Complications for Pension Plans

Federal law limits in-service distributions from retirement plans (or retirement payments to employees who are still working for the plan sponsor). DC retirement plan participants are not allowed to collect plan payments based on their own contributions before leaving the employer, unless they are at least age 59 and one-half. Until recently, federal law forbade DB pension plans from paying benefits to employees before separation unless they had reached the plan's normal retirement age (which varies across plans but is typically 65). The Pension Protection Act of 2006 (PPA) facilitated in-service distributions by allowing plans to pay benefits to active employees beginning at age 62. The IRS issued final phased retirement regulations in May 2007 that effectively ruled out in-service distributions before age 62 for DB plan participants. Because few workers can afford to partially retire unless they receive retirement benefits, these regulations effectively rule out phased retirement before age 59 for DC plan participants and before age 62 for DB plan participants.

Phased retirees in DB pension plans who are not collecting benefits often lose significant pension wealth when they move to part-time employment. Most DB plan benefit formulas tie payments to earnings received near the end of the career, typically average earnings over the last three or five years on the job. DB plan participants would receive retirement benefits based on relatively low earnings if they reduced their work hours in the last years of their career.

Instead of phasing from full-time employment to part-time work, retirees could leave the employer and then return part-time. If they return as employees (instead of consultants, say), any DB pension payments they are receiving may be suspended if they work too many hours (such as more than 40 hours in a calendar month). If they return as independent contractors or consultants, they may have to wait several months before returning to their original employer, because tax laws are unclear as to what qualifies as a termination of employment for purposes of receiving pension or retirement benefits. Several large employers, including MITRE and the Aerospace Corporation, rehire retirees who continue to collect pension benefits (Eyster, Johnson, and Toder 2008).

Deferred retirement option plans (DROPs). DROPs are one way of getting around the work disincentive effects of DB plan formulas. Under a DROP, workers who reach retirement age can continue working and receive contributions to a retirement fund equal to the pension benefit they would have received if retired. Workers do not receive cash pension benefits, but the amount contributed to the DROP account accrues interest until they actually retire. Upon retirement, employees start collecting the same annual pension benefit they would have received if they had terminated employment at the retirement age, plus they can withdraw the DROP account funds either as a lump sum or as an actuarially equivalent retirement annuity. In effect, the addition of a DROP makes the DB plan age-neutral because the present value of the employee's lifetime retirement benefit does not depend on the retirement date. Additionally, the employee does not receive any cash pension benefits until retirement.

Under some plan designs, DROPs can be used to force out employees, especially if the plan is available only between the earliest retirement age specified in the plan and the normal retirement age (Calhoun and Tepfer 1998). Furthermore, private sector employers considering DROPs must deal with a host of complex legal issues under the tax law and the Employee Retirement Income Security Act (ERISA) relating to rules against back-loading pension benefits and against discrimination favoring highly compensated employees. These legal complications have limited the use of DROPs in the private sector.

However, several states and municipalities have adopted DROPs, particularly to deal with public school teacher shortages. Arkansas, California, Louisiana, and Ohio offer them to at least some of their teachers (U.S. General Accounting Office 2001). In Arkansas, teachers who continue working in "critical need" areas such as math, science, foreign languages, and special education receive more benefits than teachers in noncritical subjects who remain at work. California offers bonuses to teachers who stay on the job once they qualify for retirement. Ohio uses the DROP program to recruit 10 percent of its teachers from its retirees. The City of Philadelphia also offers a DROP to its employees. The city's plan allows employees with 10 years of credited pension service who have reached their normal retirement age to accumulate their monthly service retirement benefit in an interest-bearing account for up to four years and to remain employed by the city (City of Philadelphia Personnel Department 2007). The program has led municipal employees to delay retirement by 1.25 years, on average, but has also substantially increased the city's pension costs (Alva, Coe, and Webb 2010).

An alternative approach to reducing the work disincentives created by DB pension plans and making phased retirement more appealing to workers in those plans is to modify the plan design. Employers could switch from a traditional DB plan to a cash balance or other hybrid plan that is essentially age-neutral. In cash balance plans, employers set aside a given percentage of salary for each employee and credit interest on these contributions. Interest credit rates are generally tied to some benchmark, such as the U.S. Treasury bill rate. Benefits are expressed as an account balance, as in DC plans, but these balances are only bookkeeping devices. Plans pay benefits from commingled funds invested in a pension trust on behalf of all participants. As with DC plans, cash balance plans do not create strong retirement incentives because they express benefits as account balances that can continue to grow throughout the worker's career (Johnson and Uccello 2004).

Complications for Other Benefits

Phased retirement also complicates health benefits. Retirees eligible for retiree health benefits can generally receive those benefits if they phase into retirement from full-time employment or return to part-time work. However, questions could arise about how these benefits wrap around Medicare coverage for phased retirees age 65 or older. Medicare's secondary payer rules identify Medicare as the primary payer for retirees with employer-provided health insurance but as the secondary payer for active workers with employer coverage. Thus, employers could experience unusually high health care costs for phased retirees age 65 and older receiving health benefits.

Phased retirees younger than 65 with employers that do not offer retiree health benefits may have trouble obtaining health insurance coverage (at least until health insurance exchanges are established in 2014). Many employers do not provide health benefits to part-time employees, and making an exception for older workers could violate antidiscrimination rules. Most employers are required to offer continuation coverage to former employees for up to 18 months after separation (or 36 months for disabled former employees), with the health plan participant covering the full premium (plus 2 percent to cover administrative expenses). This coverage, however, might not last until the retiree qualifies for Medicare at age 65. Those rehired as independent contractors or consultants would also be ineligible for health benefits.

Other types of benefits might also be eliminated or reduced for older workers who phase into retirement and move to part-time employment. For example, some employers provide life insurance and long-term disability coverage only to full-time employees. Even when phased retirees are able to maintain coverage, benefits usually decline because they are typically tied to earnings. Life insurance and long-term disability benefits, for instance, are usually computed as multiples of current salary.

The Role of Antidiscrimination Rules

Another challenge in the implementation of phased retirement programs is that they could conflict with the antidiscrimination provisions of benefit law and the Age Discrimination in Employment Act (ADEA). Employer benefit programs are governed by ERISA and the tax code. ERISA, enacted in 1974 and amended many times since then, sets minimum standards for most private sector pension and health plans to protect plan participants. The tax code also has authority because many fringe benefits enjoy special tax advantages. The value of employer-provided health benefits, for example, is not generally subject to the federal income tax, and income taxes on pension and retirement cash benefits are generally deferred until beneficiaries receive their payments, as long as they are provided through what are known as qualified plans. In return for these tax advantages, the federal government requires employers to distribute tax-qualified fringe benefits equitably across the workforce. The tax code includes several nondiscrimination tests to verify that employer benefits do not unduly favor highly compensated employees at the expense of lower-paid employees, preventing employers from using fringe benefits simply as a way to avoid taxes. However, these tests can make it difficult for employers to implement phased retirement programs.

One of the tax code's most relevant nondiscrimination rules for phased retirement plans is the benefits, rights, and features test. It stipulates that all the benefits, rights, and features of a plan must be available to all participants. A particular component of a qualified plan meets this test if the share of non–highly compensated employees benefiting from this component equals at least 70 percent of the share of highly compensated employees benefiting. In other words, a phased retirement program must not attract a much larger share of highly compensated employees than lower-paid employees.

Many formal phased programs may have difficulty meeting this test, because employers may gear phased retirement toward highly compensated workers. Employers typically use phased retirement programs to retain highly skilled and experienced workers and managers who may be difficult to replace. These employees are usually well compensated. Employers may be more reluctant to offer phased retirement to less skilled, lower-paid workers who may not be worth the expense of retaining. Moreover, low-paid employees may be unwilling to participate in a phased retirement program that does not allow for in-service distributions from pension and retirement plans because they may be unable to live on a part-time salary alone.

Congress could ease the benefits, rights, and features nondiscrimination test for formal phased retirement programs to promote flexible, part-time employment by older workers (Workplace Flexibility 2010a). It could exempt phased retirement programs from the test, for example, since the original intent of the standard was to deter tax avoidance, not promote equal access to part-time employment. Or Congress could reduce the 70 percent rule, making it easier for employers to meet the benefits, rights, and features test. Weakening the nondiscrimination test, however, could reduce low-paid workers' access to phased retirement.

Age discrimination law further complicates phased retirement. The ADEA protects workers age 40 and older from employment discrimination by employers with twenty or more employees. It outlaws discrimination on the basis of age with respect to any term, condition, or privilege of employment, including hiring, firing, promotion, layoff, compensation, benefits, job assignments, and training. Because many employers may choose to offer phased retirement only to certain employees deemed to possess essential skills, the establishment of formal phased retirement programs could expose the employer to ADEA claims, especially if it denies enrollment to relatively old employees (Workplace Flexibility 2010b).

ADEA lawsuits may claim disparate treatment (e.g., employees were treated differently and with discriminatory intent because of their age) or disparate impact (e.g., certain actions led to worse outcomes for older workers, even if the employer did not intend to discriminate). Recent case law suggests that both types of claims would be difficult to prove with regard to phased retirement programs (Workplace Flexibility 2010b). Under the disparate treatment argument, workers denied phased retirement would have to demonstrate that they qualified for the program (presumably because of their skills and experience), that they were denied because of their age, and that their denied requests to transition from full-time work to part-time work constitute an "adverse employment action." Employers could argue that phased retirement is merely a request for a change in schedule and that decisions on these matters do not qualify as adverse employment actions. Even if workers prevail on these counts, employers can refute ADEA claims by simply showing legitimate, nondiscriminatory reasons for denying enrollment in phased retirement programs. For example, the employer could argue that the employees in question lack the essential skills it needs in phased retirees.

Instead of pursuing a disparate treatment claim, plaintiffs could allege that a phased retirement program violates the ADEA because it harms older workers, even if the program was not designed to discriminate against them. However, employers could successfully refute such disparate impact claims by presenting "reasonable factors other than age" that guided their enrollment decisions. For example, employers could point to employees' performance, skills, technical background, seniority, and so on.

Another potential ADEA complication for phased retirement is that ADEA protects workers age 40 and older, yet most employers offer phased retirement only to workers in their 50s and 60s. As a result, workers in their 40s could have claimed that a phased retirement program illegally discriminated against them on the basis of age. However, in response to a recent Supreme Court ruling, the U.S. Equal Employment Opportunity Commission issued new regulations in July 2007 clarifying that the ADEA does not prohibit employers from favoring older workers over younger workers (even when the younger workers are age 40 or older).

It would generally be difficult for employees to prove that formal phased retirement programs violated the ADEA, under either a disparate treatment argument or disparate impact argument. However, the legal uncertainties that continue to surround these types of age discrimination claims may be enough to discourage employers from establishing formal phased retirement programs (Penner, Perun, and Steuerle 2002). Legal costs make lawsuits expensive, even when the defendant prevails, and many employers may choose to forgo phased retirement to limit their legal exposure, no matter how small the risk.

Employer Efforts to Promote Phased Retirement

Several surveys have examined the extent to which employers are taking steps to retain older workers. Many firms report that they are concerned about losing talent when baby boomers retire. In a series of AARP state surveys of about 400 to 700 employers, between 55 and 73 percent reported that they were likely to experience a shortfall of qualified workers in the subsequent five years (AARP 2005a, 2006, 2007a, 2007b, 2007c, 2007d). Similarly, an Ernst & Young survey of 151 Fortune 1000 companies found that 62 percent of employers believe that future retirements will lead to labor or skill shortages. However, fewer employers (between 19 and 37 percent) are taking active steps to prepare for boomer retirements, according to the same AARP surveys and a nationally rep-resentative survey of 400 employers by the Center on Aging and Work at Boston College (Pitt-Catsouphes et al. 2007).

Many employers report a willingness to allow phased retirement, but few actu-ally do so. According to a nationally representative survey of 950 employers conducted by the School of Industrial and Labor Relations at Cornell University, 73 percent of employers indicated that "something could be worked out" if a full-time white-collar worker age 55 or older asked to switch to part-time work (Hutchens 2003). Employers were less likely to allow phased retirement if they were part of large parent organizations, highly unionized, in the public sector (excluding education or social services), less dependent on part-time employees, or more dependent on older workers. Only 36 percent of employers reporting that they would allow white-collar workers to reduce their hours, however, had any phased retirees in the past three years. Other surveys suggest employers may be less likely to offer phased retirement to blue-collar than white-collar employees. The AARP and Center on Aging and Work surveys, which did not specifically ask about white-collar workers, found that 23 to 42 percent of employers offer phased retirement.

While many employers are willing to offer older workers the opportunity to reduce their hours, fewer are willing to offer additional inducements such as full health benefits or in-service pension benefits. For example, in the Cornell survey, only 26 percent of employers allowing phased retirement would provide the same health benefits to workers after they reduced their hours. About two-fifths of employers allowed phased retirement in the Cornell survey, but only 9 percent of employers in the Ernst & Young survey allowed in-service pension benefits.

Currently, most phased retirement opportunities are informal arrangements, not formal programs. Seventy-six percent of employers reporting they would allow phased retirement in the Cornell survey said these arrangements would be informal, as did 83 percent of such employers in the AARP Boston survey (AARP 2006) and 94 percent of those in the AARP Oregon and New York surveys (AARP 2007a, 2007d).

Conclusions

Providing older employees with flexible work options could encourage them to work longer and delay retirement. As workers approach traditional retirement ages, they often prefer to reduce their hours, shift into less demanding positions, and work flexible schedules, especially if they have accumulated substantial savings or can access retirement benefits so they can afford the pay reductions that usually accompany downshifting. The inclination toward workplace flexibility is often driven by emerging personal obligations, such as the need to care for frail parents, disabled spouses, or young grandchildren; worsening health; declining physical energy; or a growing preference for more leisure after a lifetime of work.

Retaining older workers provides important benefits to employers. The organization loses valuable skills, experience, and accumulated knowledge when seasoned workers and managers retire—attributes that are often difficult to replace from within and sometimes impossible to bring in from the outside. The retention of senior talent is becoming increasingly critical as the population ages. Unless older adults work more, the slow growth in the size of the younger population will lead to a stagnant labor force, making it increasingly difficult for employers to meet their staffing needs and limiting economic growth.

Phased retirement programs that allow older workers to reduce their hours and responsibilities and pursue more flexible work schedules could satisfy both the employee's desire for flexibility and the employer's need to maintain an experienced workforce. However, employers face several obstacles in setting up formal programs. Some of the most difficult issues involve benefit plans, especially DB pension plans. Employers may not provide in-service distributions to workers younger than 62, yet relatively few workers can afford to reduce their work schedules without access to retirement benefits. Also, DB plan participants usually lose substantial pension wealth if they reduce their earnings in the years immediately before retirement, because pension benefits are generally tied to earnings near the end of the career. Phased retirement complicates the provision of other types of benefits as well, including health insurance, life insurance, and disability. Many employers do not provide benefits to part-time workers, and antidiscrimination rules make it difficult to provide exceptions for older workers.

Antidiscrimination rules designed to protect low-income employees and older workers further complicate phased retirement. Federal law requires that benefits provided through tax-qualified plans be fairly evenly distributed between highly compensated and lower-paid employees. It would generally be difficult for formal phased retirement programs to meet these standards because most employers gear them toward well-paid workers, who tend to have the specialized skills and knowledge that employers value and who can generally afford to reduce their work schedules. Federal law also prohibits employment discrimination against workers age 40 and older. Employers tend to be selective about which employees they offer phased retirement, and those denied enrollment in the program may sue on grounds of age discrimination. Even if these claims would be difficult to prove, the threat of expensive litigation may discourage many employers from implementing phased retirement programs.

Several policy reforms could promote phased retirement, but many of these changes would conflict with other policy objectives. For example, pension law could be changed to allow employers to grant in-service DB plan distributions to employees younger than 62, but that would undermine the notion that pension benefits go only to retirees. Such a change could also encourage some workers to collect benefits early, permanently reducing their annual benefits for the rest of their lives. Congress could weaken or eliminate the so-called benefits, rights, and features test for phased retirement plans, mandating that enrollees include both highly compensated and non–highly compensated employees. This change, however, could leave relatively few lower-paid older workers with access to flexible work arrangements. Congress could state that the ADEA does not apply to phased retirement programs, but that would weaken employment protections and could expose some older workers to discriminatory behavior.

Additional research is needed to better understand older adults' demand for workplace flexibility and employers' apparent reluctance to establish formal phased retirement programs. For example, how will the aging of the workforce affect employers? How many older workers would work longer if they were offered flexible work schedules, and how many are unable to obtain flexible schedules? What employee traits do employers look for when deciding to which workers to offer phased retirement? How does phased retirement vary by industry and occupation? And what factors drive employer reluctance to offer phased retirement? Answers to these questions could help guide policy choices and ensure that employers get the most out of their aging workforces.

Notes

1. Most people can increase lifetime Social Security benefits by delaying benefit take-up, even if they do not work any additional years (Coile et al. 2002). The system increases monthly payments for those who wait to collect benefits to offset the reduction in the number of payments they receive over their lifetime. But as life expectancy has increased, these bonuses now exceed the actuarially fair amount, overcompensating beneficiaries who delay claiming.

2. There is some evidence, however, that the trend toward better health in late midlife has ended and perhaps reversed. For example, the share of surveyed adults age 51 to 56 reporting health problems increased between 1992 and 2004 (Soldo et al. 2007), and disability rates at age 40 to 49 increased between 1984 and 2000 (Lakdawalla, Bhattacharya, and Goldman 2004).

3. DB plans continue to dominate in the public sector, however. In 2010, 79 percent of state and local government employers participated in DB pension plans (BLS 2010), and the federal government offers a DB plan to nearly its entire workforce.

4. As married women's average lifetime earnings increase relative to men's, however, more married women are receiving benefits based on their own earning histories.

References

Alva, Samson, Norma B. Coe, and Anthony Webb. 2010. The impact of a DROP program on the age of retirement and employer pension costs. CRR Working Paper No. 2010-11. Chestnut Hill, MA: Center for Retirement Research at Boston College.

AARP. 2002. *Staying ahead of the curve: The AARP work and career study*. Washington, DC: AARP.

AARP. 2005a. *American business and older employees: A focus on midwest employers*. Washington, DC: AARP.

AARP. 2005b. *Attitudes of individuals 50 and older toward phased retirement*. Washington, DC: AARP.

AARP. 2006. *Preparing for an aging workforce: A focus on Massachusetts businesses*. Washington, DC: AARP.

AARP. 2007a. *AARP Oregon poll of employers in the state on age 50+ employees*. Washington, DC: AARP.

AARP. 2007b. *Employment planning for an aging workforce: Results from an AARP California survey of employers*. Washington, DC: AARP.

AARP. 2007c. *Looking toward an older workforce: A focus on New Mexico employers*. Washington, DC: AARP.

AARP. 2007d. *Preparing for an aging workforce: A focus on New York businesses*. Washington, DC: AARP.

AARP. 2007e. *Staying ahead of the curve: The AARP work and career study*. Washington, DC: AARP.

Buchmueller, Thomas C., Richard W. Johnson, and Anthony T. Lo Sasso. 2006. Trends in retiree health insurance, 1997 to 2003. *Health Affairs* 25 (6): 1507–16.

Bureau of Labor Statistics. 2010. *National Compensation Survey: Employee benefits in the United States, March 2009. Bulletin 2752*. Washington, DC: U.S. Department of Labor.

Bureau of Labor Statistics. 2011. *Labor force statistics from the Current Population Survey*. Washington, DC: U.S. Department of Labor.

Butrica, Barbara A., Richard W. Johnson, Karen E. Smith, and C. Eugene Steuerle. 2004. *Does work pay at older ages?* Washington, DC: The Urban Institute.

Butrica, Barbara, Karen Smith, and Eugene Steuerle. 2007. Working for a good retirement. In *Government spending on the elderly*, ed. Dimitri B. Papadimitriou, 141–74. New York, NY: Palgrave Macmillan.

Calhoun, Carol V., and Arthur H. Tepfer. 1998. *Deferred retirement option plans ("DROP plans")*. Washington, DC: Calhoun Law Group, P.C.

Calvo, Esteban. 2006. *Does working longer make people healthier and happier?* Work Opportunities for Older Americans Series 2. Chestnut Hill, MA: Center for Retirement Research at Boston College.

City of Philadelphia Personnel Department. 2007. *City of Philadelphia personnel department*. Philadelphia, PA: City of Philadelphia. Available from www.phila.gov/personnel/welcome2.htm.

Coile, Courtney, Peter A. Diamond, Jonathan Gruber, and Alain Jousten. 2002. Delays in claiming Social Security benefits. *Journal of Public Economics* 84 (3): 357–85.

Eyster, Lauren, Richard W. Johnson, and Eric Toder. 2008. *Current strategies to employ and retain older workers*. Washington, DC: The Urban Institute.

Federal Interagency Forum on Aging-Related Statistics. 2008. *Older Americans 2008: Key indicators of well-being*. Washington, DC: Government Printing Office.

Frazis, Harley, Maury Gittleman, and Mary Joyce. 1998. Correlates of training: An analysis using both employer and employee characteristics. *Industrial and Labor Relations Review* 53 (3): 443–62.

Friedberg, Leora, and Anthony Webb. 2005. Retirement and the evolution of pension structure. *Journal of Human Resources* 40 (2): 281–308.

Hutchens, Robert. 2003. *The Cornell study of employer phased retirement policies: A report on key findings*. Ithaca, NY: Cornell University, School of Industrial and Labor Relations.

Johnson, Richard W. 2007. *What happens to health benefits after retirement?* Chestnut Hill, MA: Center for Retirement Research at Boston College.

Johnson, Richard W., Amy J. Davidoff, and Kevin Perese. 2003. Health insurance costs and early retirement decisions. *Industrial and Labor Relations Review* 56 (4): 716–29.

Johnson, Richard W., Gordon B. T. Mermin, and Matthew Resseger. 2011. Job demands and work ability at older ages. *Journal of Aging and Social Policy* 23 (2): 101–18.

Johnson, Richard W., and Corina Mommaerts. 2011. *Age differences in job loss, job search, and reemployment*. Washington, DC: The Urban Institute.

Johnson, Richard W., and Eugene Steuerle. 2004. Promoting work at older ages: The role of hybrid pension plans in an aging population. *Journal of Pension Economics and Finance* 3 (3): 315–37.

Johnson, Richard W., and Cori E. Uccello. 2004. Cash balance plans: What do they mean for retirement security? *National Tax Journal* 57 (2, Part 1): 315–28.

Kaiser Family Foundation and Health Research and Educational Trust. 2010. *Employer health benefits: 2010 annual survey*. Menlo Park, CA: Kaiser Family Foundation and Health Research Educational Trust.

Lahey, Joanna N. 2008. Age, women, and hiring: An experimental study. *Journal of Human Resources* 43 (1): 30–56.

Lakdawalla, Darius N., Jayanta Bhattacharya, and Dana P. Goldman. 2004. Are the young becoming more disabled? *Health Affairs* 23 (1): 168–76.

Laschober, Mary. 2004. *Trends in Medicare supplemental insurance and prescription drug benefits, 1996–2001.* Menlo Park, CA: Henry J. Kaiser Family Foundation.

Mermin, Gordon B. T., Richard W. Johnson, and Dan Murphy. 2007. Why do boomers plan to work longer? *Journal of Gerontology: Social Sciences* 62B (5): S286–94.

MetLife Mature Market Institute. 2005. *The MetLife survey of American attitudes toward retirement: What's changed.* Westport, CT: MetLife Mature Market Institute.

National Center for Health Statistics. 2010. *Trends in health and aging.* Hyattsville, MD: National Center for Health Statistics. Available from http://209.217.72.34/aging/TableViewer/tableView .aspx?ReportId=313.

Penner, Rudolph G., Pamela Perun, and Eugene Steuerle. 2002. *Legal and institutional impediments to partial retirement and part-time work by older workers.* Washington, DC: The Urban Institute.

Pension and Welfare Benefits Administration. 2001–2002. *Private pension plan bulletin: Abstract of 1998 Form 5500 annual reports.* Washington, DC: U.S. Department of Labor.

Pitt-Catsouphes, Marcie, Michael A. Smyer, Christina Matz-Costa, and Katherine Kane. 2007. *The national study report: Phase II of the national study of business strategy and workforce development.* Chestnut Hill, MA: Center on Aging and Work at Boston College.

Reynolds, Scott, Neil Ridley, and Carl E. Van Horn. 2005. *A work-filled retirement: Workers' changing views on employment and leisure.* Worktrends 8.1. New Brunswick, NJ: John J. Heldrich Center for Workforce Development, Rutgers University. Available from www.heldrich.rutgers.edu/uploadedFiles/ Publications/WT16.pdf.

Rogowski, Jeannette, and Lynn Karoly. 2000. Health insurance and retirement behavior: Evidence from the Health and Retirement Survey. *Journal of Health Economics* 19 (4): 529–39.

Rosen, Benson, and Thomas H. Jerdee. 1995. *The persistence of age and sex stereotypes in the 1990s: The influence of age and gender in management decisionmaking.* Public Policy Institute Issue Brief 22. Washington, DC: AARP.

Sheaks, Chantel, Marcie Pitt-Catsouphes, and Michael A. Smyer. 2006. *Legal and research summary sheet: Phased retirement.* Washington, DC: Georgetown Law. Available from http://workplaceflexibility2010 .org/images/uploads/Phased%20Retirement.pdf.

Soldo, Beth J., Olivia S. Mitchell, Rania Tfaily, and John F. McCabe. 2007. Cross-cohort differences in health on the verge of retirement. In *Redefining retirement: How will boomers fare?* eds. Brigitte Madrian, Olivia S. Mitchell, and Beth J. Soldo, 138–58. New York, NY: Oxford University Press.

Steuerle, C. Eugene, Christopher Spiro, and Richard W. Johnson. 1999. *Can Americans work longer?* Straight talk on Social Security and retirement Policy 5. Washington, DC: The Urban Institute.

Stock, James H., and David A. Wise. 1990. The pension inducement to retire: An option value analysis. In *Issues in the economics of aging,* ed. David A. Wise, 205–29. Chicago, IL: University of Chicago Press.

U.S. General Accounting Office. 2001. *Older workers: Demographic trends pose challenges for employers and workers.* Washington, DC: U.S. General Accounting Office.

Workplace Flexibility 2010a. *Benefits, rights, and features nondiscrimination testing and phased retirement programs.* Washington, DC: Georgetown Law. Available from http://workplaceflexibility2010 .org/images/uploads/Nondiscrimination%20Outline%20v8.pdf.

Workplace Flexibility 2010b. *Phased retirement and the Age Discrimination in Employment Act.* Washington, DC: Georgetown Law. Available from http://workplaceflexibility2010.org/index.php/ stakeholders/older_workers/.

Workplace Flexibility and Worker Agency: Finding Short-Term Flexibility within a Highly Structured Workplace

By
LAWRENCE S. ROOT
and
ALFORD A. YOUNG JR.

"Worker agency"—the idea that workers have free will and will exercise it to meet their needs—is a fundamental part of organizational psychology and the sociology of work. Drawing on qualitative research conducted in a midwestern factory, the authors examine how workers create opportunities for short-term flexibility within a workplace characterized by shift work, strict production quotas, and team organization. Coping mechanisms involve sympathetic supervisors and supportive coworkers. Workers also describe taking independent action when the structure does not permit them to meet obligations to their families. These exercises in worker agency can be understood in terms of their legitimacy in the workplace and their potential for disruption of work. Worker agency also can be a positive factor in the workplace. Workers describe a supportive work environment as a critical factor that promotes loyalty and a willingness to go beyond workplace requirements for the good of the organization.

Keywords: work-family; flexibility; worker agency; unions; shift work; childcare; blue-collar employment

The lack of flexibility in work schedules is a defining feature in many workplaces. Workers are often expected to function in

Lawrence S. Root is a professor of social work at the University of Michigan and formerly directed the university's Institute of Labor and Industrial Relations. His research focuses on the intersection of employment and social welfare, including employee benefits and social insurance, services for workers experiencing personal problems, joint labor-management programs, and work-family issues.

Alford A. Young Jr. is Arthur F. Thurnau Professor and chair of the Department of Sociology at the University of Michigan (and jointly appointed in the Center for Afroamerican and African Studies). He has published The Minds of Marginalized Black Men: Making Sense of Mobility, Opportunity, and Future Life Chances (Princeton University Press 2004) and researches the experiences of African Americans in the world of work.

DOI: 10.1177/0002716211415787

accordance with highly structured timelines and schedules as well as firm guide-lines and expectations. Flexibility in most jobs is a function of the nature of work processes and protocols, values of management, and needs of workers. Unlike other developed countries that have implemented public policies to support fam-ily leave, the Family and Medical Leave Act, the principal federal legislation in the United States, provides only very basic protections for workers seeking to balance family responsibilities with those at work. When the demands of personal and family life come up against rigidity, workers often feel compelled to maneuver around these formal bounds, thus allowing them to attend to and resolve emer-gencies, crises, and unexpected, yet important, family and personal matters. The myriad ways in which workers respond to these external demands invite further exploration of how worker agency unfolds within the context of inflexibility at the worksite.

Although the term "worker agency" is a recent coinage, "free will," the under-lying idea, is fundamental to organizational psychology and the sociology of work. Frederick W. Taylor, in his seminal 1911 book on scientific management, pro-vides an early example of how worker agency impacts management decisions. He describes an employer's dilemma in setting productivity expectations for workers. In large part, this dilemma arises because workers have "the deliberate object of keeping their employers ignorant of how fast work can be done" (Taylor 1911, 21).

> It evidently becomes for each man's interest, then, to see that no job is done faster than it has been in the past. The younger and less experienced men are taught this by their elders, and all possible persuasion and social pressure is brought to bear upon the greedy and selfish men to keep them from making new records which result in temporarily increasing their wages, while all those who come after them are made to work harder for the same old pay. (p. 22)

Taylor's approach is often criticized as an overly mechanistic view of workers (Braverman 1974; Jurgens, Malsch, and Dohse 1993; Locke 1982; Waring 1991). But worker agency—the acknowledgment that workers are not passive actors in the workplace—is fundamental to his analysis and highlights a crucial point of attention for the present analysis of how workers negotiate work schedules in employment sectors where time at work is highly regulated.

This article draws on this perspective in examining how the demanding struc-ture of a work environment can result in significant obstacles to workplace flex-ibility and explores how employees have incorporated informal but durable mechanisms for managing work-family conflicts in the face of structural rigidity. The examples are from a manufacturing context, but the imperatives of coverage responsibilities and shift work in many service-sector jobs create similar tensions (Golden 2001). The durability and intensity of commitment to such informal mechanisms call for reconsideration in policy and research communities of how the scheduling of work in that sector has been implemented by management, how worker agency can counter efforts at control, and the implications for manage-ment seeking to create stable and productive workplace structures.

In the following sections, we first describe the research undertaken. We then explore the challenges to balancing work and family responsibilities in a specific manufacturing environment. We then turn to family events that call for short-term flexibility. We examine how the lack of formal flexibility can lead to informal ways of coping with work-family conflicts—ways that are often problematic for workers and their employers. In this way, worker agency provides an important dimension that is often not a part of management decision-making about work-family flexibility. Essentially, if worker agency is not considered, an important aspect of the management situation and the realities of the workplace are missing from the discussion. As we illustrate below, omitting such a consideration has consequences not only for worker satisfaction but also for understanding how the production process, itself, unfolds. Finally, we offer suggestions for remedying the tensions involved in balancing work and family demands by focusing on the crucial role that supervisors and other on-the-ground managers play in negotiating flexibility into this highly regulated employment sector.

"Sylvania" as a Site for Work-Family Research

Our discussion of work-family arrangements and the centrality of worker agency in achieving some measure of short-term flexibility is based on research at a mid-sized factory that we call "Sylvania." For more than two years, a research team interviewed employees, reviewed documents, and engaged in participant observation at this midwestern auto-parts plant. Our goal was to explore a range of issues related to how workers think about and deal with their work, their family, and community situation, and the conflicts experienced in meeting family obligations in the face of the demands of the workplace. Researchers observed shop floor operations, "job-shadowed," participated in workplace events (e.g., factory-wide meetings, new employee orientation, and open houses for families), worked on the line, and attended union meetings and other union-based activities.

The researchers also conducted fifty-nine open-ended interviews with salaried (management) and hourly workers.[1] Fifty-two of those interviewed were randomly selected; the other seven were included because of their leadership roles in the company or the union. The demographics of the sample are presented in Table 1. The goal of the sampling was to have a representative sample, although not one from which the researchers intended to extrapolate quantitatively to the workforce as a whole (Teddlie and Yu 2007). To avoid the bias associated with convenience sampling, a random sample was drawn, oversampling for women and salaried employees (meaning workers who do not perform assembly line duties and would usually be classified as white-collar employees). The addition of several local union and management leaders increased the number of older white men in the sample. The resulting sample roughly reflects the demographics of the workforce at Sylvania.

TABLE 1
Demographic Characteristics of Interviewees

	N	Percentage
Age[a]		
20 to 29	9	15.3
30 to 39	8	13.6
40 to 49	14	23.7
50 to 59	25	42.4
60 and older	3	5.1
Race		
White	44	74.6
African American	13	22.0
Other	2	3.4
Gender		
Male	41	69.5
Female	18	30.5
Job		
Hourly production	25	42.4
Hourly skilled trades	13	22.0
Salaried	20	33.9
Other	1	1.7

a. Percentages in the age category total 100.1. This is a result of the approximation involved in rounding the individual category percentages to one decimal place.

Almost two-thirds of those interviewed were United Auto Workers (UAW), although these hourly workers constitute a larger proportion of the overall workforce at Sylvania. Most of the union leaders who were included were in the skilled trades, so that increased the proportion of that group among the hourly UAW interviewees. Because of the oversampling of women, the percentage in the sample (30.5 percent) is somewhat higher than in the overall workforce; approximately one-quarter of the workforce was female.

The interviews generally lasted from 60 to 90 minutes. The interviews were recorded, transcribed, and entered into a qualitative software program (Atlas.ti) for coding and analysis. The semistructured interview schedule addressed a range of topics related to employment and family issues. For this article, we explore and document issues of work-family balance in a setting characterized by team-based operations, shift work, and challenging production quotas. Although drawing on a manufacturing worksite, this article is not about the experiences of manufacturing workers per se, but rather about workers whose time at work, and the timing of that work, is directly managed if not uniformly observed.

Work-family issues often turn on the nature of workplace flexibility. In this context, Christensen and Schneider (2010, 4) identify five types: short-term flexibility;

flexibility in scheduling full-time employment; alternatives to full-time, full-year employment; extended time off; and alternative career paths and timing. In the course of our research at Sylvania, workers provided examples of each of these types of flexibility. The most obvious was the challenge of childcare in the face of full-time employment, which is compounded at Sylvania because of a shift schedule that had many workers starting before dawn or ending in the middle of the night—a pattern that raises particular problems for childcare (Presser 2003). Ten of the forty-seven interviewees who had children identified childcare as being or having been a serious problem. Not surprisingly, seven of the ten were women, reflecting the secular trend of increasing labor force participation among women of traditional childbearing and childrearing age (Blau 1998; U.S. Bureau of Labor Statistics 2009). Among the men who had children but did not report childcare as a problem, most referred to their wives as taking primary responsibility for childcare. Both men and women also talked about getting assistance from other family members.

For those who reported problems with childcare, the long hours and shift schedules were a major theme in this problem. Research suggests that the proportion of the national workforce that works 50 or more hours per week has steadily increased (Jacobs and Gerson 1998). When the auto economy was strong, Sylvania hummed with activity throughout the day and most of the night.[2] There were two shifts for production and a third "midnight" shift that was primarily for maintenance. In principle, the eight-hour "day shift" would be roughly from 7:30 a.m. to 4:00 p.m. (eight hours plus one half-hour for an unpaid lunch period). The "afternoon shift" was from 3:30 p.m. to midnight. In practice, however, most people worked longer shifts. Workers routinely were scheduled for 10-hour or 12-hour shifts. When overtime was scheduled, it usually meant an earlier starting time rather than staying later. A 12-hour "day shift" might begin at 3:30 in the morning and end at 4:00 in the afternoon.

Jan, a single mother in her 40s, described in her interview the complexities of childcare that she experienced in blue-collar positions with shift work.[3] When her daughter was born, before she began working at Sylvania, she was working in a position that started early in the morning—much earlier than regular childcare programs opened:

> I found a lady while I was pregnant. She had been referred to me. I asked her and told her I was expecting and asked her when I had my daughter if she would babysit for me and she said "yeah." We corresponded and talked during my whole pregnancy. So after it was time for me to like really have the baby, she came over to meet the baby and everything. I said, "Well, is this the part where I have to grovel?" She said, "What do you mean?" I said, "Well, I never told you what time I went to work. Nobody opens before 6:00." She goes, "Well, what time do you go to work?" I said, "Well, I need to drop my daughter off by 4:00." And her face just kind of crumbled and I told her, "I'd pay you. I'd bribe you. I promise to change her, feed her and have a bottle ready at your door when I drop her off." She says, "Well, we can try it and see how it works out." Well, you know, kids kind of grow on you. So that's what happened and she continued to keep her. She kept her until she was almost two.

When Jan began at Sylvania, she was working on the day shift, which formally began at 7:30 a.m., earlier when overtime was scheduled. She had to allow a half-hour to an hour (depending on the weather) for the drive from her home and additional time to walk from the parking lot to her department, stopping to change clothes and prepare for her time on the line. In addition to the challenges of daycare, her schedule allowed only limited time for sleep so she would try to find a few hours to nap:

> If I'm really lucky, some days I can come back and get two to three hours more later [sleep] in the day before I go in. You find that people here take a lot of No-Doz or over-the-counter stuff to keep you awake. But all that does is, eventually it wears off and then you're really tired [chuckles]. So it's not a good thing. I try not to do it.

At the time Jan was interviewed, her shift at Sylvania had been changed to afternoons, which disrupted her already-tenuous work-family balance. "I've been playing charades ever since and now I'm not doing too well. Childcare is a nightmare now." Jan's afternoon shift, usually a 12-hour shift, started at 3:30 in the afternoon and ended at 4:00 in the morning. As she described her daily routine for caring for her daughter, Astra, the interviewer became confused about the timing and, at one point, asked her whether she was talking about 4:00 a.m. or 4:00 p.m. Jan responded, "When you work my shift, there is no a.m. and p.m. It all blurs together."

Jan's regular 24-hour weekday is presented in Figure 1. Her 12-hour shift starts at 3:30 p.m., which means that she has to leave her home by 2:00 to make the drive and be at her work station and ready to work by 3:30. Astra's father is retired and comes to Jan's house in the afternoon to be there when Astra comes home from school. He stays there until Jan gets home from work around 4:30 in the morning. Jan sleeps for about two hours, then wakes to get Astra ready for school. She brings Astra to school around 7:30 a.m. and returns to bed for another two hours before getting up. Sometimes Astra's father will stay around to drive her to school, in which case Jan can return to sleep a little earlier. Jan gets up around 10:00 a.m. to do housework, shopping, and errands, and prepare dinner for Astra and her father. If she does not have a dinner prepared, she cannot depend on Astra's father to provide a nutritious meal: "Her dad can cook. Once in a while, he will."

Jan's childcare arrangements are predicated on help from Astra's dad, but that can sometimes be problematic:

> It depends on the mood he's in. He's moody. That's another problem that I have. . . . He does it every day, but if I tick him off, then I don't have no babysitter. Then he'll tell me, "I'm not keeping her." So then what do you do? [chuckles] It's like you can't just leave her. My mother is 74. I'm well over 40. It's not good.

Jan reported that she might be able to switch to days, but with her lack of seniority, she would run the risk of being subsequently "bumped" back to the afternoon shift by someone with more seniority.

FIGURE 1
Jan's Work and Home Schedule

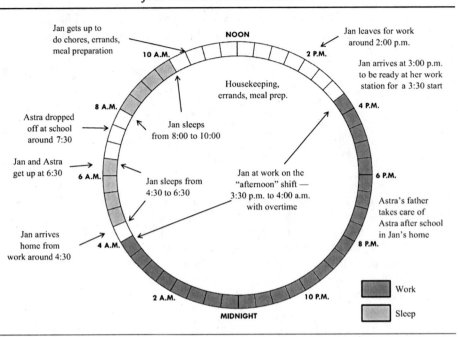

[The day shift] would be better for me. The thing is by them taking my seniority, I don't have enough seniority here to hold it. I could go to days right now and in three or four months when they had bump season, they'd bump me right back to afternoons. So to keep from switching childcare arrangements back and forth, that's—you know, children need a little stability and a little routine.

Work schedules in auto plants have long been recognized as raising serious problems for childcare. The 1999 contract negotiations between UAW and Ford included a plan for a network of family service and learning centers that would provide round-the-clock childcare to accommodate this shift structure. One of these new centers was near the Sylvania plant, but soon after its opening, the center had a long waiting list. In practice, the 24-hour schedule was never actually implemented, and the vision for the centers was never fully realized. In the face of economic pressures and the reorganization of the American auto industry, all of the UAW-Ford centers that were created eventually closed.

Despite the issues raised thus far, it must be noted that shift work itself—working an alternative to the traditional 9-to-5 job—is not always a problem for work-family balance. In some cases it can be an advantage in coordinating responsibilities. For example, one worker talked about the convenience of not having to start work until the afternoon:

If I need to do something during the day, I can get it done. All businesses are operating during the day, so most things shut down after 5:00 as far as business. Like your bills, you need to call somebody or do whatever, I can get that done during the day. I can, you know, go or do anything I need to during the day and still go to work. And when I come home if there's still something I need to go shopping for, Meijer's is 24-hours [chuckles].

I like having that morning time or whatever, to do whatever I want to do. And I don't like feeling like I have to be rushed to come to work. A big disadvantage, I believe, as far as day shift, is how their overtime is scheduled. They have to come in earlier. If they're only working nine hours they start at 6:00 or 7:00. But if they are working 11 or 12, they'll be starting at 3:00 or 4:00. So that sleep fluctuation, I couldn't do that.

Some Sylvania workers described how working the afternoon shift allowed them to share childcare responsibilities with a spouse who worked a different shift. One woman, whose husband also worked at Sylvania, talked about how they literally handed the baby off to each other in the parking lot at the shift change (Rudd and Root 2008). In fact, national statistics suggest that about one in six of those working an afternoon shift and one in ten working evenings say that they do so for family or childcare reasons. (U.S. Bureau of Labor Statistics 2005, Table 6).

Worker Agency: Creating Short-Term Flexibility in a Rigid Environment

When talking about problems of work-family balance, women interviewed at Sylvania tended to talk about childcare as a problem; men talked about not having enough time with their children, especially when their children were older and involved in school-based and other extracurricular activities. Regardless of the shift, long work hours were singled out as a problem. A supervisor commented on the toll that this takes on family life for men in the plant:

I don't know [pause] how their kids know who they are. I have no idea. And that's sad to me. Another guy that does work here, his father, you know, when he was growing up his father worked in the automotive industry and he's like, "I never knew my dad."

Workers talked about missing out on key activities in the lives of their children. In this regard, the dominant view at Sylvania—which corroborates earlier research— was that the afternoon shift is the worst for family life (Brayfield 1995). Employees are away from home from the early afternoon until well into the night:

If your kids are in school, it's even worse. You don't see them except on the weekends. They're in school all day. You might see them in the morning. You get up in the morning and take them to school. But by the time they get out of school, you're at work and by the time you get home from work, they're in bed. So you see them in the morning to take them to school and that's it. See, there's no time. There's no family time, other than the weekend. And of course, as your kids get a little older they have friends and things they want to do on the weekends. . . . You have to really make an effort to put [in] that time with them.

One father talked about his grown son who is now a swimming coach, but whom he was never able to watch compete in high school. "I never got to see him do any of his extracurricular activities because most of my time I spent on the number three [afternoon] shift." Because seniority is a major determinant of work assignments, younger workers—those who are more likely to have children at home—tended to be on the afternoon shift. Hence, these workers were most susceptible to experiencing instability in contact hours with their children while these children were at ages where they would be in most need of such contact.

In the course of our interviewing and observations, we found that particular types of worker agency were a major part of dealing with work-family conflict. Such exercises of worker agency might be sanctioned or unsanctioned. Sanctioned exercises of worker agency were those choices and actions made within the normal operating rules governing job assignments and scheduling. Although these aspects of work at Sylvania were often constrained by seniority rules, we encountered situations in which workers were able to adjust their work assignments to meet family obligations, such as childcare. For example, one woman whose husband also worked at Sylvania was able to transfer to a less desirable job on the day shift so that they as a couple could coordinate childcare (Rudd and Root 2008).

When flexibility was not present, however, we found that workers developed informal coping mechanisms to meet pressing family obligations—an exercise in "unsanctioned agency." An interview early in the research triggered interest in this aspect of worker agency, particularly the situation of parents wanting to be a part of the organized sports lives of their children (Root and Wooten 2008).

James, a long-term employee, described how he was always involved in organized sports with his children, coaching their teams to be more directly involved in an important activity in their lives:

> I had two boys and two girls and they all were on one of my teams or another. So I always had basketball, football, softball, Branford Raiders, flag football, or whatever. All year 'round. Whatever it was, my kids were always on the team. So when I came home, they came home with me.

Unlike others we interviewed, James was usually able to work on the day shift, freeing up his afternoons and evenings for these activities with his children. One time, however, he was asked to work on a Saturday when his team was playing its championship game. He said that he could work a half-day, but had to leave in the afternoon.

> I told that foreman on Monday of that week that we got the championship game, which is like a super bowl, our league against the other league—the top team. We got this super bowl game Saturday. I got to leave no later than 12 or I'm not goin' come that Saturday at all. He said, "Well, come on in, and I'll make sure you get off."
>
> I get there that Saturday mornin', I'll never forget that. I said, "Phil, you know I gotta leave at 12." "I can't let you go" [he said]. I said, "Phil, I told you about it." "Yeah, but I gotta run this job, I can't—no, no." All right. So I go to lunch at 11. I go left to the pay phone, stick my little money in, call back in, and say, "Hey, my car fell in a ditch. I'm

waitin' for AAA to come. I don't know how long they gonna' be." Okay. I said, "I may be back and I may not." So to the game I go.

Come back in that Monday and, at that time, I was workin' off the line doin' shock repair. I was just repairin' shocks on the side. Just take 'em off the line and, don't nothin' come of it, set 'em down. I come back that Monday, he posted my job on the board [so that other workers could "bid" on his job]. Now here's a man put in for it with 20 more years' seniority than me. Now I'm back on the [assembly] line.

When there was not a sanctioned way of getting the short-term flexibility he needed, James acted on his own. His exercise of "worker agency"—disappearing with an unconvincing excuse—did not go unpunished. He was transferred to a much less desirable job and the worksite was left shorthanded. The situation led to a lose-lose situation for him and for the plant.

Because of the nature of the production process at Sylvania, which included assembly lines, work teams, coverage demands, and high production targets, we were particularly struck by the challenges involved in getting short-term time off. Short-term flexibility is particularly problematic for lower-status workers in this work environment. Managers and professionals tend to have greater control of their time, in the sense that although they may work long hours, they more often can flex their time. As they supervise lower-tier workers, they typically may be charged with issuing directives and enforcing policies concerning production but not with actually generating that production. In contrast, those in line positions and with coverage responsibility—whether in manufacturing or service jobs—have the particular challenge of producing the goods or services (Baltes et al. 1999). Hence, short-term flexibility is something more than a minor inconvenience in these worksites. Instead, it can be a source of considerable disruption of the production process itself.

Work-family problems associated with the afternoon shift came up in a number of interviews, particularly around the problems of getting time off for occasional family events or commitments. Workers talked about finding informal ways to gain some short-term flexibility even within the demanding production structure. There were a number of examples of workers on the afternoon shift who talked about the importance of being a part of their children's participation in organized sports (Root and Wooten 2008). In the face of the rigidity of the organizational structure, workers' coping strategies reflected three general approaches: making informal arrangements with sympathetic supervisors, getting the support of their coworkers, and taking independent actions (such as James's decision not to return to work after he left for his Saturday lunch break).

The importance of supportive supervisors for coping with work-family balance is broadly recognized (Brunetto et al. 2010; Friedman and Johnson 1997; Scandura and Lankau 1997), and it has been identified as having specific import for those who experience the impacts of shift work (Pisarski et al. 2008). As one individual at Sylvania put it, "My boss was great. [He] knew what my issues were with my wife. . . . His family values are strong like mine. The family comes first. He has never given me a hard time for taking time off for my family." Another worker described how he would arrange to leave temporarily during his shift to have a glimpse of his daughter's cheerleading: "I'd give up Friday night, a couple hours, and tell my boss to stop my pay. I'd go to football games and watch her cheer, come back and go to work. As long as you're in an off-line job in the afternoon shift, the bosses are fairly flexible." In contrast, there were other supervisors who "want to make a name for themselves" as tough managers: "They're not very good 'people persons' like they should be. You can spot them. You can look at the numbers and spot them right off the bat where all the trouble is. Where's the absenteeism? Where's the [disciplinary reports]? They will follow that person around."

In other cases, supportive coworkers were the key to informal arrangements—a situation that has been documented in many work settings (Hodson 1997). One worker described how he was able to leave early on days when his son was playing his high school baseball games. He was working a 12-hour day shift at the time and arranged for a coworker who wanted more overtime to come in early on those days. He would put in eight hours, starting at 3:00 a.m., and then leave in time to go to the games:

> I was supposed to be working from 3:00 to 3:30 [p.m.], but the guy on afternoons was complaining about he wasn't making enough. So I just told the foreman, "Hey, I'll work from 3:00 to 11:30 and by the time my son's game come up, I'll be there to watch him." I didn't have no problem. I was at my son's games.

The reliance on coworkers to assist in the informal implementation of worker flexibility is rooted in the culture of the workplace (Bailyn 1997). In explaining that culture, many workers said that the plant maintained a "family" atmosphere. Coworkers would simply work out a way to cover for someone who wanted to slip out briefly to make an appearance at a child's event:

> It's nice here because if you're on afternoons and you have a kid, a lot of guys will let you sneak out. Not that it's right, but they'll let you sneak out to go see your son play a football game or whatever, and sneak back in. They'll cover you in that respect. So that's kind of nice. That's part of the family aspect here. A couple of guys have said that. They've been stuck on afternoons and their son was at a football game. They were determined to go see it, so they worked it out with the buddies. "I'm just going to be gone for an hour, just so I can go see him and wave to him and let him know I'm there." And then they come back.

Aside from flexibility gained through informal agreements with supervisors or with the collegial support of coworkers, there were independent actions taken by workers to meet family obligations. James's story is one example. Another highlights how a worker "worked" the system, with her doctor's help. A supervisor was unwilling to grant a leave when her husband's father was hospitalized in northern Michigan:

> My father-in-law had Parkinson's that he had been diagnosed with probably six–eight years before that. We were up there at the two-week shutdown [a periodic temporary systemwide closing of the plant] and he had taken a turn for the worse. They had him

in the hospital and didn't know if he was gonna make it or not. We had spent two solid weeks [during the shutdown] at the hospital in Marquette every day with him. They had admitted him and, like I say, they didn't know if he was going to live or die.

Well, when it come time to comin' back to work, the Family Medical Leave Act was in effect. My husband could take it because it was his father. In-laws are not considered immediate family, so I was not allowed to take the FMLA. I called my boss, told my boss what was going on. And he said, "Mrs. Dougherty, you will be back to work on Tuesday." I had called him on Monday. I said, "Jim, I can't make it back." "Mrs. Dougherty, I'm tellin' you, you will be back to work on Tuesday." I said, "Jim, I've gotta do what I've gotta do." And I hung up from him, called my family doctor, explained the situation I was under. He says, "Sounds like it's stress to me." He put me off on two weeks' medical [leave].

In this example, a worker's family care situation did not fit within the requirements of the federal law, and her supervisor showed no willingness to work with her in finding a way to care for her father-in-law. Facing this, she used her ingenuity and, with her doctor's cooperation, found a way to address her family's needs.

Other workers talked about the leverage they had, as workers, to gain the agreement of management. For example, supervisors have to "make the numbers"—meet specific production goals—and the workers in the department could subtly decrease output. Such individual or concerted group efforts are a topic in the literature, identifying a range of activities from inaction and slowdowns to wasting materials to outright sabotage (Analoui 1995; Roscigno and Hodson 2004). One worker at Sylvania told of single-handedly slowing down production on his single-operator machine in response to new restrictions on overtime. Another person remarked that if his supervisor did not authorize altering his work schedule so he could attend his son's "Bible quiz" tournament, he could leave his machine out of adjustment in a way that would make it very hard for anyone else to fix:

I [could] mix it up a little bit to where the guy came in on the next shift couldn't put it back together and be sittin' there waiting for me to put it back together [laughs]. . . . You gotta know your machine—machinery—well enough to be able to do it that way. You're really not sabotaging the machine. . . . It's just that "Oh, I guess I should have put it back that way."

Although he did not say he actually had done this, he felt his supervisor knew that he could take these kinds of retaliatory actions if his request for flexibility was not approved.

The coping mechanisms described above—expressions of worker agency—suggest different levels of legitimacy and control, reflecting the tension between conflict and cooperation (Edwards and Bélinger 2008). Figure 2 displays the examples of worker agency discussed as falling on a continuum that ranges from actions that are not under the control of management (and, hence, have greater potential for disruption) to those with greater management involvement. Having the cooperation of a supportive supervisor, even when it involves going against the rules, tends to be the least disruptive to the operations of the organization. Although it may go against formal rules, it acknowledges the authority of the supervisor, and presumably, the involvement of the supervisor ensures that such actions

FIGURE 2
Examples of Human Agency at Sylvania

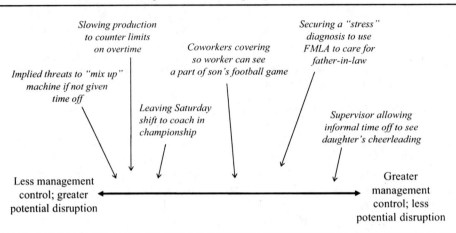

are not excessively disruptive in terms of the work that needs to be done. Hence, both worker satisfaction and production can remain high.

Creating flexibility by getting coworkers to help "cover" during an absence has less management control and a greater potential for disruption in the workplace. It also may reinforce a sense of competitiveness between workers and management. In this case, workers may find themselves generally satisfied with the workplace (at least as far as relations with coworkers is concerned) but less satisfied with management. This kind of consistent tension has the capacity to inhibit productivity. Finally, the third method discussed—workers taking independent actions, possibly in direct defiance of the rules—has the least legitimacy within the workplace and the greatest potential to be seriously disruptive. This condition can severely cripple production while also sustaining, and potentially enhancing, worker dissatisfaction with the workplace.

Implications for Work-Family Policy and Practice

Our emphasis on worker agency in regard to the tensions involved in managing the work-family balance is not an affirmation of sabotage or coercion as a critical resource for workers. Rather, we are highlighting both the impact that constraints place on a certain sector of workers in their effort to manage the tenuous balance of work-family obligations and how a lack of workplace flexibility can result in individual and group responses that can have negative impacts on the workplace. Workers in an inflexible environment will seek to create their own flexibility when pressured by competing obligations.

Our discussion of worker agency has focused on its exercise against constraints in the workplace. But we should not neglect the positive aspects of worker agency that arise from a sense of commitment to the organization—loyalty and the willingness to go beyond the basics of what is required for a job. When workers at Sylvania talked about the characteristics of a "good job," they most frequently mentioned factors that we typically associate with job satisfaction: pay levels that are considered fair, good working conditions, and a sense of accomplishment. But they also talked about how the quality of their relationship to supervisors influenced their commitment to their work. The importance of the "workplace culture" and the nature of relationships were suggested in our earlier discussion of the "family" environment that facilitated informal flexibility. Interviews suggested the depth of feeling—at least for some workers—about the nature of supervision as a key to how they feel about their work.

> For me what distinguishes one job from another is really the people. And for me, I need to feel appreciated. If I don't—because I've had an experience in my career where I didn't feel appreciated and I felt unproductive and it didn't motivate me one single bit. So a good job to me is when you have leadership that you would do anything for. And that's what I—the kind of job I enjoy the most. So it doesn't really matter what it is content-wise. But it's more the way it's run. The way it's run and if you have a good leader who appreciates you as a valuable member of the team, that's a good job.

Another worker, talking about a "good job," emphasized the importance of the support she received that helped her to get through a difficult period in her life:

> And before, it was, at work they didn't want to hear about anything at home. They don't care about anything at home. "When you're at work, you're at work. Don't bring your [home issues up]." But you can't help it. When it's in your head and in your heart. . . . And especially if you're having a tough time, whether it be a divorce or the loss of a loved one or an illness or something, before you weren't allowed to bring that to work with you. And now they're realizing that um, that is part of your life and you do have to deal with that when you're at work. And if just having some benefit of the Family Medical Leave, you know, the person can take off for a month or whatever and get their life back in order, they're glad to come back. They didn't really want to leave. You know, they really just need a small amount of time or consideration or something to get through this. They don't want to give up their job and things like that. I think that's often great.

Conversely, unresolved work-family tensions are associated with a negative sense of job satisfaction (Frye and Breaugh 2004; Kossek and Ozeki 1998). A salaried worker talked about how his sense of his employer changed after the insensitive response of his supervisor at his previous job:

> My brother-in-law committed suicide just before I left [my earlier job]. I got an emergency phone call one morning from my nephew, his son, that he had shot himself. And when I told my boss, he said, "Why do you have to leave? It's just your brother-in-law." [pause] That was a hard thing to do. In fact, that was probably one of the things that led me to leave.

As we stated in the introduction to this article, some broad-based commitments to flexibility in the workplace have already garnered significant public attention and have been inspired by policy formation. The Family and Medical Leave Act of 1993 (FMLA) provided employees of medium and large companies up to 12 weeks of unpaid leave during any 12-month period. Leaves can be taken for a number of reasons, including the birth or adoption of a child; the care of spouse, son, daughter, or parent of an employee who has a serious health condition; or a serious health condition that makes the employee unable to perform the essential functions of his or her position. The creation and implementation of this act signaled a major transformation in formal policy concerning workplace flexibility but, as is the case more generally with federal government policy, was an initiative imposed from outside of the workplace.

From the perspective of government policy, the scope of the FMLA is generally limited to medical care and time off related to birth or adoption. Several states have passed their own family leave statutes that extend FMLA's coverage to smaller employers and to additional relatives (e.g., parents-in-law, rather than only biological parents, and domestic partners). Some states have also added provisions for short-term flexibility, such as for addressing issues related to domestic violence (Women's Legal Defense and Education Fund 2011). For the most part, however, short-term flexibility is largely a function of the internal policies of the firm. Although federal government policy concerning workplace flexibility has a direct impact on many worksites, its effect on smaller employers and on work-family conflicts other than those identified by the legislation in other employment arenas may be only psychological, calling attention to the importance of the issue.

Our research suggests that there may be important advantages for companies that seek to create an environment in which there are options for informal flexibility. Worker agency should be an important factor in considering policies and practices concerning workplace flexibility and work-family balance more generally. Management has a primary responsibility for maintaining an effective workplace. Accordingly, initiatives that target the behavior of middle-level managers—what may best be called manager and supervisor "agency"—extend the possibilities for the transformation of the workplace. Implementing such initiatives serves the objectives of enhancing a workplace culture that both advances worker satisfaction with and commitment to the workplace and leads to increased productivity.

In focusing on managers and supervisors, it must be kept in mind that attempts at control can be thwarted when they do not give adequate attention to the real pressures facing workers and the pressures on workers to actively seek ways to meet competing demands of work and family. How employers deal with these issues can go a long way toward influencing the positive dimensions of worker agency—commitment to the job, loyalty, and willingness to take initiatives beyond the basic requirements of the job. Rather than solely emphasizing the creation and implementation of formal policies, an important step toward the transformation of the workplace so that worker flexibility can be more fruitfully incorporated is to recognize and encourage flexibility on the part of employers, managers, and frontline supervisors. In the case of manufacturing firms, a change-from-within approach rests not solely on a moral foundation of fairness to workers but also on the basis that such efforts may benefit the workplace more generally by enhancing both productivity and employee commitment.

Although middle-level managers and supervisors are critical to implementing this cultural change, it is important that cultural changes take place first for this level of management. This article emphasizes that flexible responses to emerging employee crises and short-term family commitments are crucial for achieving worker satisfaction and commitment to productivity. Government policies and top-down mandates concerning employee behavior and production outcomes will be most effective if the agency of these managers and supervisors is recognized as a pivotal factor at the workplace. Accordingly, such managers must be informed, encouraged, and possibly formally trained to recognize the need for worksite flexibility and the methods of effectively employing it. This may ultimately mean that the reward system for such managers (whether it be in terms of material/economic rewards or advancement/heightened recognition for leadership in the workplace) should include the incorporation of flexibility systems into the workplace along with the traditional criteria for managerial advancement. Ultimately, then, for flexibility to take hold in employment sectors where rigid regulation of time at work is directly related to the goals and objectives of firms, a human resource approach is needed that accepts flexibility as an essential tool and is implemented in a way that avoids to the extent possible forcing employees to choose between work and family.

Notes

1. This research was generously supported by the Alfred P. Sloan Foundation and its University of Michigan Center for the Ethnography of Everyday Life. During the course of the study, seven individuals participated as part of the research team: Bob Bowen, Dilli Dehal, Tom Fricke, Pete Richardson, Larry Root, Elizabeth Rudd, and Alford Young Jr. Most of the semistructured interviews were carried out by Root and Rudd.

2. During the course of this research, Sylvania experienced decreased orders and steady downsizing. Eventually, after the recession took hold in 2008, the plant closed.

3. All names of research subjects used in this article are pseudonyms.

References

Analoui, Farhad. 1995. Workplace sabotage: Its styles, motives, and management. *Journal of Management Development* 14 (7): 48–65.

Bailyn, Lotte. 1997. The impact of corporate culture on work-family integration. In *Integrating work and family: Challenges and choices in a changing world*, eds. Saroj Parasuraman and Jeffrey H. Greenhaus, 209–19. Westport, CT: Quorum Books.

Baltes, Boris B., Thomas E. Briggs, Joseph W. Huff, Julia A. Wright, and George A. Neuman. 1999. Flexible and compressed workweek schedules: A meta-analysis of their effects on work-related criteria. *Journal of Applied Psychology* 84 (4): 596–13.

Blau, Francine. 1998. Trends in the well-being of American women. *Journal of Economic Literature* 36 (1): 112–65.

Braverman, Harry. 1974. *Labor and monopoly capital: The degradation of work in the twentieth century*. New York, NY: Monthly Review Press.

Brayfield, April. 1995. Juggling jobs and kids: The impact of employment schedules on fathers' caring for children. *Journal of Marriage and the Family* 57 (2): 321–32.

Brunetto, Yvonne, Rod Farr-Warton, Sheryl Ramsey, and Kate Shakloc. 2010. Supervisor relationships and perceptions of work-family conflict. *Asia Pacific Journal of Human Resources* 48 (2): 212–32.

Christensen, Kathleen, and Barbara Schneider. 2010. Introduction: Evidence of the worker and workplace mismatch. In *Workplace flexibility: Realigning 20th-century jobs for a 21st-century workforce*, eds. Kathleen Christensen and Barbara Schneider, 1–14. Ithaca, NY: Cornell University Press.

Edwards, Paul, and Jacque Bélinger. 2008. Generalizing from workplace ethnographies: From induction to theory. *Journal of Contemporary Ethnography* 37 (3): 291–313.

Friedman, Dana E., and Arlene A. Johnson. 1997. Moving from programs to culture change: The next stage for corporate work-family agenda. In *Integrating work and family: Challenges and choices for a changing world*, eds. Saroj Parasuraman and Jeffrey H. Greenhaus, 209–19. Westport, CT: Quorum Books.

Frye, N. Kathleen, and James, A. Breaugh. 2004. Family-friendly policies, supervisor support, work-family conflict, family-work conflict, and satisfaction: A test of a conceptual model. *Journal of Business and Psychology* 19 (2): 197–220.

Golden, Lonnie. 2001. Flexible work schedules: What are we trading off to get them? *Monthly Labor Review* 124 (3): 50–67.

Hodson, Randy. 1997. Group relations at work: Solidarity, conflict, and relations with management. *Work and Occupations* 24 (4): 426–52.

Jacobs, Jerry, and Kathleen Gerson. 1998. Who are the overworked Americans? *Review of Social Economy* 45 (4): 442–59.

Jurgens, Ulrich, Thomas Malsch, and Knuth Dohse. 1993. *Breaking from Taylorism: Changing forms of work in the automobile industry*. Cambridge: Cambridge University Press.

Kossek, Ellen E., and Cynthia Ozeki. 1998. Work-family conflict, policies, and the job-life satisfaction relationship: A review and directions for organizational behavior-human resources research. *Journal of Applied Psychology* 83 (2): 139–49.

Locke, Edwin A., 1982. The ideas of Frederick W. Taylor: An evaluation. *Academy of Management Review* 7 (1): 14–24.

Pisarski, Anne, Sandra A. Lawrence, Philip Bohle, and Christine Brook. 2008. Organizational influences on the work life conflict and health of shiftworkers. *Applied Ergonomics* 39 (5): 580–88.

Presser, Harriet B. 2003. *Working in a 24/7 economy: Challenges for American families*. New York, NY: Russell Sage Foundation.

Root, Lawrence S., and Lynn Perry Wooten. 2008. Time out for families: Work, fathers, and sports. *Human Resource Management* 47 (3): 481–99.

Roscigno, Vincent I., and Randy Hodson. 2004. The organizational and social foundations of worker resistance. *American Sociological Review* 69 (1): 14–39.

Rudd, Elizabeth, and Lawrence S. Root. 2008. "We pass the baby off at the factory gates": Work and family in the manufacturing Midwest. In *The changing landscape of work and family in the American middle class*, eds. Elizabeth Rudd and Lara Descartes, 61–85. Lanham, MD: Lexington Books.

Scandura, Terri A., and Melenie J. Lankau. 1997. Relationships of gender, family responsibilities and flexible work hours to organizational commitment and job satisfaction. *Journal of Organizational Behavior* 18 (4): 377–91.

Taylor, Frederick W. 1911. *Principles of scientific management*. New York, NY: Harper Brothers.

Teddlie, Charles, and Fen Yu. 2007. Mixed methods sampling: A typology with examples. *Journal of Mixed Methods Research* 1 (1): 77–100.

U.S. Bureau of Labor Statistics. 2005. Economic news release: Workers on flexible and shift schedules in May 2004. Available from www.bls.gov/news.release/History/flex.txt.

U.S. Bureau of Labor Statistics. 2009. Labor force participation of women and mothers, 2008. Available from www.bls.gov/opub/ted/2009/ted_20091009.htm.

Waring, Stephen P. 1991. *Taylorism transformed: Scientific management theory since 1945*. Chapel Hill: University of North Carolina Press.

Women's Legal Defense and Education Fund. 2011. *State law guide: Employment rights for victims of domestic or sexual violence*. Available from www.legalmomentum.org/assets/pdfs/employment-rights.pdf.

The Human Face of Workplace Flexibility

This article reviews several recent studies on working families and discusses the importance of why workplace flexibility needs to become a standard of the U.S. workplace. Most children reside in households with either two employed parents or an employed single parent. The inflexibility of work and school schedules is a pressure that working parents feel on a daily basis and one that affects their work-related productivity, health, and family life. Whether employed in a white-collar job or in a low-wage one, employed parents often experience anxiety and guilt as they face the obligations of work and family. Parent-role overload and time deprivations are particularly acute problems that many employed mothers and fathers cope with on a daily basis. Overall, work-family conflict leads to decreased psychological well-being. Parents need to work to meet the needs of their families, yet their lives show signs that the current situation is untenable. A new balance needs to be achieved between work and home for working families.

Keywords: workplace flexibility; working families; work-family conflict; multitasking; family stress; family well-being

By
BARBARA SCHNEIDER

U.S. families are experiencing serious time constraints as the demands of work and family life increasingly require more attention and involvement. Confronted with workplaces and educational institutions that have rigid schedules governing where and when one has to be at work or school, the predictable and unpredictable nature of daily life is taking a major toll on the emotional well-being of parents and their children. Most working parents have the daily worry of arranging their schedules to accommodate the demands of *time* needed not only for work-related activities but also to adequately

Barbara Schneider is the John A. Hannah Distinguished Professor in the College of Education and the Department of Sociology at Michigan State University. Her research focuses primarily on the social context of families and schools and their relationship to adolescent development. She codirected the Center on Parents, Children and Work at the University of Chicago, which resulted in the book Being Together, Working Apart: Dual-Career Families and the Work-Life Balance *(Cambridge University Press 2005).*

DOI: 10.1177/0002716211415824

supervise and be actively engaged in their children's lives (Christensen, Schneider, and Butler forthcoming).

We cannot see it or touch it, yet we all are keenly aware when an hour passes. How we spend our time provides a window into the priorities and activities of our daily lives. Time diary studies, such as the American Time Use Survey (ATUS) and the National Survey of Parents (Bianchi, Robinson, and Milkie 2006), provide robust estimates of the time spent by working parents and the activities they engage in when at work, at home, and in public places. However, these studies do not contain information regarding how parents feel when working overtime or on the weekends, being caught in traffic and missing their children's school events, or performing household tasks such as cooking or cleaning. Examining not only the amount of time spent on activities but how parents feel when engaged in them can provide a deep understanding of why the structures of workplaces are increasingly incompatible with the changing dynamics of working families. This article relies on findings from multiple studies (including data from the 500 Family Study, which collected information on the subjective experiences of working families) and discusses the importance of workplace flexibility and why it should become a standard for work, especially for working families.

Why We Need to Care about Time

The majority of children under the age of 18 reside in households with either two employed parents or with an employed single parent (Bureau of Labor Statistics 2010). Recent U.S. estimates indicate that these employed fathers and mothers spend, on average, approximately 64 hours per week on paid and unpaid work combined (Bianchi, Robinson, and Milkie 2006). For parents in professional jobs, these numbers are considerably higher. Jacobs and Gerson (2004) estimate that mothers and fathers in managerial positions work at their paid jobs well over 40 hours a week.

Looking specifically at mothers and fathers employed full-time in various types of jobs, mothers spend on average eight hours per day on work, whereas fathers spend about nine hours (Allard and Janes 2008). Figure 1 shows the hours spent in a typical day for a working mother and father.

The time mothers are not working outside the home is spent disproportionately on gender-specific tasks. Mothers allocate more time to household management and childcare (2.9 hours per day vs. 1.6 hours per day for fathers) and spend less time in leisure than fathers (2.3 hours per day vs. 2.9 hours per day, respectively).

What Figure 1 does not indicate is how daily work hours correspond to the hours that parents are responsible for their children's care. Clearly, children too young to be enrolled in regular school need supervision the entire time their parents are at work. However, school-aged children also need supervision, and the rigid schedules of elementary and secondary schools do not overlap with the

FIGURE 1
Average Time Allocations per Day for Working Parents

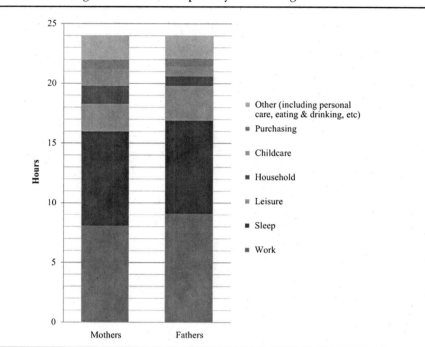

Source: Author's tabulations from data presented in Allard and Janes (2008).

standard workday of most employed parents (see Christensen and Schneider [2010] for further discussion of this argument). School days are shorter than the average workday, and children are in school for far fewer days than parents working full time are at the workplace.

Few of us think about how the length of the school year and school day conflicts with working parents' schedules. Most states require that children spend a minimum of 180 days in school; however, several states require less than 175 days (National Center for Education Statistics [NCES] 2008). This means that parents have at least 185 days when they have to solely manage their children's care (see Figure 2). If parents' jobs do not occur over the weekend, they still are responsible for at least 81 weekdays during the year when their children are not in school. School holidays and vacation breaks including those long months of summer require working parents to make arrangements for their children's care and supervision.

Most full-time jobs allow workers two weeks of vacation and some personal days. Taking these times into account, there are approximately 55 days per year that parents are responsible for their children's care when they have to work. This 55-day estimate does not include the days when there are parent-teacher conferences (which vary by state and school district) or other times when schools are closed unexpectedly for weather and other circumstances.

FIGURE 2
Number of Unsupervised Days for School-Age Children of Working Parents

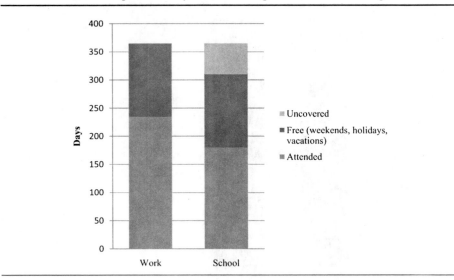

Source: Author's tabulations.

Breaking down these days into hours, children are in school approximately 6.5 hours each weekday (NCES 2008). A full-time working parent spends approximately 8 hours at the job and commutes slightly less than an hour to and from work each day (U.S. Census Bureau 2004). This means that, at a minimum, on an average school day there are approximately 2.5 hours that parents are responsible for the direct care of their children when they are at work and their children are not in school.

For the parents whose workdays begin before school, this means ensuring that someone is responsible for taking care of breakfast and transporting their children to school. Similarly, if parents have to work late, someone has to manage care after school and provide dinner for their children. A study by the NCES examining before- and after-school care for kindergarteners through eighth graders found that 20 percent of children have scheduled nonparent arrangements before school, and 50 percent of them have such arrangements after school (Carver, Iruka, and Chapman 2006). While these statistics are for younger children, it is also the case that teenagers (especially those unable to drive) often require transportation services and supervision. And for all children, the presence or absence of a family dinner has been shown to be critical for family and children's well-being (Ochs et al. 2010).

It does not take too much imagination to understand why working parents, in the struggle to meet work and family commitments, report keeping priorities straight and managing their time as serious concerns (Schneider and Waite 2005). The responsibilities of arranging for care when needing to leave for work early or having to stay late, and covering those unpredictable times when traveling, are now an integral part of working parents' lifestyles. This lifestyle requires working parents to be actively involved in the extensive management and scheduling of family time. Additionally, parents have to be available to provide care for those unpredictable times when a child or relative is sick or becomes injured. The Centers for Disease Control estimates that on average a child can expect to miss three to five days of school a year due to illness or injury (Blackwell and Tonthat 2003). Parent stress related just to these fairly typical events has been shown to result in being distracted at work and anxious about work at home (Barnett 2010).

The pressure and responsibility of providing direct supervision seems overwhelming from a strategic planning perspective, but parenting today is much more than supervision. Most parents desire to improve their child's educational performance and enhance his or her psychological well-being (Schneider and Waite 2005). Being directly involved in their child's education has become a norm of behavior that parents, especially those in the middle class, are anxious to fulfill. The popular media has helped to create a standard of "good parenting" that emphasizes the importance of parents' helping with homework; arranging for extracurricular activities, summer camps, and academic programs; hiring tutors and coaches; and being instantaneously accessible via phone or text messaging. The media also emphasizes the negative consequences if parents fail to help their children in these ways, including falling behind in academic performance and failing to be admitted to the college of one's choice.

Navigating the U.S. educational system, by selecting the best schools, right teachers, and recognizing and remediating the negative consequences of mediocre test scores, is normative among middle-class parents. For parents of adolescents, there is the added responsibility and commitment of time, effort, and resources to assist their children in the college selection and admission processes. The familiar phrase of "helicopter parents" hovering over the lives of their college students, ready to intervene on a moment's notice, now applies not only to postsecondary but all school-aged children.

The time necessary to supervise children and be actively involved in their educational careers often collides with parents' work schedules. Being available to help with homework, volunteer in school, and address potential academic problems requires time, which is in short supply for many parents who work long hours and have little or no flexibility to change their schedules for when their children are at home. The inflexibility of work and school schedules is a pressure that working parents feel on a daily basis. These emotional experiences affect worker health and productivity and family life, creating resentment among adolescents when their parents miss and are not involved in sport and school activities (Marchena 2005) and stress and strain on a marriage (Nielsen 2005).

For low-wage workers, these problems are even more salient. These workers are often in jobs with inflexible work arrangements, such as the ability to take personal days for child or relative care, and unpredictable work schedules that interfere with their children's school schedules (Heymann and Earle 2000). Holding jobs with little flexibility and having limited financial resources to find alternative care, these parents have to rely on relatives or institutional care (Offer 2005). Adolescents in these families often have to assume the parenting role: babysitting younger siblings and taking full responsibility for meals and personal care (Csikszentmihalyi and Schneider 2000). With respect to interfacing with the school or undertaking activities (e.g., tutors or special programs) that would support their children's success, lack of informational networks, resources, and the flexibility to interact frequently with teachers all contribute to a challenging situation for these parents and their families. Although the parents may believe the schools are taking full responsibility for their children's educational needs and their own involvement is less important, the schools often view these parents as uncaring or disinterested (Hassrick and Schneider 2009).

Subjective Experiences of Working Families

Whether working in a white-collar job or in a low-wage one, employed parents often experience anxiety and guilt as they face the obligations of work and family. As discussed above, parent-role overload and time deprivations are particularly acute problems that many employed mothers and fathers cope with on a daily basis. Two of the most common concerns of working parents are not being able to spend enough time with their children and spouse (Milkie et al. 2004; Roxburgh 2006) and the desire to work less (Clarkberg and Moen 2001; Galinsky, Kim, and Bond 2001; Weston et al. 2004; Reynolds 2005). Jacobs and Gerson (2004), for example, estimate a 10-hour gap between the number of hours parents of young children actually work and ideally wished they could work each week.

Other studies of working parents also show that the majority of mothers would prefer to work part time and that unemployed mothers looking for work would prefer part-time jobs (Christensen 2005; Hart 2003). However, the part-time option is often not pursued even in workplaces where this type of flexibility practice is offered (Hewlett 2010). Studies indicate that mothers working full time are concerned that their careers will be damaged by engaging in part-time work or jobs that offer flexible working arrangements (Galinsky et al. 2010). In contrast, fathers are less likely to desire part-time work but instead prefer jobs that would be more accommodating to the lives of their families. These accommodations include working less overtime, traveling less, and having more control over when they have to work (Christensen 2005).

It is not only family demands for greater time that have created pressures for working parents but also the increasing time demands experienced on the job. Using data from two national surveys, Nomaguchi (2009) found that employed parents increasingly feel that they do not have enough time to get things done at their jobs. This heightened sense of time pressure at work is significantly associated with an increase in the report of work-family conflict since the 1970s. Feeling stress from the combination of work and family responsibilities, some parents are seeking new jobs that can relieve the strains associated with work-life conflict (Moen and Huang 2010).

Research has consistently shown a negative relationship between work-family conflict and health and well-being (Allen et al. 2000; Bellavia and Frone 2005). Working parents, in struggling with work and family commitments, describe feelings of stress; emotional and psychological pressure; and a lack of energy to cope with their spouses, children, and jobs (Offer and Schneider 2010)—feelings that can adversely affect their health and productivity. For example, an estimated one-third of the workforce experiences stress about their children's after-school time, leading to decreased productivity and increased absenteeism (Barnett and Gareis 2006; McGuire, Kenny, and Brashler 2006).

Recognizing the relationship between long hours of work and well-being, analyses of subjective dimensions of time use can produce rich understandings of how mothers, fathers, and children are feeling throughout the day and can reveal varying levels of positive and negative emotions in different social contexts. Several studies funded by the Alfred P. Sloan Foundation have examined these issues using a wide range of methodologies. One of these is the 500 Family Study, a multimethod investigation of the work-life balance among U.S. middle-class families, two hundred of which have kindergarten-age children and three hundred of which have adolescents (Schneider and Waite 2005). This study obtained information on families living in eight urban and suburban communities across the United States.

Although not a sample of all families in the United States, the 500 Family Study does comprise a representative group of middle-class, dual-earner parents and their children (Hoogstra 2005; Jeong 2005). The definition of what is considered "middle class" is somewhat contentious, as job status, earnings, assets, and values are often not well aligned. In this study, parents were considered middle class if at least one parent held a postsecondary degree. The majority of the parents in the five hundred families are employed in management positions, such as account executives; however, there are also teachers, librarians, and nurses in the sample. Given the types of jobs these parents hold, it is not unexpected that they work long hours, on average more than 45 hours per week.

Several methods were used to examine the family and work experiences of the parents and children in the 500 Family Study, including surveys, in-depth interviews, and time diaries.[1] These data collection methods were designed to be complementary and provide detailed information about work, marriage, childcare, parent supervision, allocation of household tasks, and psychological well-being. In addition, several items from national studies were included, enabling comparisons of findings from this study to those with larger representative samples.

One unique aspect of the 500 Family Study was the use of the experience sampling method (ESM). Developed by Mihaly Csikszentmihalyi and his colleagues (Hektner, Schmidt, and Csikszentmihalyi 2007), the ESM, like traditional time diaries, examines how individuals spend their time, whom they are with, and the activities in which they are engaged. However, the ESM also provides detailed information on individuals' subjective interpretations of their experiences at particular moments over the course of a day and week. In the 500 Family Study, the

ESM operated through a preprogrammed watch that emitted several signals in the form of faintly audible beeps during the course of a day over a given week. When beeped, respondents completed a series of items that described their activities and subjective emotions. Obtaining repeated reports of positive and negative emotions over time makes it possible to estimate an individual's overall subjective emotion, as well as identifying those instances when that emotion, like stress, anger, or happiness, increases or decreases (for further information on the study design and methods, see Hoogstra 2005). Another advantage of the ESM is its ability to assess how individual family members subjectively experience time spent alone and with others, including coworkers, spouses, and children.

Emotions experienced while working during the day, in the evenings, and on weekends are real, not responses to laboratory-simulated events. ESM emotions capture more than the single global assessment elicited by a survey item, which asks, for example, "How stressed do you feel at work?" By examining how one feels throughout a day, it is possible to determine differences in the levels of stress experienced when at work from those at home. This is especially relevant for working mothers, who, studies show, are often responsible not only for the actual housework but for the mental labor of planning, organizing, and managing family life.

How individuals feel and react to specific situations is often viewed as being dispositional, genetic-, or personality-dependent, rather than being influenced by the situations they are in or whom they are with. Males and females are often thought to have different emotional responses, which are often assumed to be the consequence of gender. Certainly there are gender differences; however, there are also internal variations in daily experiences, and these occur both within individuals and across situations. Since the 500 Family Study involves both parents and children, it is possible to match ESM data from each family member and determine not only what a mother was doing and thinking at a point in time, but also what her spouse and children were doing at the same time and how each felt about their activities. Thus, the ESM provides an opportunity to examine, for example, how mom feels while getting dinner ready and helping with homework, how her adolescent feels doing homework and talking to her, and how dad at the same time feels while driving home from work and listening to the news.

Coping with Limited Time

The National Survey of Parents (Bianchi, Robinson, and Milkie 2006) shows that married couples in 2000 spent nearly 130 hours a week on market and non-market work combined, an approximately 10-hour increase since the mid-1960s. This does not include mental tasks such as organizing activities, planning events, and coordinating schedules (Darrah, Freeman, and English-Lueck 2007; Devault 1999). Time- and energy-consuming, yet often taken for granted, mental tasks can be thought of as the control panel that navigates the schedule for juggling work and family demands. As discussed earlier, parent involvement for school-age children has become a scheduling problem of managing and organizing time for transportation, lessons, and other after-school activities (Ochs et al. 2010).

Overall, perceptions of time deprivation and a sense of overworking have encouraged working families to set new priorities and develop coping strategies to manage their lives. Some parents have turned to purchasing services in the market, such as childcare, takeout meals, and cleaning services (Bianchi et al. 2000; Stuenkel 2005). Others have changed the amount of time they are willing to devote to cooking, cleaning house, or participating in leisure activities to maximize time with their children (Bianchi, Robinson, Milkie 2006). Multitasking constitutes yet another mechanism working families use to cope with the pressures of the "time squeeze."

Multitasking

Undertaking several activities at once, or the rapid alternation between them, is often viewed as a way for parents to get more accomplished within a limited time period. Using this definition and data from time diary studies conducted over several decades, Bianchi, Robinson, and Milkie (2006) report that multitasking almost doubled for working parents between 1975 and 2000. Results from their time diary studies show that the number of multitasking hours per week increased from 42 to 81 for married mothers and from 40 to 78 for married fathers (Bianchi, Robinson, and Milkie 2006). With the increase in cell phone use and texting since 2006, one might expect that these numbers would increase substantially. There is some evidence from the collaborative study of the University of Michigan and Pew Research Center's Internet and American Life Project that the number of times a day that adolescents and their parents are contacting each other has increased dramatically within the past three years (Lenhart 2010). Ninety-eight percent of the parents of cell-owning teenagers report that the major reason their children have a phone is so they can be in touch no matter where they are. Teens also report that they use their phones to call their parents and text primarily to contact friends. For both parents and teenagers, the cell phone has become one of the mechanisms by which it is possible to multitask in a variety of locations.

Notwithstanding that working parents seem more likely to multitask today than in the past, how they feel when engaged in such activities is less understood. Most time diary studies include information about respondents' main activity at a particular point in time (i.e., primary activity); few ask respondents to record both their main activity and any other activity they might be engaged in simultaneously (i.e., secondary activity). Time studies that include secondary activities tend to focus on broad domains, such as childcare (Bianchi, Robinson, and Milkie 2006; Craig 2006; Ironmonger 2004; Zick and Bryant 1996), leisure (Bittman and Wajcman 2000), and housework (Lee and Waite 2005; Williams and Donath 1994). Using these broad types of categories presents a somewhat limited view of multitasking and makes it difficult to identify the roles that multitasking may be playing in the everyday lives of contemporary working families.

One exception is recent work by Offer and Schneider (2010) that relies on ESM data from the 500 Family Study. In this study, the researchers selected a subsample that included mothers and fathers who completed both the ESM and survey questionnaires. This subsample selection produced 368 mothers who responded to 16,878 beeps and 241 fathers who responded to 9,482 beeps, resulting in ESM response rates of 78 percent for mothers and 73 percent for fathers. Analyses comparing the subsample with the larger 500 Family sample showed no bias between ESM and survey completers and noncompleters. Missing items were assigned with multiple imputation techniques (see Offer and Schneider 2010).

Extending their initial work on multitasking, Offer and Schneider (n.d.) have undertaken several new analyses. These new analyses broaden the scope of multitasking, creating several different measures that classify multitasking into seven broad categories, including work, housework, childcare, personal care, communication, transportation, and mental labor. To assess the relationship between psychological states and evaluation of life quality, five composite measures of well-being outcomes were constructed from the ESM. These constructs include positive affect (feeling good about oneself, cheerful, relaxed), negative affect (feeling irritated, frustrated, and nervous), stress (feeling stressed and strained), productive (feeling hardworking, productive, active, and successful), and focus (feeling in control, concentrating, and able to deal with the situation at hand). Additionally, a number of items were examined from the surveys, including psychological distress, perceived stress, work-family conflict, and family time guilt. Multivariate analysis included the context in which multitasking occurred and whom the parent was with. Work and family characteristics were also included.

Results showed that both mothers and fathers multitask slightly more than half of their waking time. Some of this time is during leisure activities and when commuting. When such periods of time are excluded, multitasking as it relates to work and home activities occurs a little less than a third of the time when parents are awake. Overall, mothers are more likely to multitask than fathers. When at home, mothers multitask more than fathers; however, fathers multitask more than mothers at work. When at work, fathers are more likely to be engaged in two work-related activities; this combination is less likely for mothers. Both mothers and fathers multitask more at home than at work. Not unexpectedly, when mothers multitask at home, they are substantially more likely than fathers to be with their children.

Multitasking reaches its peak in the early evening hours around 7:00 p.m. Other peak moments occur in the early morning around 8:00 a.m., when the family is getting ready for work and school, and at 4:00 p.m., when school ends and children need to be transported to their afternoon activities. When multitasking at home, both mothers and fathers typically engage in two housework-related activities, although mothers are more likely than fathers to be engaged in multiple housework-related activities. Mothers and fathers rarely report work-related tasks as the primary activity while multitasking. However, parents, especially those who report high levels of stress, are more likely to report working alone in the evenings when at home.

The subjective experiences accompanying multitasking are somewhat contradictory. When multitasking at both work and home, mothers and fathers report feeling more productive than when engaged in a single activity. Yet while multitasking may create a sense that things are getting done more efficiently, it comes with other emotional costs. Both mothers and fathers report an increased sense of negative affect and stress when multitasking. These feelings are more pronounced for mothers when at home. Among mothers, multitasking is associated with higher levels of frustration, irritation, and stress. Mothers are also more likely to report greater work-family conflict than fathers when multitasking.[2] Multitasking for mothers at home becomes more positive when in the presence of their children. As Bianchi, Robinson, and Milkie (2006) find, when mothers are engaged in some household tasks, they are also likely to be engaged with their children in a leisure activity, such as eating a snack or playing a game. Multitasking in these instances allows mothers to spend more time with their children in activities they find pleasurable while accomplishing a less enjoyable task at the same time.

Being at Work

The 500 Family Study was conducted during 2002 and 2003, before the recent economic slowdown. Even in the best of economic times, working families were coping with issues of job security, health care, and other benefit packages that they perceived as unsustainable in the near- and long-term future. Over a third of the five hundred families in the early 2000s experienced a job change, job loss, or shift in job status from full to part time, or attempted to reenter the labor force during the two-year period of the study. Parents, even those with stable jobs, and their children expressed in interviews and surveys a sense of job and career instability. This sense of cautionary concern with the future was often associated with a desire on the part of some parents to work even harder, putting in long hours at night and over the weekend even though they expressed guilt and stress about spending time away from their families. A subset of the five hundred parents (twenty-two mothers and fifty-five fathers), who worked more than 45 hours a week, were identified as "unconditional workers"—they were willing to work long hours even though they felt emotionally compromised.

Why are they working?

When both parents work, some of the primary extrinsic reasons for doing so are salary and benefits (Buchmueller and Valletta 1996, 1998). One area of concentration in the 500 Family Study was why mothers working full time stayed in their jobs given that most preferred to work part time. To understand why women work full time (over 35 hours a week), specific attention was placed on the perceived value of benefits since health care and retirement plans are rarely available to those who work part time. Results from a series of multivariate analyses show that mothers who are working long hours at their jobs are often motivated to do so to qualify for job benefits such as health insurance, paid absences, and retirement plans (Martinez 2005). Benefits were shown to be more important than salary when examining why mothers were working full time. Among the 500 Family Study, mothers working full time and fathers were concerned that one health care plan tended to provide inadequate coverage for spouses and children and would prove deficient if one partner were terminated or laid off from a job for long periods of time.[3]

Working at work

One typical comment of employees is that they feel much of what they do at their job is not related to the actual work for which they were hired. How do people spend their time at work, how do they feel about it, and how is it different from when they are at home? Sexton (2005), using survey and ESM data from the 500 Family Study and information from the *Occupational Handbook* (Bureau of Labor Statistics 2000), separated primary tasks from secondary tasks among fourteen of the most common jobs held by the parents. Time spent at work was then classified in one of four categories: primary work, work-related, preparation to work, and personal care. Analyses show that, on average, half of the workday is spent on work-related activities and a fourth of the day is spent on work preparation and personal tasks. Only one-quarter of the workday is actually spent on core activities related to one's occupation, confirming to some extent the idea that little time spent at work is on primary tasks (this does not vary by gender or occupation).

When mothers and fathers are involved in primary activities, they feel more engaged and satisfied than when spending time on work-related tasks or preparing to work. The more time people spend doing primary work, the more satisfied they are with their jobs and the less likely they are to bring negative feelings home, even if their jobs are complex and demanding. For many of these parents, work provides a challenging and interesting environment not found elsewhere, but home offers emotional benefits not found in the workplace. Parents employed in occupations that allow them some autonomy and flexibility are more engaged at work and at home. These findings suggest that the emotional effects of work and home are complex and not necessarily consistent across contexts. Perhaps engagement in work tasks is essential to increasing both positive feelings and subsequent job satisfaction but is not a requirement for feeling positive at home. Sexton (2005) found that parents (especially fathers) feel more relaxed at home and much more engaged when at work. These findings suggest that sources of worker dissatisfaction may be associated with the types of work they perform, the control they exercise in their jobs, and their general outlook.

Sexton's (2005) ESM results were supported by another analysis that included biomarkers.[4] Using cortisol samples obtained from family members, Adam (2005) found that parents experience greater feelings of productivity and higher levels of involvement (both mothers and fathers) and enjoyment (mothers only; fathers experience more enjoyment at home) when they are at work than when they are at home. Results show that momentary stresses of parents' daily working lives are related to small increases in cortisol. These results are worrisome, particularly if such momentary reactivity is sustained over time, as prolonged exposure to increased cortisol levels has been shown to have harmful long-term effects on health (see Adam et al. 2010).

Being at Home

There are emotional benefits that occur at work that are not necessarily duplicated at home. Being at home is a different emotional experience from being at work, and it varies by gender. Time spent at home with family is positive for mothers and fathers, although fathers experience more positive affect and emotional benefit from being at home than their wives (Koh 2005). When at work, fathers feel significantly lower levels of positive affect and greater negative affect than when they are at home or in public places. Mothers, on the other hand, report similar levels of positive affect at work and at home. What is not consistent between mothers and fathers are their subjective experiences when in public places (such as shopping centers). When mothers are in public, they experience greater positive emotions, feel strong and proud, and report higher intrinsic motivation than when at home. It may be that public locations provide an opportunity for working mothers to get away from the demanding tasks of home and work (Koh 2005).

It is not difficult to understand why mothers would find time alone a positive experience. As discussed, when at work they are working long hours, and when at home they are multitasking, most often taking care of their children and doing housework. Although fathers are doing more housework than they did 20 years ago, they still do less than their spouse. Housework is a source of dissatisfaction among all family members. For mothers, fathers, and adolescents, when engaged in housework alone, their positive affect is significantly lower (and negative affect is significantly higher) than when engaged in other types of activities such as watching television or doing paid work. However, positive feelings regarding housework increase when all family members engage in it together. Being together as a family is one of those rare remedies for relieving stress, especially among mothers who work long hours.

Being with children

Even when both parents are working, mothers still shoulder many parenting responsibilities, including dealing with the problems their teenage children encounter on a day-to-day basis (i.e., emotional transfer). Examining the emotional transfer between parents and adolescents, Matjasko and Feldman (2005) found, as did Larson and Richards (1994), that mothers were more in-tune with their adolescents' emotions than were the fathers. Fathers may be spending more time with their adolescents as reported in the time studies (Bianchi, Robinson, and Milkie 2006), but they are not necessarily interacting with them.

Fathers returning home from work generally report increases in happiness; sometimes, however, they return from work angry. When fathers return home angry, it has less of a negative effect on adolescents' mood than when mothers return from work angry. Adolescents are more likely to report feeling angry when their mothers return from work angry than when their fathers do so. What is particularly interesting about these findings is that the biological (cortisol) and ESM findings reinforce each other, suggesting that adolescents, both girls and boys, are more likely to have emotional responses similar to their mothers but not to their fathers.

One "gendered" explanation for these findings may be that when dads return from the office angry, adolescents may see this emotion as a legitimate response given the importance teenagers place on the fathers' work roles. When mothers return home angry, adolescents may feel that such emotions are less appropriate, and what is of primary concern is their care and emotional well-being. There is some evidence that supports this conclusion. Kalil, Levine, and Ziol-Guest (2005) show that boys and girls place greater value on the occupations of their fathers; few desire to have occupations like their mothers', even when their occupations are of higher prestige and income than the fathers'. Regardless of the type of occupation, fathers are seen as having the jobs most desirable for the adolescents to pursue as adults.

Being with parents

As other researchers have shown, adolescents in the 500 Family Study expect to be part of a dual, full-time earner family. Expectations about the need to work full time are not just a parental concern about finding a way to maintain a reasonable lifestyle; such views are also held by their children. Adolescents expect to work when they become adults. However, in assessing their parents' roles in handling the work-family conflict, they report differing views about how their mothers and fathers are handling their work responsibilities. Adolescents hold their mothers responsible for managing the household. When mothers work at home, their adolescents express considerable dissatisfaction that is consistent with the view that adolescents expect their mothers to take care of their daily needs. With respect to fathers, adolescents are not accepting of their fathers' having to work long hours or having work-related obligations interfere with their presence at extracurricular activities such as sports games. The idea that fathers are working out of necessity rather than choice appears to be an outdated perception. Adolescents believe that their economic needs, including the costs of postsecondary education, are a family expense requiring the wages of both parents. Long work hours of fathers are not excusable any more than those of mothers (Marchena 2005).

Understanding Work-Family Conflict

Children need and want their parents to be actively engaged in their lives and are aware when their parents make themselves available to attend activities or engage with them in important conversations about school, friends, and acceptable and unacceptable behaviors. Working parents are also aware of their children's needs and desires, yet the pull of the workplace oftentimes places them in untenable positions. In our present economic environment, having two employed parents is a necessity, not an option, as some have suggested (Christensen and Schneider 2010). The costs of running a household and meeting basic family needs require two incomes, let alone the extras of providing funds for extracurricular activities or assisting with costs for college.

Parents are going to continue to work, and the stress and pressures of work-family conflict are only likely to increase unless more flexibility options are designed and implemented to meet the needs of today's working parents. Some have suggested redesigning schools so that they are more amenable to the schedule of working parents. Recent polls suggest that parents see this as a very undesirable option, instead preferring that the workplace become more flexible (9 percent for longer school hours vs. 51 percent for more flexible work hours/schedules, 16 percent for more paid time off, and 13 percent for better and more daycare options [Boushey and Williams 2010]). Moreover, the costs of undertaking such changes would undoubtedly become prohibitive, especially now that most public educational institutions are facing severe economic constraints.

There are essentially two types of flexibility that can help to meet the needs of today's working parents: flexible work arrangements (FWAs) that allow employees more control over when and where they work on a daily basis, and formal and informal time-off policies that allow for short-term time off (STO) (see Christensen, Schneider, and Butler [forthcoming] for a description of these types of flexibility and their impact on working families). FWAs include flextime (allowing variability in the start and end times of the workday), compressed work weeks, reduced hours, job sharing, swapping shifts, phased retirement, and part-year work. Some flextime programs have banking hours (i.e., allowing for extra hours and working longer days so that these hours can be banked for later use). Having flexibility to use these banked hours for times when children are not in school due to illness or holidays is one of the options parents prefer for greater workplace flexibility (Bond et al. 2002). STO is typically available in most large firms, and employees are permitted to have a number of days off in a year for personal or family reasons, including care for a sick child or relative, without a reduction in pay or having to take vacation days (Georgetown University Law Center 2010).

Parents need options for caring for their children when school is not in session, and changing the start and end times of work can reduce the stress and pressure of finding appropriate alternative care arrangements. This is especially important in the morning for younger children, who are sometimes left alone to get themselves and their siblings out the door for school. Research shows (Bond and Galinsky 2006) that changing the start and end times of the workday, whether a formal or informal policy, increases job satisfaction, engagement, and retention. Furthermore, employees with access to flexible workplace arrangements exhibit significantly better mental health than other employees, and low-income workers experience this positive effect even more strongly than higher earners (Bond et al. 2002).

Many companies find that flexibility is cost-efficient and have implemented flexibility programs that provide benefits to both employees and employers. The accounting firm of Deloitte & Touche calculated savings of approximately $41.5 million in turnover-related costs in 2003 due to their flexibility programs (Corporate Voices for Working Families 2005). One major study of hundreds of companies found that providing new alternatives for structuring the workplace not only led to workers' feeling more satisfied and committed to their jobs but also maximized the productivity of the companies implementing such practices (Galinsky, Bond, and Sakai 2008).

In our current downturn economy, some companies have reduced costs to allow employees to take advantage of workplace flexibility during the summer months (such as a four-day workweek). One company, KPMG LLP, an audit, tax, and advisory firm, has implemented a sabbatical program that provides partially paid leaves of 4 to 12 weeks, in which employees receive 20 percent of their regular salaries with the option to use accrued personal time-off hours to offset the pay differential (Families and Work Institute forthcoming). Since this option was made available in spring 2010, more than 450 employees have volunteered to participate in this program (Christensen, Schneider, and Butler forthcoming).

Another type of flexibility option for working parents is telecommuting, working from home. With the increased use of the Internet, Skype, and instant messaging, one might expect that many more companies and individuals would engage in such practices. This does not appear to be the case. Telecommuting remains largely perceived by companies as being uncommitted and shirking office responsibilities. One company that appears to have overcome the negative perceptions associated with telecommuting is 1-800 CONTACTS, a contact lens retailer where nearly half of the employees in the call centers work from home. The company reports that its employee turnover rates are below one-third of the national average for the call center industry (Christensen, Schneider, and Butler forthcoming).

Flagship businesses have implemented flexibility programs that provide benefits to working parents by changing the structure of the workday. However, merely changing hours and allowing individuals to job share, swap shifts, or work from home have to be accompanied by a change in the culture of the workplace. Today, the culture of work reinforces for professionals and managers a dedication to colleagues and clients that is increasingly difficult to achieve given the limited hours workers have in a day, week, or month. For those in low-wage jobs, the workplace is unduly regulatory, offering few opportunities to meet personal needs.

The culture of the workplace needs to change from one that now requires a commitment to work at the cost of families' well-being to one that establishes the highest standard of living for all employees. A new balance needs to be achieved between work and home for working families. Our social worlds have changed; working families are the human face of the American workplace. Bringing work and family life into a more reasonable alignment requires a new configuration of work that meets the needs of both businesses and families. Workplace flexibility is not an option but a critical need of working families and the businesses in which they work.

Notes

1. The 500 Family Study is unique in that it was conducted through the efforts of faculty, postdoctoral fellows, and graduate students who worked collaboratively on all aspects of the study. The separate studies referenced in this article are the result of this collaboration, with the author(s) taking primary responsibility for the analysis and writing.

2. When a correlation analysis was conducted using the survey measure on work-family conflict and multitasking, results showed that mothers were more likely than fathers to report higher levels of work-family conflict with multitasking than fathers, but the results were not significant. The negative feelings about work and family constructed from items that are more specific, such as feeling guilty about family when at work, had a more robust and significant relationship with increased levels of multitasking.

3. This information is based on interview data that probed motivations for working.

4. More recently, researchers have been investigating the complex relationships between social context and biology. In this study, we were specifically interested in examining the activities of mothers, fathers, and children with their stress-sensitive physiological system. Human saliva contains hormones, specifically cortisol, that can show increases and decreases in stress-related production in the bloodstream. Taking samples of saliva throughout everyday activities instead of in a laboratory setting can help to identify how individual levels of stress may increase or decrease by situation.

References

Adam, Emma K. 2005. Momentary emotion and cortisol levels in the everyday lives of working parents. In *Being together, working apart: Dual-career families and the work-life balance*, eds. Barbara Schneider and Linda J. Waite, 105–34. New York, NY: Cambridge University Press.

Adam, Emma K., Leah D. Doane, Richard E. Zinbarg, Susan Mineka, Michelle G. Craske, and James W. Griffith. 2010. Prospective prediction of major depressive disorder from cortisol awakening responses in adolescence. *Psychoneuroendocrinology* 35:921–31.

Allard, Mary D., and Marianne Janes. 2008. Time use of working parents: A visual essay. *Monthly Labor Review* 131(6): 3–14.

Allen, Tammy D., David E. L. Herst, Carly S. Bruck, and Martha Sutton. 2000. Consequences associated with work-to-family conflict: A review and agenda for future research. *Journal of Occupational Health Psychology* 5:278–308.

Barnett, Rosalind. 2010. Women at work: By the numbers. *Research ezine* 1(2): 9–11.

Barnett, Rosalind C., and Karen C. Gareis. 2006. Antecedents and correlates of parental after-school concern: Exploring a newly identified work-family stressor. *American Behavioral Scientist* 49:1382–99.

Bellavia, Gina M., and Michael R. Frone. 2005. Work-family conflict. In *Handbook of work stress*, eds. Julian Barling, E. Kevin Kelloway, and Michael R. Frone, 113–47. Thousand Oaks, CA: Sage.

Bianchi, Suzanne, Melissa A. Milkie, Liana C. Sayer, and John P. Robinson. 2000. Is anyone doing the housework? Trends in the gender division of household labor. *Social Forces* 79:191–228.

Bianchi, Suzanne, John P. Robinson, and Melissa A. Milkie. 2006. *Changing rhythms of American family life*. New York, NY: Russell Sage Foundation.

Bittman, Michael, and Judy Wajcman. 2000. The rush hour: The character of leisure time and gender equity. *Social Forces* 79:165–89.

Blackwell, Debra L., and Luong Tonthat. 2003. Summary health statistics for U.S. children: National health interview survey, 1999. National Center for Health Statistics. *Vital Health Stat* 10(210).

Bond, James T., and Ellen Galinsky. 2006. Using survey research to address work-life issues. In *The work and family handbook: Multi-disciplinary perspectives, methods, and approaches*, eds. Marcie Pitts-Catsouphes, Ellen E. Kossek, and Stephen A. Sweet, 411–33. Mahwah, NJ: Lawrence Erlbaum.

Bond, James T., Cindy Thompson, Ellen Galinsky, and David Prottas. 2002. *Highlights of the 2002 national study of the changing workforce*. New York, NY: Families and Work Institute.

Boushey, Heather, and Joan C. Williams. 2010. *Resolving work-life conflicts: Progressives have answers*. Available from www.americanprogress.org/issues/2010/03/work_life_conflict.html.

Buchmueller, Thomas C., and Robert G. Valletta. 1996. The effects of employer-provided health insurance on worker mobility. *Industrial and Labor Relations Review* 49:439–55.

Buchmueller, Thomas C., and Robert G. Valletta. 1998. *Health insurance and the U.S. labor market*. FBRSF Economic Letter. San Francisco, CA: Federal Reserve Bank of San Francisco.

Bureau of Labor Statistics. 2000. *Occupational outlook handbook*. Washington, DC: Bureau of Labor Statistics.

Bureau of Labor Statistics. 2010. Table 4: Families with own children: Employment status of parents by age of youngest child and family type, 2009–10 annual averages. Available from www.bls.gov/news/release/famee.t04.htm (accessed 20 August 2010).

Carver, Priscilla, Iheoma U. Iruka, and Chris Chapman. 2006. *After-school programs and activities: 2005*. NCES 2006-076. Washington, DC: National Center for Education Statistics.

Christensen, Kathleen. 2005. Achieving work-life balance: Strategies for dual-earner families. In *Being together, working apart: Dual-career families and the work-life balance*, eds. Barbara Schneider and Linda J. Waite, 449–60. New York, NY: Cambridge University Press.

Christensen, Kathleen, and Barbara Schneider, eds. 2010. *Workplace flexibility: Realigning 20th century jobs for a 21st century workforce*. Ithaca, NY: Cornell University Press.

Christensen, Kathleen, Barbara Schneider, and Donnell J. Butler. Forthcoming. Families with school age children. *The Future of Children*.

Clarkberg, Marin, and Phyllis Moen. 2001. Understanding the time-squeeze: Married couples' preferred and actual work-hour strategies. *American Behavioral Scientist* 44:1115–35.

Corporate Voices for Working Families. 2005. *Business impacts of flexibility: An imperative for expansion*. Washington, DC: Corporate Voices for Working Families.

Craig, Lyn. 2006. Does father care mean fathers share? A comparison of how mothers and fathers in intact families spend time with children. *Gender & Society* 20:259–81.

Csikszentmihalyi, Mihaly, and Barbara Schneider. 2000. *Becoming adult: How teenagers prepare for the world of work*. New York, NY: Basic Books.

Darrah, Charles N., James M. Freeman, and J. A. English-Lueck. 2007. *Busier than ever! Why American families can't slow down*. Stanford, CA: Stanford University Press.

Devault, Marjorie L. 1999. Comfort and struggle: Emotion work in family life. *Annals of the American Academy of Political and Social Science* 561:52–63.

Families and Work Institute. Forthcoming. *2010 guide to bold new ideas for making work work*. New York, NY: Families and Work Institute.

Galinsky, Ellen, James T. Bond, and Kelly Sakai. 2008. *2008 national study of employers*. New York, NY: Families and Work Institute.

Galinsky, Ellen, Stacy S. Kim, and James T. Bond. 2001. *Feeling overworked: When work becomes too much*. New York, NY: Families and Work Institute.

Galinsky, Ellen, Kelly Sakai, Sheila Eby, James T. Bond, and Tyler Wigton. 2010. Employer-provided workplace flexibility. In *Workplace flexibility: Realigning 20th-century jobs for a 21st-century workforce*, eds. Kathleen Christensen and Barbara Schneider, 131–56. Ithaca, NY: Cornell University Press.

Georgetown University Law Center. 2010. *Flexible work arrangements: Selected case studies*. Workplace Flexibility 2010. Available from http://workplaceflexibility2010.org/images/uploads/FWA_CaseStudies.pdf.

Hart, Peter D. 2003. *Imagining the future of work: A strategic research study conducted for the Alfred P. Sloan Center*. Washington, DC: Peter D. Hart Research.

Hassrick, Elizabeth, and Barbara Schneider. 2009. Parent social networks: Securing a school advantage for their children. *American Journal of Education* 115:195–225.

Hektner, Joel M., Jennifer A. Schmidt, and Mihaly Csikszentmihalyi. 2007. *Experience sampling method: Measuring the quality of everyday life*. Thousand Oaks, CA: Sage.

Hewlett, Sylvia A. 2010. Keeping engaged parents on the road to success. In *Workplace flexibility: Realigning 20th-century jobs for a 21st-century workforce*, eds. Kathleen Christensen and Barbara Schneider, 95–109. Ithaca, NY: Cornell University Press.

Heymann, S. Jody, and Alison Earle. 2000. Low-income parents: How do working conditions affect their opportunity to help school-age children at risk? *American Educational Research Journal* 37:833–48.

Hoogstra, Lisa. 2005. The design of the 500 Family Study. In *Being together, working apart: Dual-career families and the work-life balance*, eds. Barbara Schneider and Linda J. Waite, 18–38. New York, NY: Cambridge University Press.

Ironmonger, Duncan. 2004. Bringing up Betty and Bobby: The inputs and outputs of childcare time. In *Family time: The social organization of care*, eds. Nancy Folbre and Michael Bittman, 93–109. New York, NY: Routledge.

Jacobs, Jerry A., and Kathleen Gerson. 2004. *The time divide: Work, family, and gender inequality*. Cambridge, MA: Harvard University Press.

Jeong, Jae-Gea. 2005. Appendix A: Obtaining accurate measures of time use from the ESM. In *Being together, working apart: Dual-career families and the work-life balance*, eds. Barbara Schneider and Linda J. Waite, 461–82. New York, NY: Cambridge University Press.

Kalil, Ariel, Judith Levine, and Kathleen Ziol-Guest. 2005. Following in their parents' footsteps: How characteristics of parental work predict adolescents' interest in parents' jobs. In *Being together, working apart: Dual-career families and the work-life balance*, eds. Barbara Schneider and Linda J. Waite, 422–42. New York, NY: Cambridge University Press.

Koh, Chi-Young. 2005. The everyday emotional experiences of husbands and wives. In *Being together, working apart: Dual-career families and the work-life balance*, eds. Barbara Schneider and Linda J. Waite, 169–89. New York, NY: Cambridge University Press.

Larson, Reed W., and Maryse H. Richards. 1994. *Divergent realities: The emotional lives of mothers, fathers, and adolescents*. New York, NY: Basic Books.

Lee, Yun-Suk, and Linda J. Waite. 2005. Husbands' and wives' time spent on housework: A comparison of measures. *Journal of Marriage and Family* 67:328–36.

Lenhart, Amanda. 2010. *Cell phones and American adults: They make just as many calls, but text less often than teens*. Washington, DC: Pew Internet and American Life Foundation.

Marchena, Elaine. 2005. Adolescents' assessment of parental role management in dual-earner families. In *Being together, working apart: Dual-career families and the work-life balance*, eds. Barbara Schneider and Linda J. Waite, 333–60. New York, NY: Cambridge University Press.

Martinez, Sylvia. 2005. Women's intrinsic and extrinsic motivations for working. In *Being together, working apart: Dual-career families and the work-life balance*, eds. Barbara Schneider and Linda J. Waite, 79–101. New York, NY: Cambridge University Press.

Matjasko, Jennifer L., and Amy F. Feldman. 2005. Emotional transmission between parents and adolescents: The importance of work characteristics and relationship quality. In *Being together, working apart: Dual-career families and the work-life balance*, eds. Barbara Schneider and Linda J. Waite, 138–58. New York, NY: Cambridge University Press.

McGuire, Jean F., Kaitlyn Kenny, and Phyllis Brashler. 2006. *Flexible work arrangements: The fact sheet*. Available from http://workplaceflexibility2010.org/images/uploads/FWA_FactSheet.pdf.

Milkie, Melissa A., Marybeth J. Mattingly, Kei M. Nomaguchi, Suzanne M. Bianchi, and John P. Robinson. 2004. The time squeeze: Parental statuses and feelings about time with children. *Journal of Marriage and Family* 66:739–61.

Moen, Phyllis, and Qinlei Huang. 2010. Customizing careers by opting out or shifting jobs: Dual earners seeking life-course "fit." In *Workplace flexibility: Realigning 20th-century jobs for a 21st-century workforce*, eds. Kathleen Christensen and Barbara Schneider, 73–94. Ithaca, NY: Cornell University Press.

National Center for Education Statistics (NCES). 2008. Table 166. *Digest of Education Statistics*. Available from http://nces.ed.gov/programs/digest/d08/tables/dt08_166.asp.

Nielsen, Mark R. 2005. Couples making it happen: Marital satisfaction and what works for highly satisfied couples. In *Being together, working apart: Dual-career families and the work-life balance*, eds. Barbara Schneider and Linda J. Waite, 196–216. New York, NY: Cambridge University Press.

Nomaguchi, Kei M. 2009. Change in work-family conflict among employed parents between 1977 and 1997. *Journal of Marriage and the Family* 71:15–32.

Ochs, Elinor, Merav Shohet, Belinda Campos, and Margaret Beck. 2010. Coming together at dinner: A study of working families. In *Workplace flexibility: Realigning 20th-century jobs for a 21st-century workforce*, eds. Kathleen Christensen and Barbara Schneider, 57–70. Ithaca, NY: Cornell University Press.

Offer, Shira. 2005. Overview. In *Being together, working apart: Dual-career families and the work-life balance*, eds. Barbara Schneider and Linda J. Waite, 227–28. New York, NY: Cambridge University Press.

Offer, Shira, and Barbara Schneider. 2010. Multitasking among working families: A strategy for dealing with the time squeeze. In *Workplace flexibility: Realigning 20th-century jobs for a 21st-century workforce*, eds. Kathleen Christensen and Barbara Schneider, 43–56. Ithaca, NY: Cornell University Press.

Offer, Shira, and Barbara Schneider. n.d. *Revisiting the gender gap in time-use patterns: Multitasking and well-being among mothers and fathers in dual-earner families.* Manuscript in progress.

Reynolds, Jeremy. 2005. In the face of conflict: Work-life conflict and desired work hour adjustments. *Journal of Marriage and Family* 67:1313–31.

Roxburgh, Susan. 2006. "I wish we had more time to spend together . . ." The distribution and predictors of perceived family time pressures among married men and women in the paid labor force. *Journal of Family Issues* 27:529–53.

Schneider, Barbara, and Linda J. Waite, eds. 2005. *Being together, working apart: Dual-career families and the work-life balance.* New York, NY: Cambridge University Press.

Sexton, Holly R. 2005. Spending time at work and at home: What workers do, how they feel about it, and how these emotions affect family life. In *Being together, working apart: Dual-career families and the work-life balance*, eds. Barbara Schneider and Linda J. Waite, 49–71. New York, NY: Cambridge University Press.

Stuenkel, Carolyn P. 2005. A strategy for working families: High-level commodification of household services. In *Being together, working apart: Dual-career families and the work-life balance*, eds. Barbara Schneider and Linda J. Waite, 252–72. New York, NY: Cambridge University Press.

U.S. Census Bureau. 2004. *Journey to work: 2000.* Washington, DC: U.S. Census Bureau.

Voydanoff, Patricia. 2004. The effects of work demands and resources on work-to-family conflict and facilitation. *Journal of Marriage and Family* 66: 398–412.

Weston, Ruth, Matthew Gray, Lixia Qu, and David Stanton. 2004. Long work hours and the wellbeing of fathers and their families. *Australian Journal of Labour Economics* 7:255–73.

Williams, Ross, and Sue Donath. 1994. Simultaneous uses of time in household production. *Review of Income and Wealth* 40:433–40.

Zick, W. Keith, and Cathleen D. Bryant. 1996. An examination of parent-child shared time. *Journal of Marriage and the Family* 58:227–37.

Workplace Flexibility and Daily Stress Processes in Hotel Employees and Their Children

By
DAVID M. ALMEIDA
and
KELLY D. DAVIS

This research aims to understand the consequences of inadequate workplace flexibility through the lens of daily stress processes. Using a sample of hourly paid hotel employees with children ages 10 to 18 who participated in a daily diary study, the authors compared workers with low and high flexibility on stressor exposure, reactivity, and transmission. The findings showed a consistent pattern of hourly workers with low flexibility having greater exposure to work stressors in general and to workplace arguments in particular. Workers with low flexibility were also more emotionally and physically reactive to work stressors. There was some evidence of stressor transmission to children when parents had low flexibility. Increasing workplace flexibility could serve as a protective factor in exposure and reactivity to stressors experienced in daily life.

Keywords: workplace flexibility; daily stress; stressor exposure; stressor reactivity; stress transmission

In recent years, there has been increasing recognition that workplace flexibility affords individuals the opportunity to manage the responsibilities of employment and caregiving as well as personal needs. Flexibility has been defined in a variety of ways, because it can represent a range of options. Flexible work arrangements

NOTE: This research was supported by the Alfred P. Sloan Foundation and conducted as part of the Work, Family and Health Network, which is funded by a cooperative agreement through the National Institutes of Health and the Centers for Disease Control and Prevention, National Institute of Child Health and Human Development (Grant nos. U01HD051217, U01HD051218, U01HD051256, U01HD051276), National Institute on Aging (Grant no. U01AG027669), Office of Behavioral and Social Sciences Research, and National Institute for Occupational Safety and Health (Grant no. U01OH008788). The contents of this publication are solely the responsibility of the authors and do not necessarily represent the official views of these institutes and offices. Special acknowledgment goes to Extramural Staff Science collaborators, Rosalind Berkowitz King, PhD, and Lynne Casper, PhD, for designing the original Workplace, Family, Health and Well-Being Network Initiative.

DOI: 10.1177/0002716211415608

encompass latitude in the scheduling of hours worked, the number of hours worked, and the location of work (Georgetown University Law Center 2010). The ability to have one's schedule and workplace adapt to life's demands can make filling multiple roles less stressful, whereas rigid work schedules and location expectations can be stressful in day-to-day life.

Our research aims to understand the consequences of inadequate workplace flexibility through the lens of daily stress processes. Using daily stress and emotional stress paradigms, we examined the extent to which hourly workers with low flexibility were exposed to more stressors, were more reactive to those stressors, and transmitted these stressful experiences to their children more often compared to workers with high flexibility. We did so by using a sample of hourly hotel employees and their children ages 10 to 18 who participated in a daily diary study.

Hotel Work and Well-Being Study

This work was initiated through a program officer's grant from the Alfred P. Sloan Foundation to learn about work and family issues in the hotel industry. Our discussions with industry leaders as well as with hotel employees and their spouses indicated that some common stressors were linked to the health of employees and possibly of their family members, including long and unpredictable work hours; schedules that do not dovetail well with family schedules, routines, and rituals (e.g., weekend and holiday work); permeable family boundaries (e.g., ubiquitous pagers, cell phones, etc.); unexpected snafus that require immediate attention (e.g., overbooked rooms, employees who do not report to work); and stressful interactions with guests and coworkers that must be handled professionally (Cleveland et al. 2004).

Building on this information, we received additional Sloan Foundation funding and were chosen by the National Institute of Child Health and Human Development (NICHD) to be a part of the Work, Family & Health Network to carry out a larger and more systematic study to examine the effects of daily stress on hotel employees and their family members. This project uses the daily diary method as a tool for understanding the work-family interface in its dynamic complexity. In particular, our project highlights our group's interest in understanding

David M. Almeida is a professor of human development at Pennsylvania State University. His current work involves linking self-reported daily stressors to physiological indicators of well-being, including endocrine and immune functioning. He is one of the principal investigators for the Workplace Practices and Daily Family Well-Being Project. He currently serves on the editorial board of Psychology and Aging.

Kelly D. Davis is a research assistant professor at Pennsylvania State University. Her research focuses on how employees' work experiences spill over to family life and cross over to other family members' well-being. Her work has been published in the Journal of Marriage and Family, Family Relations, *and* Child Development.

the day-to-day processes through which daily stressors on the job come to shape the daily health and well-being of individual hotel employees and their family members. We argue that the daily diary method is an essential tool for research focused on workplace flexibility because it can illuminate, on a day-to-day basis, employees' utilization of workplace policies or practices, as well as whether and how such utilization patterns covary with daily indicators of work-family conflict and their links to psychological and physical health.

Daily Stress Paradigm

We designed the project to be a telephone diary study of daily stressors and health among hotel hourly workers and their children. The primary goal of this article is to examine patterns of exposure to day-to-day work and family stressors as well as individuals' physical and emotional reactivity to these stressors. Daily stressors are defined as relatively minor events arising from day-to-day living, such as the everyday concerns of work, caring for others, and commuting between work and home. They can also refer to small, more unexpected events that disrupt daily life: "little" life events such as arguments with children, unexpected work deadlines, or a malfunctioning computer. In terms of their physiological and psychological effects, daily stressors may be associated with spikes in arousal or psychological distress that day (Almeida, MacGonagle, and King 2009). In addition, minor daily stressors exert their influence by not only having separate and immediate direct effects on emotional and physical functioning, but also by piling up over a series of days to create persistent irritations, frustrations, and overloads that may result in more serious stress reactions, such as anxiety and depression (Lazarus 1999; Zautra 2003).

Stressor Pathways to Individual Health and Well-Being

There are two primary pathways through which daily stressors impact individual well-being: stressor exposure and stressor reactivity (Almeida 2005). *Stressor exposure* is the likelihood that an individual will experience a stressor based on combinations of individual and situational factors. Experiencing stressors is not simply a matter of chance or bad luck; rather, differences in stressor exposure more often emerge from individual, social, and environmental characteristics (Pearlin 1993, 1999; Wheaton 1997, 1999). There is substantial evidence that stable sociodemographic, psychosocial, and situational factors, such as gender (Almeida and Horn 2004; Hamarat et al. 2001), personality (Bouchard 2004; Penley and Tomaka 2002), and social support (Brewin, MacCarthy, and Furnham 1989; Felsten 1991), play a significant role in differences in stressor frequency, content, and appraisal. We believe that inadequate workplace flexibility limits workers' control and time to proactively plan daily responsibilities and thus increases exposure to daily stressors.

Reactivity is the likelihood that an individual will show emotional or physical reactions to the stressors he or she encounters (Almeida 2005; Bolger and Zuckerman 1995; Cacioppo 1998). In this sense, stressor reactivity is not defined as well-being (i.e., negative affect or physical symptoms), but is operationally defined as the within-person relationship between stressors and well-being. Reactivity, therefore, is a dynamic process that links stressors and well-being over time. Previous research shows that people who are more reactive to daily stressors are more susceptible to physical disease than are people who are less reactive (Cacioppo et al. 1998). Because individuals' resources and their environments (e.g., education, income, and chronic stressors) limit or enhance the possibilities and choices for coping (Lazarus 1999), reactivity to stressors is likely to differ across people and across situations (Almeida 2005). One primary goal of this article is to assess whether inadequate workplace flexibility increases exposure and reactivity to work- and home-related daily stressors.

Stressor Pathways to Family Members: Stressor Transmission

The effects of daily stressors are not limited to the individual. Family members and close others may also bear the brunt of such stressors. Larson and Almeida (1999) proposed a research paradigm to assess emotional transmission in families. Within this paradigm, the family is viewed as a nexus of daily interchanges among household members and between these members and the world outside the family. Through regular patterns of interactions with each other and outside systems, family members are affected by and affect each other. Our project focused primarily on how the work setting affects not only the employee's health, but also the child's or spouse's health (i.e., crossover) and other indicators of family functioning. For example, a worker experiencing a great deal of interpersonal tension at work may experience psychological distress that is brought home in the evening and regularly affects his or her spouse and children. Through such chain reactions, stressors enter the family through a particular family member and are transmitted to other family members in a predictable sequence. The final goal of this article is to investigate whether inadequate work flexibility predicts increased stressor transmission from hotel employees to their children.

The Daily Diary Method

The understanding of daily stressors has benefited from the development of the daily diary method, which involves repeated measurements on individuals during their daily lives. On each occasion of measurement, individuals report the stressors they experienced on that day as well as the behaviors, physical symptoms, and emotional states experienced during that same time frame. Perhaps the most valuable feature of the diary method is the ability to assess within-person processes. This method represents a shift from identifying universal, between-person patterns of association between stressors and health to charting the day-to-day fluctuations in stress and health within individuals as well as identifying their predictors, correlates, and sequelae (Reis and Gable 2000). Stress is a process that occurs within the individual, and research designs need to reflect this. For example, instead of asking whether individuals with high levels of work stress experience more physical health problems than individuals with less stressful jobs, a researcher can ask whether a worker experiences more health problems on days when he or she has too many deadlines (or is reprimanded) compared with days when work has been stress-free. As we will underscore in our concluding remarks, we think this feature of the method has enormous potential for understanding how workplace flexibility affects the daily lives of employees and their family members.

Flexibility and Daily Stress

Increasingly in the past decade, researchers have been interested in how flexibility is linked to stress and health. Flexible work policies have been associated with fewer stress-related health problems and better physical health (Butler et al. 2009; Grzywacz, Carlson, and Shulkin 2008; Halpern 2005). Little is known about the underlying mechanisms connecting flexibility and health. Flexibility could serve as a protective factor in exposure to stressors and how reactive an individual is to stressors that are inevitable in daily life. Low flexibility could exacerbate the link between stress and negative affect and health symptoms. Unfortunately, often those who need flexible work arrangements the most do not have access to them. Women, less-educated, and minority workers are less likely to have access than other workers (Golden 2001). Low-income workers and hourly paid workers are less likely to get access to flexible arrangements (Corporate Voices for Working Families 2006; Swanberg, Pitt-Catsouphes, and Drescher-Burke 2005). To address this important issue, our analyses used a sample of female minority hourly workers and one of their children ages 10 to 18. In particular, we investigated the role of flexibility in daily stress processes of female minority hourly workers by addressing the following research questions:

1. Does daily stressor exposure differ by levels of workplace flexibility?
2. Does daily stressor reactivity vary by workplace flexibility?
3. Does daily stressor transmission from mothers to children occur depending on the level of flexibility?

Method

Participants and procedure

Our research focused on the experiences of hotel employees, including the daily work experiences of individuals in different positions of the industry (e.g., general managers, department managers, hourly workers). In one component of the study, we examined work-family processes by measuring the daily experiences of hourly hotel workers and their offspring (ages 10 to 18). Specifically, hotel employees and their family members were telephoned on eight consecutive days and asked to report on their daily experiences, including time use, stressful experiences, family processes, and daily psychological and physical well-being.

For these analyses, data came from forty-seven hotel hourly employees and their biological or adopted children. After getting permission from human resource managers, research assistants set up tables (usually in the staff cafeteria at the hotel) to share information about the Hotel Work and Well-Being Study with hourly employees in full-service hotels (i.e., those with a restaurant on location) across the United States. Using this strategy, 157 hourly employees expressed an interest in participating in the study. Of those 157 employees, interviewers were able to reach 105 participants who met eligibility requirements. Criteria were that participants (1) were hourly (not salaried) staff at the hotel in housekeeping, in food and beverage, or at the front desk; (2) were proficient in English; and (3) had a child between the ages of 10 and 18 who resided at home and who would be allowed to and willing to participate. Of the 105 eligible participants, seventy-seven hotel hourly employees (73%) completed a baseline telephone survey on work and family responsibilities, health, well-being, and background information. Following the baseline survey, sixty-four children out of seventy-two possible completed the daily diary (82%). Because 80 percent of the hourly paid parents were mothers, the analyses were restricted to mothers. Thus, for the proceeding analyses, forty-seven mother-child dyads were included (N = 323 days from mothers, 331 days from children). Of the 323 days from mothers, 230 were work days.

The sample was composed of mothers with hourly positions who had mostly been in the hotel industry for eight years on average (SD = 5.72, range = 1–26). They were 39 years old on average (SD = 7.57), with 57 percent having a high school diploma or less. Median income was $25,000 ($M$ = $25,134, SD = $9,150). Seventy percent of the mothers were black or African American, 25 percent were non-Hispanic white, 4 percent were Hispanic, and 4 percent were Asian. They had three children on average (M = 2.89, SD = 1.81). Target children (the one child selected from each family to participate) were, on average, 13 years old (SD = 2.33) and in the eighth grade. A little more than half of the youth participants were boys (57 percent).

Measures

Workplace flexibility was derived from three items from Thompson, Beauvais, and Lyness's (1999) work-family culture scale included in the baseline survey.

These items specifically reference flexibility in the workplace. They are: "In your hotel it is very hard to leave during the workday to take care of personal or family matters"; "In your hotel, employees who participate in available work-family programs (e.g., job sharing, part-time work) are viewed as less serious about their careers than those who do not participate in the programs"; and "In your hotel, employees who use flextime are less likely to advance their careers than those who do not use flextime." Participants used a 5-point Likert scale to respond from (1) *strongly disagree* to (5) *strongly agree*. On average, hourly employees had neutral feelings about flexibility in their workplace ($M = 3.15$, $SD = 1.29$). To compare hourly employees with low versus high flexibility, two groups were created: The low-flexibility group (64 percent) indicated that they, on average, agreed with the items ($M = 2.38$). The high-flexibility group (36 percent) indicated that they "disagreed or strongly disagreed" with the items ($M = 4.5$). Cronbach's alpha for the three items was .75.

Hourly workers' daily stressors were measured using the Daily Inventory of Stressful Events (DISE; Almeida, Wethington, and Kessler 2002). During the daily telephone calls, interviewers asked a series of stem questions about whether the hourly employee had experienced work- and non-work-related stressors in the past 24 hours. The work-related stressors questions referred only to stressors experienced at the hotel job specifically. These included work arguments, interpersonal tensions, employee- or coworker-related stressors, stressors involving hotel guests, and general work overloads. For each stressor experienced, interviewers probed about the content, the focus of who was involved, perceived threat (e.g., disappointment, loss), severity, and appraisal (i.e., areas of life that were at risk because of stressor). Stressors outside of work included arguments with others, arguments with the target child, network stressors, home stressors, and stressors involving the target child. Only the latter two are included here. For these analyses, stressors were coded as $0 =$ no stressor that day and $1 =$ stressor. Each work stressor was tested in separate models but at both the between- and within-person levels.

Parents' negative affect was assessed using the Positive and Negative Affect Schedule (PANAS; Watson, Clark, and Tellegen 1988). Using a 5-point scale ($0 =$ *very slightly/not at all*; $4 =$ *extremely*), each day parents rated how much of the day they felt different indicators of a negative mood. Ten items reflecting negative mood (distressed, upset, guilty, scared, hostile, irritable, ashamed, nervous, jittery, and afraid) were averaged separately, so that higher scores represented experiencing that mood for more time on a given day. On average, participants reported experiencing very low negative affect; the scale was positively skewed and had to be transformed by adding a constant of one and performing a log transformation. Cronbach's alphas for parents' negative affect were .87 at the between-person level and .76 at the day level.

Children's negative affect was assessed using a shortened version of the PANAS (Watson, Clark, and Tellegen 1988) that was used for the parents. Youth rated ($0 =$ *very slightly/not at all*; $4 =$ *extremely*) how much of the time that day they felt four negative emotions (upset, irritable, nervous, and afraid). The negative affect scale was created by averaging responses on the respective items.

Similar to parents, children reported experiencing low negative affect; the scale was positively skewed and had to be transformed by adding a constant of one and performing a log transformation. Cronbach's alpha for children's negative affect was .66 at the person level and was .54 at the day level.

Parents' health symptoms were assessed using a shortened version of Larsen and Kasimatis's (1991) symptom checklist. We omitted items that overlapped with the psychological distress scale (e.g., "urge to cry"). Our version assessed aches (e.g., headaches, backaches, and muscle soreness), gastrointestinal symptoms (e.g., poor appetite, nausea/upset stomach, constipation/diarrhea), and upper respiratory symptoms (e.g., sore throat, runny nose). Each day the respondents indicated whether they had each symptom (0 = no, 1 = yes) and rated their severity (1 = *very mild*; 10 = *very severe*). We calculated the number of daily symptoms by summing the affirmative responses out of a possible twenty-one each day. This scale has been validated in the National Study of Daily Experiences (Almeida, Wethington, and Kessler 2002). Parents had a daily mean of two health symptoms (SD = 2.65, range = 0–14).

Children's health symptoms were also assessed using an adaptation of Larsen and Kasimatis's (1991) symptom checklist. Each day, children were asked how much of the time that day they experienced "a headache, backache, or muscle soreness"; "a cough, sore throat, fever, chills, or other cold symptoms"; "allergies or asthma"; and "nausea, diarrhea, poor appetite, or other stomach problems." Children responded from 1 (*all the time*) to 5 (*none of the time*). Items were reverse-coded, recoded so that 0 equaled *none of the time*, and averaged so that higher numbers represented more health symptoms that day. Children's daily responses ranged from 0 to 1.67 (*M* = 0.19, *SD* = 0.33).

The covariates included in all models were day in study, parent age, number of kids, and number of work hours. *Day in study* ranged from one to eight. Starting days of interviews varied, so that day in study and day of the week did not necessarily correspond. In models, day in study was recentered so that zero equaled day 1. *Parent age* was obtained in the hourly baseline interview and was centered at the grand mean of 39. *Number of children* was created by summing the responses to two questions in the baseline interview: "How many biological or adopted children currently live with you (at least half the time)?" and "How many step-children or foster children currently live with you (at least half the time)?" This variable was centered at the mean rounded up to the nearest whole number, three. The final covariate was *work hours*, which was assessed daily in the diary by the question, "Since this time yesterday, how many hours did you spend at your hotel job?" This variable was grand-mean centered at six hours.

Analysis plan

For the stressor exposure research question, we computed *t*-tests to compare low- and high-flexibility hourly employees on frequency of experiencing various stressors. The dependent variables were the frequency of stressors averaged across the eight days. For stressor reactivity and transmission, we used the Proc Mixed function in SAS to test multilevel models with interview days nested within families (Singer 1998).

The data necessitated the use of multilevel modeling (MLM) for several reasons. First, because the same participants completed the daily diaries for eight consecutive days (i.e., multiple observations from the same person), their responses were nonindependent, which is a violation of an underlying assumption of general linear models. The responses were also nonindependent because responses on days closer to one another (e.g., days 3 and 4) tended to be more similar than responses on days farther apart (e.g., days 3 and 8). As a result, committing a Type I error was more likely, because standard errors will be inaccurately small and significance tests will be too lenient if the days are treated as nonnested within individuals. Therefore, the datasets were constructed so that each family had eight lines of data—one line per day. Second, some participants did not complete all eight days of the daily diary. MLM uses as much data on the dependent variables provided by each person as are available, rather than deleting participants who are missing any data from the analyses as traditional ordinary least squares (OLS) regression would do. In other words, MLM models do not require the same data structure for each person. Third, MLM allows one to partition the variance into multiple levels (Bryk and Raudenbush 1992). Using MLM to analyze daily data permits researchers to add another level of interpretation beyond between-person or between-family comparisons; researchers can examine within-person (or within-family) variability (Almeida 2005). Models distinguish among fixed effects (i.e., parameter estimates that describe the overall values for the sample) and random effects (i.e., the variability or error around the fixed effects). Therefore we tested two-level models. At level one, we included day in study and stressor (person-mean centered). At level two, we included the mean occurence of a given stressor across the eight days, the categorical work flexibility variable, and the remaining covariates (age, number of kids, and work hours). In the models, intercepts were allowed to vary. Finally, two-way interactions between stressors and flexibility were included to test flexibility as a moderator in stressor reactivity and transmission.

Results

Descriptive statistics

Table 1 shows the means, standard deviations, and correlations of the stressor and well-being variables. In the table, flexibility is presented as a continuous variable to get a general picture of the associations. The variables are at the between-person (mean across days) level. As can be seen, high flexibility at work is associated with fewer arguments and fewer experiences of any stressors at work. Higher flexibility is also significantly related to lower parental negative

TABLE 1
Between-Person Means, Standard Deviations,
and Correlations between Variables (N = 47)

	1	2	3	4	5	6	7	8	9	10	11	12
Flexibility	1.00											
Arguments at work	-.53***	1.00										
Tensions at work	-.15	.33**	1.00									
Emp/coworker stressors	.04	-.06	.03	1.00								
Hotel guest stressors	.11	.04	.26*	.00	1.00							
Any work stressor	-.41***	.62***	.73***	.26*	.31**	1.00						
Home stressors	.06	.10	.10	.28*	.27*	.17	1.00					
Stressor involving child	.12	.10	.28**	-.04	.07	.20	.29**	1.00				
Parent NA (log)	-.30**	.45**	.55***	.30**	.16	.59***	.12	.12	1.00			
Parent symptoms	-.36**	.30**	.38	.01	.04	.28*	.19	-.05	.52***	1.00		
Child NA (log)	.20	-.19	-.02	-.13	-.09	-.15	-.11	.18	.16	.01	1.00	
Child symptoms	.08	-.16	.05	-.06	-.15	-.12	-.06	.11	-.25*	.07	.69***	1.00
M	3.15	0.10	0.11	0.04	0.03	0.31	0.05	0.04	0.16	2.19	0.21	0.19
SD	1.31	0.15	0.14	0.09	0.07	0.27	0.09	0.09	0.13	2.24	0.17	0.20

$^*p < .10.$ $^{**}p < .05.$ $^{***}p < .01.$

affect and fewer health symptoms. Greater frequency of work stressors was generally linked to greater negative affect and, for arguments at work, with more health symptoms.

Workplace flexibility and stressor exposure

The first research aim was to investigate whether hourly hotel workers with low flexibility were exposed to more stressors than workers with high flexibility. t-tests were computed on the mean frequency of stressors across the study days. Table 2 shows that hourly workers with low flexibility reported more work arguments than workers with high flexibility. Low-flexibility workers experienced a work argument on 13 percent of the days, whereas high-flexibility workers experienced them on only 5 percent of the days. Hourly workers with low flexibility also reported having work stressors more often (37 percent of the days) compared with workers with high flexibility (21 percent of the days). Table 2 also shows that low-flexibility workers have more physical health symptoms than do high-flexibility workers. The remaining t-test results, although nonsignificant, follow the same pattern (with the exception of employee/coworker stressors).

TABLE 2
t-Tests of Stressor Exposure and Distress by Flexibility (N = 47)

	Low Flexibility (N = 30)		High Flexibility (N = 17)		
	M	SD	M	SD	t-Test
Stressors					
Arguments at work	0.13	0.17	0.05	0.09	$t(45) = 2.33, p < .05$
Tensions at work	0.12	0.14	0.09	0.13	$t(45) = 0.63, ns$
Employee/coworker stressors	0.03	0.08	0.06	0.11	$t(45) = -0.75, ns$
Hotel guest stressors	0.03	0.08	0.03	0.06	$t(45) = 0.10, ns$
Any work stressor	0.37	0.28	0.21	0.22	$t(45) = 2.07, p < .05$
Home stressors	0.06	0.09	0.04	0.10	$t(45) = 0.60, ns$
Stressor involving target child	0.06	0.11	0.02	0.05	$t(45) = 1.44, ns$
Mother distress					
Negative affect[a]	0.17	0.13	0.13	0.13	$t(45) = 0.93, ns$
Physical symptoms	2.63	2.50	1.42	1.46	$t(45) = 2.09, p < .05$
Child distress					
Negative affect[a]	0.20	0.18	0.22	0.17	$t(45) = -0.50, ns$
Physical symptoms	0.20	0.21	0.18	0.19	$t(45) = 0.28, ns$

a. Log transformed due to skewness and kurtosis.

Workplace flexibility and stressor reactivity

The second aim of this study was to determine if flexibility buffered stressor reactivity. Results of our MLM analyses presented in Table 3 provide evidence of this buffering effect. First, there was a significant interaction between the within-person predictor of work tensions and flexibility on employees' negative affect. Having more work tensions, on average, was linked to having greater negative affect. However, controlling for this between-person effect, there was evidence of daily variability. The estimates of simple slopes for low and high flexibility revealed that having a work tension on a given day was associated with greater negative affect compared with days with no work tensions, but this was only for hourly employees with low flexibility, $Est. = .13$, $t(191) = 2.67$, $p < .01$. There was no significant within-person association for employees with high flexibility, $Est. = -.12$, $t(191) = -1.75$, ns. This interaction is displayed in Figure 1. There was also a between-person association between frequency of employee/coworker stressors and flexibility predicting negative affect, $Est. = -.93$, $t(54) = -1.98$, $p = .05$. Hourly

TABLE 3
Multilevel Models of Flexibility as a Moderator
of Hourly Workers' Reactivity to Work Tensions

	Negative Affect		Physical Symptoms	
	Est.	SE	Est.	SE
Fixed effects				
Intercept	0.08°°	0.04	1.73°°°	0.58
Day[a]	0.002	0.01	−0.21°°°	0.04
Age[b]	−0.002	0.002	0.001	0.04
Number of kids in home[c]	0.01	0.01	0.23	0.16
Daily work hours[d]	−0.01	0.01	−0.11	0.18
Flexibility[e]	0.001	0.04	0.91	0.72
Between-person (BP) work tension	0.56°°	0.22	4.28	3.62
Within-person (WP) work tension	−0.12	0.07	−0.40	0.52
BP Work Tension × Flexibility	0.25	0.26	3.30	4.31
WP Work Tension × Flexibility	0.25°°°	0.08	0.90	0.63
Random effects				
Intercept	0.01°°	0.003	2.97°°°	0.70
Residual	0.03°°°	0.003	1.79°°°	0.18

a. Day was centered at day 1.
b. Age was centered at the mean age of 39.
c. Number of kids was centered at the mean, which was three.
d. Daily work hours was centered at the mean of six hours/day.
e. Flexibility was coded as 0 = low flexibility and 1 = high flexibility.
°°$p < .05$. °°°$p < .01$.

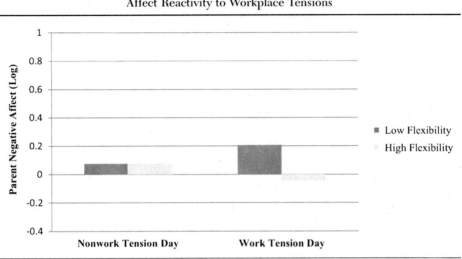

FIGURE 1
Low Workplace Flexibility Exacerbates Parents' Negative
Affect Reactivity to Workplace Tensions

employees with a high frequency of employee/coworker stressors had greater negative affect when their flexibility was high, *Est.* = .97, $t(54)$ = 2.84, p < .01. A trend-level interaction between having a stressor at home on a given day and flexibility predicting negative affect also emerged, *Est.* = –.24, $t(277)$ = –1.92, p = .06. For employees with high flexibility, having a home stressor was linked to greater negative affect compared with days when they did not have a stressor at home, *Est.* = .24, $t(277)$ = 2.30, p < .05.

There was a within-person, any work stressor by flexibility interaction predicting health symptoms, *Est.* = .97, $t(190)$ = 2.01, p = .05. Only the estimate for low flexibility was significant, *Est.* = .55, $t(190)$ = 2.01, p = .05. Having any type of work stressor on a given day was associated with more health symptoms, but only for employees with low flexibility.

Workplace flexibility and transmission of daily stress

The third and final research aim was to test whether there was evidence of flexibility as a moderator of daily stress transmission from hourly employees to their children. For these analyses, we excluded families with children who were on summer vacation during the daily diary study (n = 9), given the different structure of daily activities and time use. There was some evidence of transmission of parents' work tensions to children's negative affect (see Table 4). The more work tensions hourly workers had, the higher their children's negative affect if their jobs were low in flexibility (B = .54, SE = .29, p = .07); this did not hold for workers with high flexibility (see Figure 2).

TABLE 4

Multilevel Models of Flexibility as a Moderator of Hourly
Workers' Transmission of Work Tensions to Their Child (N = 38 Dyads)

	Negative Affect		Physical Symptoms	
	Est	*SE*	*Est*	*SE*
Fixed effects				
Intercept	0.29°°°	0.07	0.28°°°	0.07
Day[a]	−0.02°°	0.01	−0.02	0.01
Age[b]	−0.01	0.004	−0.003	0.005
Number of kids in home[c]	0.01	0.02	0.02	0.02
Daily work hours[d]	0.01	0.02	−0.01	0.02
Flexibility[e]	−0.07	0.08	−0.01	0.09
Between-person (BP) work tension	−0.52	0.38	−0.66	0.41
Within-person (WP) work tension	0.09	0.11	−0.07	0.13
BP Work Tension × Flexibility	1.06°°	0.47	0.81	0.51
WP Work Tension × Flexibility	−0.17	0.14	0.07	0.16
Random effects				
Intercept	0.02°°°	0.01	0.02°°	0.01
Residual	0.06°°°	0.01	0.08°°°	0.01

a. Day was centered at day 1.
b. Age was centered at the mean age of 39.
c. Number of kids was centered at the mean, which was three.
d. Daily work hours was centered at the mean of six hours/day.
e. Flexibility was coded as 0 = low flexibility and 1 = high flexibility.
°$p < .10.$ °°$p < .05.$ °°°$p < .01.$

Discussion

Flexible work arrangements benefit employees across multiple levels. Extant research has shown that giving flexibility to employees can even benefit employers due to lower health costs and turnover of employees (Halpern 2005). More research, however, is needed to understand the benefits of flexible work arrangements for employees themselves. The present study examined whether flexibility can provide a context for less stressor exposure, reactivity, and transmission in employees' daily lives.

In terms of the first research aim, there was some support showing that hourly workers with low flexibility have greater stressor exposure, particularly exposure to work arguments. The rest of the results follow the pattern that hourly workers with low flexibility are more susceptible to experiencing daily stressors. Arguments at work could be related to the topic of flexibility, as some of our open-ended responses have revealed, or could be due to the lack of flexibility and potentially other less desirable job conditions.

FIGURE 2
Low Workplace Flexibility Exacerbates Transmission of Parents' Work Tensions to Children's Negative Affect

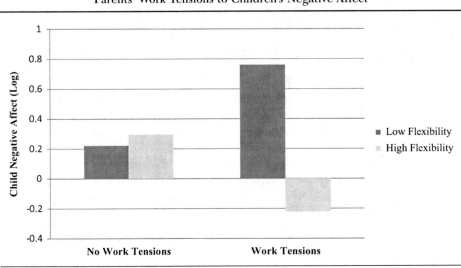

For the second research aim, overall, most findings support the notion that low flexibility exacerbates stressor reactivity for hourly hotel employees. In conditions of low flexibility, daily workplace tensions were associated with higher negative affect, and experiencing any work stressor was linked to more health symptoms on the same day. Such stressor reactivity was not apparent when employees had high flexibility. Thus, it seems that low flexibility can make coping with daily hassles at work more difficult, whereas high flexibility would be a protective factor. The following description of a workplace tension from one of our hourly employees illustrates this situation:

> There are request forms for employees to fill out when they need to request a day off. I put in a request to have the 16th off. My supervisor said she could not give me the day off. I explained to my supervisor that I wanted to go to the dentist that day and I have had to put it off twice already. I decided not to argue, because I need my job. This was very stressful and I was very angry.

Another description from an hourly employee shows how schedule inflexibility can be stressful as it relates to parenting responsibilities:

> I avoided an argument with my boss today. The schedule came out and she scheduled me for a night shift when I can only work mornings because I have to be home for the kids. This was stressful and I was somewhat angry and nervous. This made me want to leave my job but this would risk my financial situation.

A counterintuitive finding did emerge, however: among employees with high flexibility, high frequency of stressors involving coworkers had greater negative affect. This could be a sporadic finding, but it brings up an interesting notion—in some cases, high flexibility may not be protective. Perhaps employees in highly flexible contexts find themselves covering for their coworkers who are flexing their work schedules. Future research should examine when high flexibility can be protective and to what point.

The third aim was to determine if stressor transmission from parents to children depends on parents' flexibility on the job. There was some evidence of stressor transmission when parents had low flexibility. Specifically, when parents had low flexibility and more work tensions, their child's negative affect was greater. Future research should continue to explore the possibility of how parents' work experiences can be transmitted or "cross over" to children and how flexibility may be a resource when faced with negative work experiences.

Although only a first step, the present analyses show the utility of a daily diary design in studying workplace flexibility. Future research would benefit from a more comprehensive measure of flexibility than used here. Although even with this measure, some interesting findings emerged. These findings make the case that we need to help employees manage day-to-day life. One way to do that is to change work practices, particularly work schedule flexibility. Moen, Kelly, and Chermack (2009) followed the implementation of a workplace initiative at Best Buy called ROWE, the Results-Only Work Environment. The initiative involved shifting the focus from face time in the office to productivity for white-collar workers. By increasing employees' sense of control over their work time, they reported improvements in health and commitment to the job. Lambert (2009) designed a study to increase schedule predictability and flexibility in a retail store. More predictable work schedules were related to lower stress and less interference between work and family responsibilities. Researchers should continue to assess these initiatives at global and daily levels for workers at all levels.

Another way to help employees manage daily life is to change the work attitudes and workplace culture. One way to do this is to encourage supervisors to be more supportive and accommodating to employees' family needs. Kossek and Hammer (2008) trained grocery store managers to be more sensitive to and to be able to handle employees' work-life issues. Compared to a year prior to the training, employees had lower blood pressure and had better sleep quality and overall health. Employees were also more satisfied with their jobs. Flexibility can improve employees' lives but also help to retain talented employees, a positive outcome for businesses. In sum, helping employees manage day-to-day life can lead to a healthier workplace, healthier employees, and healthier families.

References

Almeida, David M. 2005. Resilience and vulnerability to daily stressors assessed via diary methods. *Current Directions in Psychological Science* 14:64–68.

Almeida, David M., and Melanie C. Horn. 2004. Is daily life more stressful during middle adulthood? In *How healthy are we? A national study of well-being at midlife*, eds. Orville Gilbert Brim, Carol D. Ryff, and Ronald C. Kessler, 425–51. Chicago, IL: University of Chicago Press.

Almeida, David M., Katherine MacGonagle, and Heather King. 2009. Assessing daily stress processes in social surveys by combining stressor exposure and salivary cortisol. *Biography and Social Biology* 55:219–37.

Almeida, David M., Elaine Wethington, and Ronald C. Kessler. 2002. The Daily Inventory of Stressful Experiences (DISE): An interview-based approach for measuring daily stressors. *Assessment* 9:41–55.

Bolger, Niall, and Adam Zuckerman. 1995. A framework for studying personality in the stress process. *Journal of Personality and Social Psychology* 69:890–902.

Bouchard, Thomas J., Jr. 2004. Genetic influences on human psychological traits: A survey. *Current Directions in Psychological Science* 13:148–51.

Brewin, Chris R., Brigid MacCarthy, and Adrian Furnham. 1989. Social support in the face of adversity: The role of cognitive appraisal. *Journal of Research in Personality* 23:354–72.

Bryk, Anthony S., and Stephen W. Raudenbush. 1992. *Hierarchical linear models*. Thousand Oaks, CA: Sage.

Butler, Adam B., Joseph G. Grzywacz, Susan L. Ettner, and Bo Liu. 2009. Workplace flexibility, self-reported health, and health care utilization. *Work and Stress* 23:45–59.

Cacioppo, John T. 1998. Somatic responses to psychological stress: The reactivity hypothesis. In *Advances in psychological science*, eds. Michel Sabourin, Fergus Craik, and Michele Robert, 87–114. East Sussex, UK: Psychology Press.

Cacioppo, John T., Gary G. Berntson, William B. Malarkey, Janice K. Kiecolt-Glaser, John F. Sheridan, Kirsten M. Poehlmann, Mary H. Burleson, John M. Ernst, Louise C. Hawkley, and Ronald Glaser. 1998. Autonomic, neuronendocrine, and immune responses to psychological stress: The reactivity hypothesis. *The Annals of the New York Academy of Sciences* 840:664–73.

Cleveland, Jeanette, John O'Neill, Ann C. Crouter, and Robert Drago. 2004. *Hotels and home lives*. New York, NY: Alfred P. Sloan Foundation.

Corporate Voices for Working Families. 2006. *Workplace flexibility for lower wage workers*. Washington, DC: Corporate Voices for Working Families.

Felsten, Gary. 1991. Hostility, stress and symptoms of depression. *Personality and Individual Differences* 21:461–67.

Georgetown University Law Center. 2010. *Flexible work arrangements: A definition and examples*. Workplace Flexibility 2010. Available from http://workplaceflexibility2010.org/images/uploads/general_information/fwa_definitions examples.pdf.

Golden, Lonnie. 2001. Flexible work schedules: Which workers get them? *American Behaviorist Scientist* 44:1157–78.

Grzywacz, Joseph G., Dawn S. Carlson, and Sandee Shulkin. 2008. Schedule flexibility and stress: Linking formal flexible arrangements and perceived flexibility to employee health. *Community, Work & Family* 11:199–214.

Halpern, Diane F. 2005. How time-flexible work policies can reduce stress, improve health, and save money. *Stress and Health* 21:157–68.

Hamarat, Errol, Dennise Thompson, Karen M. Zabrucky, Don Steele, Kenneth B. Matheny, and Ferda Aysan. 2001. Perceived stress and coping resource availability as predictors of life satisfaction in young, middle-aged, and older adults. *Experimental Aging Research* 27:181–96.

Kossek, Ellen E., and Leslie B. Hammer. 2008. Forethought frontline workers: Supervisor work/life training gets results. *Harvard Business Review* 86:36.

Lambert, Susan. 2009. Making a difference for hourly employees. In *Work-life policies that make a real difference for individuals, families, and organizations*, eds. Ann C. Crouter and Alan Booth, 169–96. Washington, DC: Urban Institute Press.

Larsen, Randy J., and Margaret Kasimatis. 1991. Day-to-day physical symptoms: Individual differences in the occurrence, duration, and emotional concomitants of minor daily illnesses. *Journal of Personality* 59:387–423.

Larson, Reed, and David M. Almeida. 1999. Emotional transmission in the daily lives of families: A new paradigm for studying family process. *Journal of Marriage and the Family* 61:5–20.

Lazarus, Richard S. 1999. *Stress and emotion: A new synthesis*. New York, NY: Springer.

Moen, Phyllis, Erin Kelly, and Kelly Chermack. 2009. Learning from a natural experiment: Studying a corporate work-time policy initiative. In *Work-life policies that make a real difference for individuals, families, and organizations*, eds. Ann C. Crouter and Alan Booth, 97–131. Washington, DC: Urban Institute Press.

Pearlin, Leonard I. 1993. The social contexts of stress. In *Handbook of stress: Theoretical and clinical aspects*, eds. Leo Goldberger and Shlomo Breznits, 305–15. New York, NY: Free Press.

Pearlin, Leonard I. 1999. The stress process revisited: Reflections on concepts and their interrelationships. In *Handbook of sociology of mental health*, eds. Carol S. Aneshensel and Jo C. Phelan, 395–415. Dordrecht, the Netherlands: Kluwer Academic.

Penley, Julia A., and Joe Tomaka. 2002. Associations among the Big Five, emotional responses, and coping with acute stress. *Personality and Individual Differences* 32:1215–28.

Reis, Harry T., and Shelly L. Gable. 2000. Event-sampling and other methods for studying everyday experience. In *Handbook of research methods in social and personality psychology*, eds. Harry T. Reis and Charles M. Judd, 190–222. New York, NY: Cambridge University Press.

Singer, Judy D. 1998. Using SAS PROC MIXED to fit multilevel models, hierarchical models, and individual growth models. *Journal of Educational and Behavioral Statistics* 24:323–55.

Swanberg, Jennifer E., Marcie Pitt-Catsouphes, and Krista Drescher-Burke. 2005. A question of justice: Disparities in employees' access to flexible schedule arrangements. *Journal of Family Issues* 26:866–95.

Thompson, Cynthia A., Laura L. Beauvais, and Karen S. Lyness. 1999. When work-family benefits are not enough: The influence of work-family culture on benefit utilization, organizational attachment, and work-family conflict. *Journal of Vocational Behavior* 54:392–415.

Watson, David, Lee Anna Clark, and Auke Tellegen. 1988. Development and validation of brief measures of positive and negative affect: The PANAS scales. *Journal of Personality and Social Psychology* 54:1063–70.

Wheaton, Blair. 1997. The nature of chronic stress. In *Coping with chronic stress*, ed. Benjamin H. Gottlieb, 43–73. New York, NY: Plenum.

Wheaton, Blair. 1999. The nature of stressors. In *A handbook for the study of mental health: Social contexts, theories, and systems*, eds. Allan V. Horwitz and Teresa L. Scheid, 176–97. New York, NY: Cambridge University Press.

Zautra, Alex J. 2003. *Emotions, stress and health*. New York, NY: Oxford University Press.

Keeping Women in the Science Pipeline

Premier science largely depends on the quality of the pool of future scientists. Women now represent a large part of the talent pool in the United States, but many data sources indicate that they are more likely than men to "leak" out of the science pipeline before obtaining tenure at a college or university. The authors' research examines this issue in detail, drawing on multiple sources, including the Survey of Doctorate Recipients and several original surveys. Their findings show that family formation—most important marriage and childbirth—accounts for the largest leaks in the pipeline from graduate school to the acquisition of tenure for women in the sciences. The authors also find that researchers receive limited benefits when it comes to family responsive policies, such as paid maternity and parental leave, and that young scientists receive the least. Together, federal agencies and universities can make headway in solving this systemic problem.

Keywords: women; science; family formation; researchers; universities; federal agencies; family policies

By
MARC GOULDEN,
MARY ANN MASON,
and
KARIE FRASCH

Marc Goulden is the director of Data Initiatives, Academic Affairs, at the University of California, Berkeley. He studies career-life experiences among academics. His most recent work (with Mary Ann Mason and Karie Frasch), funded by the Alfred P. Sloan Foundation, examines the role of federal funding, gender, and family in academic research careers.

Mary Ann Mason is a professor and faculty codirector of Berkeley Law's CHEFS at the University of California, Berkeley. As dean of the Graduate Division from 2000 to 2007, she and her research team pioneered work on the effect of family formation on the careers of men and women PhDs and more recently on women scientists.

Karie Frasch is director of Faculty Equity and Welfare, Office for Faculty Equity in Academic Affairs, at the University of California, Berkeley. She has worked on or managed research projects funded by the Alfred P. Sloan Foundation, including the UC Faculty Family Friendly Edge, since 2005.

NOTE: Portions of this article have been reproduced from Marc Goulden, Karie Frasch, and Mary Ann Mason, *Staying Competitive: Patching America's Leaky Pipeline in the Sciences* (Berkeley Center on Health, Economic, & Family Security and The Center for American Progress 2009). The authors wish to thank the Alfred P. Sloan Foundation for generously funding this research.

DOI: 10.1177/0002716211416925

Premier science largely depends on the quality of the pool of future scientists. For this reason, the United States has made a major effort over the past 30 years to attract more outstanding U.S. students, particularly women, into research science (Congressional Commission on the Advancement of Women and Minorities 2000, 20; Burke and Mattis 2007). Women have risen to the challenge with significant increases in all physical sciences and engineering, and they have made a huge advance in the life sciences, where they now receive more than 50 percent of all PhDs (U.S. Census Bureau 2008; National Science Foundation [NSF] 2009).

Women now represent a large part of the talent pool for research science, but many data sources indicate that they are more likely than men to "leak" out of the pipeline in the sciences before obtaining tenure at a college or university (Long 2001; Mason and Goulden 2002, 2004a, 2004b; American Council on Education 2005; Nelson 2007; Committee on Maximizing the Potential of Women 2007; Ceci, Williams, and Barnett 2009; Goulden, Frasch, and Mason 2009). The loss of these women, together with serious increases in European and Asian nations' capacity for research, means the long-term dependability of a highly trained U.S. workforce and global preeminence in the sciences may be in question (Hill et al. 2007; Committee on Prospering in the Global Economy 2007; Kazmierczak, James, and Archey 2005, 2007; Galama and Hosek 2008; Lane 2008; Adams 2009).

Our research addresses the effect of family formation on both when and why women and men drop out or opt out of the academic science career path and on those who remain on the path. It offers an extensive examination of the experiences of researchers as well as the role that institutions of higher education and federal granting agencies play in regard to the leaky pipeline in the sciences.

We collected and analyzed data from a number of sources: a national longitudinal survey, the Survey of Doctorate Recipients (SDR), sponsored by the NSF and other federal agencies,[1] and several original surveys. Our surveys covered four academic researcher populations in the University of California system, including doctoral students, postdoctoral scholars, academic researchers, and faculty; a survey of the sixty-two-member institutions of the Association of American Universities, a nonprofit organization of leading public and private research universities in the United States and Canada;[2] and a survey of ten of the major federal granting agencies.[3]

The United States Is a Global Leader in Science, but We Risk Losing Our Edge

Since the end of World War II, major research universities, federal agencies, and the private industry have built a scientific infrastructure across the United States of an unprecedented nature. Working together, we have established ourselves as the premier science nation; the master of innovation in areas such as information technology and processing, nanotechnology, biotechnology, genetics, semiconductor electronics, weapons technology, and engineering; and the standard by which other nations measure themselves. Our stellar programs in the sciences attract graduate students and postdoctoral scholars from around the globe, and our commitment to funding both basic and applied science has served as a model for aspiring nations (Jackson 2003; Galama and Hosek 2008; Lane 2008).

Although recent debate is divided on whether we are maintaining our global preeminence in the sciences, certain patterns are generally accepted. Nations such as South Korea and China are experiencing relatively faster growth than the United States, and the European Union as a whole has achieved a magnitude similar to if not greater than our own. Other nations are also investing heavily in higher education, including providing incentives for students to obtain science and engineering degrees (Hill et al. 2007; Kazmierczak, James, and Archey 2005, 2007; Committee on Prospering in the Global Economy 2007; Galama and Hosek 2008; Lane 2008; Adams 2009; National Science Board 2010).

Perhaps more troubling, multiple sources of evidence suggest that younger generations of Americans begin their educational careers with interest in science but all too often sour on the enterprise, opting out along the way in pursuit of more attractive endeavors. This trend appears particularly acute among girls and women and among underrepresented minorities (Long 2001; Mason and Goulden 2002, 2004a, 2004b; American Council on Education 2005; Nelson 2007; Committee on Maximizing the Potential of Women 2007; Ceci, Williams, and Barnett 2009; Goulden, Frasch, and Mason 2009).

This general pattern of domestic attrition in the sciences has received greater attention in recent years, but the periodic sounds of alarm seem to have been subdued because our labor supply of talented scientists has been back-filled with large numbers of newly minted international PhDs and postdoctoral fellows (Committee on Policy Implications of International Graduate Students and Postdoctoral Scholars 2005; Davis 2005). This so-called "brain drain" from other countries that has so greatly benefited the United States appears to have suppressed our concern about the loss of some of our domestic populations from the science pipeline.

Increasingly, however, as high-tech regions have become established in other nations—India, Ireland, China, and South Korea, to name a few of the best-known examples—and research universities around the world are seemingly closing the gap in regard to institutional excellence, the long-term dependability of this supply of a highly trained, readily available international workforce is in question.

Demographic Shifts in the U.S. Academic Science Workforce

Our domestic supply of highly trained scientific researchers and scholars has undergone a tectonic shift in the past 40 years. Women, who once composed a tiny fraction of our domestic PhDs in the sciences, are becoming the majority

FIGURE 1
Women as a Percent of Doctoral Recipients in the United States (U.S. Citizens Only),
Sciences, 1966–2006

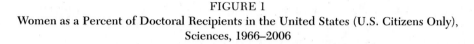

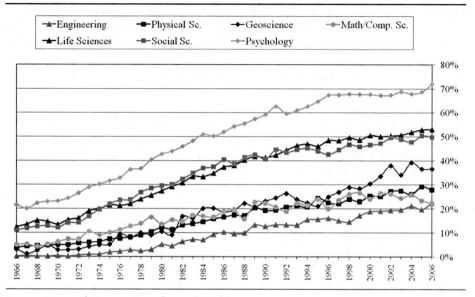

Source: National Science Foundation (2008b).

population in large segments of the sciences: psychology; the social sciences; and, perhaps most important, the large and rapidly expanding life sciences—the cornerstone of the new age of biology.

The gender split between the more human-centric and nonhuman-centric sciences remains, with women predisposed toward pursuits that tie more directly to human experience (Jacobs 2005; Lubinski and Benbow 2006; Rosenbloom et al. 2008), but even these lines are blurring. Women have made impressive gains in the least tractable of the sciences, breaking through into the once homogeneous fields of physical sciences, technology, engineering, and mathematics (NSF 2008b). Over the past four decades (see Figure 1), the relative proportion of women PhD recipients has increased more than one hundred–fold in engineering (from a scant 0.2 percent in 1966 to 22.5 percent in 2006), twelve-fold in the geosciences (3 percent to 36.6 percent), and eight-fold in the physical sciences (3.7 percent to 27.9 percent). Since these general trends appear unabated and women are outperforming men at the baccalaureate and master's level of education in the United States (U.S. Census Bureau 2008), it seems reasonable to conclude that further gains will occur.

Despite this fundamental shift, federal agencies and academic institutions as a whole have been slow to understand some of the implications of a labor supply that is increasingly composed of women. The "leaky pipeline" for women in the sciences, sometimes referred to as the "pool problem," because of the low number of women in job applicant pools relative to their rates of doctoral degrees granted, has become a point of debate in recent years. Discussions about the reasons for the leaks range from "chilly" institutional and departmental climates to gender bias and discrimination, from innate differences in cognition to lack of mentoring to the role of marriage and children (Valian 1998; Massachusetts Institute of Technology 1999; Committee on Maximizing the Potential of Women 2007; Committee on Gender Differences 2009; American Association of University Professors 2001; Mason and Goulden 2002, 2004a, 2004b; Ward and Wolf-Wendel 2004; Van Anders 2004; Wolfinger, Mason, and Goulden 2008; Goulden, Frasch, and Mason 2009). This debate was perhaps best brought to national attention in the aftermath of comments by former Harvard University President Lawrence Summers in 2005, when he referenced theories that women might have less intrinsic aptitude to excel at academic science careers (Jaschik 2005).

The story is becoming clearer. A recent report from the National Academy of Sciences, *Gender Differences at Critical Transitions in the Careers of Science, Engineering, and Mathematics Faculty* (Committee on Gender Differences 2009), discusses in detail the underrepresentation of women in many of the scientific disciplines at academic institutions across the country, particularly in the higher faculty ranks. The report confirmed that women who received PhDs in the sciences were less likely than men to seek academic research positions—the path to cutting-edge discovery—and they were more likely to drop out before attaining tenure if they did take on a faculty post. However, the report stated that their surveys did not shed light on many of the potential reasons why women were more likely to drop out. It states: "The report does not explore the impact of children and family obligations (including elder care) on women's willingness to pursue faculty positions in R1 institutions or the duration of postdoctoral positions" (Committee on Gender Differences 2009, 3).

Data from both the National Institutes of Health (NIH) and NSF (see Figure 2)—the two agencies providing the greatest amount of funds to researchers in U.S. universities and colleges—also suggest that the leaky pipeline is not an aspect of the past. Women compose a much larger proportion of the predoctoral fellowships given by these agencies than they do postdoctoral fellowships and competitive faculty grants. The drop off in relative proportion is dramatic, with women composing 63 percent and 54 percent of NIH's and NSF's predoctoral awards in 2007, respectively, but just 25 percent and 23 percent of the competitive faculty grants awarded in the same year (NSF 2008a, 2009; NIH Office of Extramural Research 2008b; Schaffer 2008). The recent demographic surge in the proportion of women PhDs may account for some, but not all, of this dramatic drop.

The Effect of Family Formation on Faculty Careers in the Sciences

The best way to assess what is truly going on in the pipeline for women in the sciences is to conduct careful longitudinal analyses that follow the same individuals over time, from PhD receipt onward. The SDR that NSF and other federal

FIGURE 2
Problems in the Pipeline: Women as a Percent of NIH and NSF Awards[*], by Level of
Award (2007)

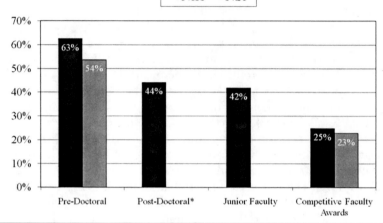

Sources: NSF (2008); NSF (2009); NIH (2008b); Schaffer (2008).
*The postdoctoral award information for NSF is missing significant data (39% of awards were
to women, 47% to men, and 14% of the sample was unknown in 2007). We chose not to include
the data point because it is not comparable to the others.
Source: Fae Korsmo, Senior Advisor, Office of the Director, NSF.

agencies sponsored makes this analysis possible. The SDR—a longitudinal, biennial, nationally representative survey of PhD recipients' postdegree employment
status with almost 170,000 participants under age 76 from 1973 to 2003—has
included family related questions since 1981 and is therefore the ideal data source
to measure the effects of gender and family on men's and women's academic
career progress (Clark 1994; NSF 1995, 2010).

Most well-known scholarly studies on faculty rank advancement and academic
productivity have used other data sources (Cole and Zuckerman 1987; Long,
Allison, and McGinnis 1993; Jacobs 1996; Perna 2001). Only more recently have
scholars turned their attention to the SDR as a significant data source for exploring the diversity of the doctoral scientific workforce (Ginther 2001; Long 2001;
Mason and Goulden 2002, 2004a, 2004b; Wolfinger, Mason, and Goulden 2008;
Goulden, Frasch, and Mason 2009).

Building on this existing work, and using discrete-time event history analyses
(Allison 1995), we have modeled the effects of gender and family on the likelihood of individuals leaking out of the pipeline in the sciences, including the
physical sciences, biological sciences, and social sciences, from (1) PhD receipt
to entering a tenure-track position and (2) entering a tenure-track position to
the achievement of tenure (see Figure 3). These analyses control for disciplinary fields within the sciences, age, ethnicity, PhD calendar year, time to PhD

FIGURE 3
Leaks in the Pipeline to Tenure for Women PhDs in the Sciences*

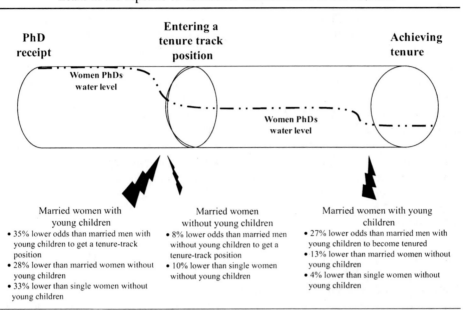

PhD receipt	Entering a tenure track position	Achieving tenure

Married women with young children
- 35% lower odds than married men with young children to get a tenure-track position
- 28% lower than married women without young children
- 33% lower than single women without young children

Married women without young children
- 8% lower odds than married men without young children to get a tenure-track position
- 10% lower than single women without young children

Married women with young children
- 27% lower odds than married men with young children to become tenured
- 13% lower than married women without young children
- 4% lower than single women without young children

*Results are based on survival analysis of the *Survey of Doctorate Recipients* (a national biennial longitudinal dataset funded by the National Science Foundation and others, 1981 to 2003) in all sciences, including social sciences. The analysis takes into account discipline, age, ethnicity, PhD calendar year, time-to-PhD degree, and National Research Council academic reputation rankings of PhD program effects. For each event (PhD to TT job procurement, or TT job to tenure), data are limited to a maximum of 16 years. The waterline is an artistic rendering of the statistical effects of family and gender. Note: The use of NSF data does not imply the endorsement of research methods or conclusions contained in this report. Person-year N for entering tenure track=140,275. Person-year N for achieving tenure=46,883. TT = tenure track.

degree, and National Research Council PhD degree program reputation ranking. Moreover, our analysis uses survey weights designed to adjust for attrition and thereby yield a sample that is comparable to the overall U.S. population of scientists.[4]

Our findings show that family formation—most importantly marriage and childbirth—account for the largest leaks in the pipeline between PhD receipt and the acquisition of tenure for women in the sciences. Specifically, women who are married with children in the sciences are 35 percent less likely to enter a tenure-track position after receipt of their PhD than married men with children, and they are 27 percent less likely than their male counterparts to achieve tenure upon entering a tenure-track job.

Early Career Decisions among Young Scientists

Young scientists often make decisions about their career path while still in training. Our doctoral student and postdoctoral scholar surveys provide unparalleled data on these students' experiences in the University of California (UC) system (Goulden and Mason 2006; Goulden, Frasch, and Mason 2008). We have found that the problems in the science pipeline are not restricted to the post-PhD pursuit of tenure—they start early and are persistent along the way. In particular, career-life issues in regard to future career goals are of pressing concern to many aspiring academics, particularly women in the sciences.

Our data from both the UC doctoral student survey and UC postdoctoral scholar survey[5] indicate that both populations in aggregate report a shifting away from the career goal of professor with research emphasis, with the women's move being more pronounced (Goulden, Frasch, and Mason 2009). A recent study of NIH postdoctoral fellows observed a similar pattern (Martinez et al. 2007). Professors with a research emphasis are arguably key players in our national science infrastructure, both from the knowledge building and discovery perspective and in training our future scientific labor force. Although private industry plays a significant role, particularly in development, scientists at academic institutions often receive funding to push forward basic research in areas that industry is less likely to pursue because of technical or financial risks (National Science Board 2010).

In both surveys, we asked individuals who had shifted their career goal away from professor with research emphasis what factors were important in their decision-making process. Among doctoral students in the sciences, negative experiences as a PhD student were most commonly cited as very important in their decision. After this item, however, career-life issues populated the remaining top five most commonly cited factors, including other life interests, professional activities being too time-consuming, issues related to children, and geographical location issues (frequently considered a career-life issue because of proximity to family and impact on various quality-of-life issues, such as housing and schools [Goulden, Frasch, and Mason 2009]).

In all cases, women doctoral students were statistically more likely than men to cite these career-life issues as very important in their decision-making process. In the most dramatic example, they were more than twice as likely as men to cite issues related to children (44 percent vs. 20 percent) as very important in their decision to shift their career goal away from professor with research emphasis.

The factors that men and women postdoctoral scholars cited for shifting their career goal away from professor with research emphasis show both similar patterns and notable differences to those of doctoral students. In aggregate, career issues related to advancement, job market, security, and money populate four out of the top five issues most commonly cited as very important (unlike doctoral students), but there are major gender divisions among postdoctoral scholars. Issues related to children was the only career-life issue in the top five that both

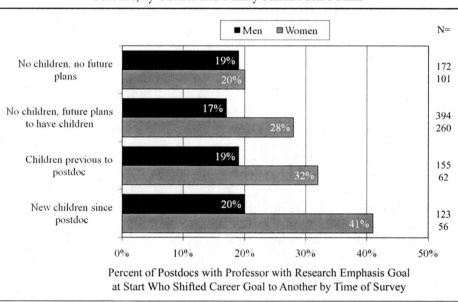

FIGURE 4

Shifting Career Goal Away from Professor with Research Emphasis: UC Postdoctoral Scholars, by Gender and Family Status/Future Plans

Percent of Postdocs with Professor with Research Emphasis Goal
at Start Who Shifted Career Goal to Another by Time of Survey

Source: Goulden, Frasch, and Mason (2008).

men and women cited, but for women it was the most important reason for shifting their career goal away from professor with research emphasis (Goulden, Frasch, and Mason 2009).

The issue of children is quite dramatic in influencing UC postdoctoral women's decisions to abandon professorial career goals with research emphasis. Among postdoctoral scholars with no children and no future plans to have them, women and men are essentially equally likely to indicate that they shifted their career goal away from professor with research emphasis, with roughly one in five doing so (see Figure 4). Future plans to have children, however, affect female and male postdoctoral scholars differently, with women more likely to shift their career goal (28 percent of women vs. 17 percent of men). Having children prior to entering a postdoctoral position in the UC system and having a new child since entering the position appear to ratchet up the pressure further on women to drop their professor with research emphasis career goal, but does not do so for men. Women postdoctoral scholars who had children after they became a postdoctoral scholar in the UC system were twice as likely as men who experienced a similar life-changing event to change their career goal (41 percent vs. 20 percent) and twice as likely to do so as women with no children and no future plans to have children (41 percent vs. 20 percent [Goulden, Frasch, and Mason 2009]).

Similarly, female doctoral students who became new mothers and were paid from federal grants at the time of the birth/adoption event displayed an intensified flight response away from professorships with research emphasis. In the case of this small population (only forty-five women in the UC system survey), the reported career shift was particularly marked, with 46 percent of these women indicating that they wanted to pursue a career goal of professor with research emphasis at the beginning of their doctoral studies but just a mere 11 percent still reporting this goal at the time of the survey. Men, too, showed a large decline in relative proportion (from 59 percent to 45 percent from start to time of survey), but it paled in comparison to the relative decline among women (Goulden, Frasch, and Mason 2009).

We asked the women in this group to explain in their own words why they had changed their career goal. Thirteen out of the sixteen new mothers chose to explain what had led to their career shift (a notably high rate of response to this particular open-ended question). Overwhelmingly these individuals cited family life issues in their decision to alter their career goals. For example, one woman wrote, "I think it might be easier to balance work and family in a faculty position where the emphasis is on teaching." And another said, "I feel that for me, research demands too much time away from my family. Also, as a woman, I don't feel as if the current academic environments are any more supportive of women with families."

Among our UC postdoctoral scholars and doctoral students in the sciences, research-intensive careers in university settings have a bad reputation. They are viewed as the least family friendly of a range of possible career choices (including tenure-track careers at teaching-intensive institutions, non-tenure-track faculty positions, policy and managerial careers inside and outside academia, and research careers within and outside academia). Specifically, only 36 percent of postdoctoral women and 52 percent of postdoctoral men view tenure-track careers at research-intensive institutions as family friendly, compared with the majority who consider policy or managerial careers outside of academia to be family friendly (77 percent of postdoctoral women and 73 percent of postdoctoral men). Doctoral students in the sciences also cast a skeptical eye toward tenure-track careers at research-intensive universities, with just 28 percent of the women and 44 percent of the men viewing these careers as family friendly. In contrast, about three-fourths of female doctoral students and male doctoral students in the sciences view research careers and policy or managerial careers outside academia as family friendly.

Since most UC postdoctoral scholars (89 percent of women and 83 percent of men) and doctoral students in the sciences (86 percent of women and 76 percent of men) indicate that they are very or somewhat concerned with the family friendliness of possible career paths, these findings on the perception of the family friendliness of career types bode ill for fast-track academic careers. Unless a concerted effort is undertaken by research universities and federal agencies to remedy the current situation, women with familial concerns are likely to disproportionately leak out of the science pipeline to the detriment of our future global competitiveness (Goulden, Frasch, and Mason 2009).

FIGURE 5
Family Status of Tenured Faculty in the Sciences*

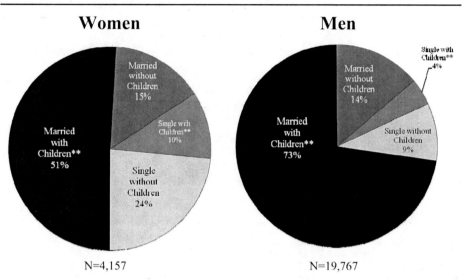

*PhDs from 1978–1984 who are tenured 12 years out from PhD in Phys., Bio., Health Sc., Eng., Math, & Tech.
**Had a child in the household at any point post-PhD to 12 years out.
Source: NSF, *Survey of Doctorate Recipients*. Sciences, 1979-1999.
Note: The use of NSF data does not imply the endorsement of research methods or conclusions contained in this report.

Of course, in part, the concern that these young women express simply reflects the familial patterns that they can readily observe among science faculty in their own institutions and the United States. Our data from the UC doctoral student survey illustrate the fact that among female doctoral students, the perception of how family friendly tenure-track careers are at research-intensive universities is strongly associated with how common they think it is for female faculty to have children (Mason, Goulden, and Frasch 2009). Furthermore, our analysis of SDR data has demonstrated that the life trajectories of tenured female scientists differ from those of tenured males (see Figure 5). Tenured male scientists are far more likely to be married with children (73 percent) than tenured female scientists (51 percent). And women are nearly three times more likely than men to be single without children (NSF 2010). The divorce rate among tenured female faculty is also high; more than 50 percent higher than that of tenured men (Mason and Goulden 2004a).

Of course, not all women want children or marriage. As one colleague put it, "Motherhood would only keep me from my passion: science." And many men and women enjoy partnerships not revealed by this traditional survey, which inquires only about marriage.

FIGURE 6
Provision of *Paid Maternity Leave* for Academic Populations at Association of American Universities (AAU) (62 total)

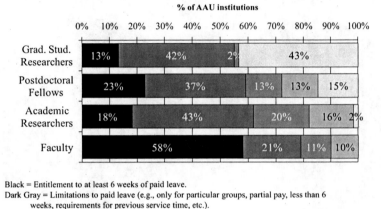

Black = Entitlement to at least 6 weeks of paid leave.
Dark Gray = Limitations to paid leave (e.g., only for particular groups, partial pay, less than 6 weeks, requirements for previous service time, etc.).
Medium Gray = Paid leave depends on sick and/or vacation leave accruals.
Light Gray = Delay in availability of sick and/or vacation leave accruals, ie., FMLA.
Off-White = Less, ad hoc, or no paid leave available.

Source: Frasch, Goulden, and Mason (2008b).

America's Researchers and Family Responsive Benefits

Compounding these concerns, America's researchers receive limited benefits when it comes to family responsive policies, such as paid maternity and parental leave. Young scientists early in the pipeline are the least likely to receive these benefits (family responsive policies also include benefits such as modified duties, stopping the clock, flex time, and part-time work, among others).

Our in-depth analysis of these trends and surveys of the sixty-two-member institutions of the Association of American Universities (AAU) and ten of the major federal granting agencies (Frasch, Goulden, and Mason 2008a, 2008b) indicate that a significant contributor to these issues is the under-benefiting of America's researchers. A lack of coordination between research universities and federal agencies in providing America's researchers with family responsive policies appears to be a major part of the problem (Goulden, Frasch, and Mason 2009).

Federal agencies that fund the lion's share of research activities at universities across the nation defer to the local personnel policies of institutions for fringe benefits, including family responsive policies, based on Office of Management and Budget (OMB) Circular A-21, *Cost Principles for Educational Institutions* (OMB 2000). Although this approach has the clear advantage of protecting the autonomy of local institutions—a hard-fought-for and protected principle among universities and colleges—the lack of guidance and oversight has resulted in porous benefiting of America's researchers that unintentionally reinforces the sense or current reality that fast-track academic careers, particularly those in the sciences, are not family friendly. There are compelling reasons for federal agencies to take a proactive role in ensuring family responsive policies that will help women scientists to achieve their career goals. First, there is the public commitment of federal agencies to assure gender equity in the science pipeline; and second, there is the mandated role of federal agencies in assuring Title IX compliance by federal grant-contract recipients, including research universities (Goulden, Frasch, and Mason 2009).

Based on our survey of AAU institutions, the benefiting of America's researchers through baseline family responsive policies—specifically paid maternity and parental leave at the time of a birth event or adoption event in the case of new parents—is erratic at best.[6] As seen in the black bars in Figure 6, faculty are the only population of researchers to which a majority of the AAU universities (58 percent) provide what can be considered a baseline family responsive maternity leave policy: at least six weeks of guaranteed paid leave following childbirth, *without limitations*. Only a fraction of research universities offer this level of paid maternity leave to graduate students, postdoctoral scholars, and academic researchers, with only 13 percent of universities making this baseline policy available to graduate students (43 percent of them offer only ad hoc paid leave, or no paid leave at all). Six weeks is typically considered to be a minimum normal period of recovery from childbirth (for cesarean sections the length is at least eight weeks [Cunningham et al. 2009]). Less than one-quarter of the research universities offer this standard to graduate student researchers, postdoctoral scholars, and academic researchers (a mere 13 percent of universities offer this baseline policy to graduate students, 23 percent to postdoctoral scholars, and 18 percent to academic researchers).

Many universities do provide some maternity leave, but the limitations associated with this policy significantly affect contingent classes of researchers, such as graduate students, postdoctoral scholars, and academic researchers. These limitations include a limit on the number of individuals who qualify for the policy, limitations on the length of the policy or the percentage of salary paid, and limitations focused on the accrual of sick and/or vacation leave.

Policies that depend on the accrual of sick or vacation leave can be especially problematic, particularly for contingent workers. Since accrual requires time, many of these classes of researchers are unlikely to have enough accrued time available (particularly in the case of pregnant women at institutions that provide no paid leave *prior* to childbirth, requiring women to use existing sick or vacation leave if they want or need that time). For example, a typical full-time postdoctoral birth mother would have to work for about one full year (if she earns one day of sick leave per month and one and a half days of vacation leave per month) with no previous use of this time to have the baseline six weeks of maternity leave.

If university policies for these populations model Family and Medical Leave Act (FMLA) eligibility requirements, many graduate student researchers,

FIGURE 7

Provision of Paid Parental Leave for Academic Populations at Association of American Universities (AAU) (62 total)

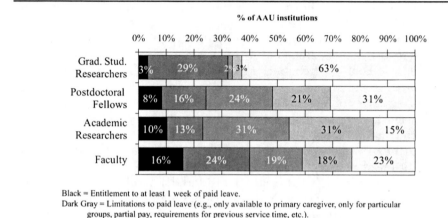

Black = Entitlement to at least 1 week of paid leave.
Dark Gray = Limitations to paid leave (e.g., only available to primary caregiver, only for particular groups, partial pay, requirements for previous service time, etc.).
Medium Gray = Paid leave depends on sick and/or vacation leave accruals.

Source: Frasch, Goulden, and Mason (2008b).

postdoctoral scholars, and even academic researchers may not qualify because of their contingent nature. In general, few if any graduate students satisfy the FMLA requirement of having worked for one full year and at least 1,250 hours over the year. Newly appointed postdoctoral fellows, newly appointed academic researchers, and part-time academic researchers are not likely to satisfy this requirement either. In fact, FMLA was purposefully designed to exclude contingent and most part-time employees from its protections, which makes it a poor choice to use for designing family responsive policies for nonfaculty academic researchers (Goulden, Frasch, and Mason 2009).

The level of paid parental leave is even less encouraging—only a tiny number of institutions provide a baseline of at least one week of guaranteed paid parental leave without limitations to any of the four populations (see Figure 7). Using this standard, a paltry 3 percent of institutions offer paid leave to graduate student researchers and a lackluster 16 percent offer it to faculty. For family responsive policies to be viewed as a normal part of the academic experience, this low level of paid parental leave needs to be increased; or paid maternity leave will stand as the only visible policy, and mothers who use it may be at an increased risk of being stigmatized for doing so. Ideally, both women and men need access to family responsive policies that are equitable and take into account both the biological and caregiving components of family formation, most notably childbirth.

Some Universities May Not Be in Compliance with Title IX Requirements

According to findings from our AAU survey, some universities may not be complying with Title IX, which requires research universities receiving federal funds to (1) treat pregnancy as a temporary disability for purposes of calculating job-related benefits, including any employer-provided leave; and (2) provide unpaid, job-protected leave for "a reasonable period of time" if the institution does not maintain a leave policy for employees (Goulden, Frasch, and Mason 2009).

When asked about the provision of unpaid leave to postdoctoral birth mothers, one university respondent indicated that they do not provide it, and six indicated that they did not know whether or not it was provided. All universities and colleges should have in place a clear policy regarding unpaid leave for birth mothers. And Title IX reviews should look at these policies to ensure that universities are in compliance.

Grants and Contracts in Fast-Track Academic Science

In 2002, nearly half (48 percent) of tenure-track faculty ages 25 to 45 in the sciences and social sciences (U.S. PhDs only) had work in the previous year that was partially or fully supported by contracts or grants from the federal government, with the largest support provided by NIH or NSF (NSF 2010). Federal grants play a critical role in achieving promotion and tenure in academia; among tenure-track faculty in the sciences, support from federal grants and contracts is strongly associated with career advancement, particularly at Carnegie Research I institutions, or R1s (Goulden, Frasch, and Mason 2009).

As a result of the NSF Authorization Act of 2002, the RAND Corporation conducted and released a report examining gender differences in federal grant funding outcomes at NIH, NSF, and the U.S. Department of Agriculture (Hosek et al. 2005). While this study found few or no differences between men and women in funding requested, the probability of getting funded, or the size of the award, it did not examine the likelihood that men and women, with or without children, would secure federal funding, or the population of people who did not apply for these grants.

The RAND report did find that at NSF and NIH, female first-time applicants, whether successful or not, were less likely than men to apply again within two years. This finding is supported by research from two other studies that found that women were less likely than men to apply for funding from federal agencies (Grant and Low 1997; Blake and La Valle 2000). Analyzing the SDR (from 1981 to 2003), we found that female tenure-track faculty who were married with young children were 21 percent less likely than tenure-track men who were married with young children, 26 percent less likely than tenure-track women who were married without young children, and 19 percent less likely than single women without children to have their work partially or fully supported by federal grants or contracts on a year-to-year basis (Goulden, Frasch, and Mason 2009).

There is also great pressure on principal investigators (PIs) who hold grants that support young scientists. In our focus groups, PIs reported that when researchers paid by grants needed family leave or modification of duties, it put them in a very difficult position in which they wanted to support the individual but also knew that their research projects would likely suffer. With no existing method for receiving remuneration for this loss, faculty PIs reported frustration with this dynamic. In fact, data from our survey of faculty PIs at UC Berkeley make clear the extent to which this is a difficult issue—32 percent reported that granting family responsive leave to researchers paid from their grants had a negative impact on their work (Zedeck, Stacy, and Goulden 2009).

Evidence from the SDR suggests that the collision course between career timing and family timing may only be getting worse. Our analysis of SDR data indicates that while the average age for tenure receipt among tenure-track faculty in the sciences was 36 in 1985, the average age extended out past 39 by 2003 (Goulden, Frasch, and Mason 2009). Similarly, the average age at receipt of the first NIH RO1-equivalent grant (major research project grant) increased from about 34 years of age in 1970 to 42 in 2007 (NIH Office of Extramural Research 2008a).

This elongated career timeline creates a host of challenges for individuals, particularly women, who want to pursue fast-track academic careers in the sciences without forgoing childbirth and child-rearing. Our data from the UC system suggest that for many years large proportions of women faculty have purposely waited to have children until they knew they would receive or already had received tenure. In fact, the most common age for women faculty in the UC system to have children is between 38 and 40 years of age (Mason, Stacy, and Goulden 2002).

As the tenure timeline pushes out, the possibility of having a child after tenure receipt but before a significant decline in fertility decreases. Given that delaying fertility is so common among fast-track academic women (only roughly 14 percent of our female UC doctoral students were parents at the time of the survey), the current strategy of delayed fertility may come under an even greater challenge. This is of great concern because even in 2002–2003, 40 percent of our UC faculty female respondents who were past the likely age of fertility indicated that they had fewer children than they wanted (compared to 20 percent of men [Mason et al. 2005]).

As all of the fast-track academic timelines have pushed out—age at PhD receipt, number of years in postdoctoral positions, and age at start of tenure-track positions—faculty PIs may find themselves in an increasingly difficult situation as the pressure on them may intensify to either deny family responsive accommodations to researchers paid from their grants or completely avoid hiring individuals they fear might end up giving birth to children. Sadly, this will undoubtedly have an additional negative impact on the earlier pipeline in the sciences, with young scholars sensing the tension experienced by the faculty PIs and knowing that choosing to have a family will be met with concern among their mentors (and yet their own career timeline pressures may argue that the time is now or never to have a child).

The Lifelong Effects of Family Formation on Career

Family responsibilities do not end with childbirth. The lockstep structure of academia is unforgiving. Parents, but particularly women, experience significant caregiving responsibilities up through age 50, making it hard for them to keep up with academic career pressures. For faculty and researchers in the sciences, the need to secure initial grant money and then pursue additional funding to continue research projects and support graduate students and postdoctoral scholars add an additional layer of unrelenting time pressure. In focus groups conducted by our research team with faculty and academic researchers with federal funding, the theme of never being able to take a break was continually returned to by participants (Goulden, Frasch, and Mason 2009). Some felt that if they took the time off that they were entitled to, they would get behind on their federally funded projects, create a productivity gap, and lessen their ability to secure future grants. Moreover, the fear of "bias against caregiving" in academia, and those who make use of family responsive policies, has been well documented (Drago et al. 2004; Williams 2000, 2004).

The time pressures of academia are unrelenting for most faculty in the sciences, who work on average about 50 hours a week up through age 62. When combined with caregiving hours and housework, UC female faculty ages 30 to 50 with children report a weekly average of over 100 hours of combined activities (compared to 86 hours for men with children [Mason, Stacy, and Goulden 2002]). Female faculty with children spend an average of more than 30 hours a week on caregiving up through age 50, while family responsive policies rarely address this long-term career-life issue.

Early Steps at Family Responsive
Policies, Benefits, and Resources

Although much remains to be done, some AAU institutions have put in place family responsive policies, benefits, and resources, including time-based policies and benefits such as stopping the clock (i.e., tenure-clock extension), various childcare supports such as on- and off-campus centers, monetary supplements such as tuition remissions, and other resources such as lactation rooms.

Federal agencies have made similar efforts, with some agencies—particularly NIH and NSF—standing above the rest. Efforts include the provision of no-cost extensions for caregiving purposes (typically providing an additional year to complete the project, with no additional funds), grant supplements to support family responsive policies or needs, gender equity workshops, formalized agency policies or statements supporting women in the academic pipeline, allowing part-time effort on fellowships or grants, and extending the fellowship period for caregiving (Goulden, Frasch, and Mason 2009). However, the lack of coordination between research universities and federal agencies creates inconsistent and inadequate coverage.

Recommendations for Federal Agencies and Universities

Promote clear, well-communicated, baseline
family responsive policies for all classes of researchers

As described in this article and our earlier report (Goulden, Frasch, and Mason 2009), America's researchers do not receive enough family responsive benefits, particularly the more junior researchers. Together, federal agencies and universities can make headway in solving this systemic problem.

Federal agencies, particularly NIH, NSF, and the nonprofit organization the American Association for the Advancement of Science (AAAS), which oversees federally funded research fellows for many of the federal granting agencies, can help by setting equitable, clearly communicated baseline family responsive policies for their fellows. At the same time, universities need to adopt baseline family responsive policies for all of their classes of researchers—not just faculty. Graduate student researchers and postdoctoral scholars receive the most limited benefits and are arguably the most important in affecting the future of U.S. science.

Provide federal agency or university
supplements to offset family event productivity loss

Without providing additional financial supplements in association with family responsive policies, faculty PIs—those with primary responsibility for the design, execution, and management of a research project—will continue to bear the brunt of supporting family related absences from their research dollars. This dynamic is unfair to PIs and may create a situation where they will find it to their advantage to avoid hiring researchers who might eventually need family responsive policies. This becomes an unintended form of discrimination against women. To avoid this structural difficulty, supplementary funding needs to be provided when researchers paid from grants take necessary leaves/modifications.

Collaboratively move toward a full package of family friendly
policies and resources that take into account the career-family life course

All major research universities should look into building a family friendly package of policies and resources, and federal agencies should provide much more than they already do. Sharing and wide-scale adoption of proven practices are necessary.

Remove time-based criteria for fellowships and productivity assessments
that do not acknowledge family events and their impact on career timing

The lockstep timing of academia needs to be more flexible. Time caps and barriers to entry—such as those that require a postdoctoral scholar position to begin within a certain number of years following receipt of the PhD—that set rigid sequential deadlines should be removed. Universities and federal agencies need to examine all of their policies in this regard and look for ways to encourage reentry into the pipeline for academic researchers who take time off for giving birth or caring for children and promote a more holistic concept of career patterns that honors the larger needs of individuals.

Collect and analyze the necessary data to make sure existing
and future policy initiatives are effective in meeting researchers'
needs and comply with Title IX

The lack of necessary data and multiyear commitments to these efforts continues to hamper our delivery of truly effective initiatives. Decisions about family responsive policies, programs, and benefits will continue to be made on intuition and anecdote if they are not tracked by systematic longitudinal data. Both federal agencies and universities need to build and maintain the necessary datasets to assess whether efforts are yielding positive results and whether Title IX requirements are being met. To achieve this, federal agencies can provide more grant programs to help determine whether efforts are working, and Title IX compliance reviews should include questions on family responsive policies.

Our current inadequate family responsive benefits for America's researchers make no economic sense. In the world of federal grants, individuals who drop out of science after years of training represent a huge economic loss and are a detriment to our nation's future excellence. Given the nation's interest in maintaining America's competitive advantage, future federal investments should be focused on patching the leaky pipeline in the sciences. Doing so will help us to preserve our competitive edge.

Notes

1. The use of NSF data does not imply endorsement of research methods or conclusions contained in that report.

2. See Association of American Universities (AAU), available at www.aau.edu/.

3. These agencies include NSF, NIH, U.S. Department of Agriculture, National Aeronautics and Space Administration, Department of Defense, Department of Energy, U.S. Agency for International Development, National Endowment for the Humanities, Department of Commerce, and the Department of Education.

4. Results are based on Survival Analysis of the SDR, 1981 to 2003 in all sciences, including social sciences.

5. The data were cut to doctoral students in the sciences because of the substantial proportion of students in nonscience fields, and the postdoctoral survey was inclusive of all respondents because of the small fraction of nonscience postdoctoral fellows.

6. We received completed surveys from fifty-six of the sixty-two AAU institutions (90 percent) and searched policy documents for the remaining six.

References

Adams, James. 2009. Is the U.S. losing its preeminence in higher education? National Bureau of Economic Research Working Paper 15233, Cambridge, MA.

Allison, Paul D. 1995. Survival analysis using the SAS system: A practical guide. Cary, NC: SAS Institute, Inc.

American Association of University Professors. 2001. Statement of principles on family responsibilities and academic work. Washington, DC: American Association of University Professors.

American Council on Education. 2005. An agenda for excellence: Creating flexibility in tenure-track faculty careers. Washington, DC: American Council on Education, Office of Women in Higher Education.

Blake, Margaret, and Ivana La Valle. 2000. Who applies for research funding? Key factors shaping funding application behaviour among women and men in British higher education institutions. London: National Centre for Social Research.

Burke, Ronald, and Mary Mattis, eds. 2007. Women and minorities in science, technology, engineering, and mathematics: Upping the numbers. Northampton, MA: Edward Elgar.

Ceci, Stephen, Wendy Williams, and Susan M. Barnett. 2009. The underrepresentation of women in science: Sociocultural and biological considerations. Psychological Bulletin 135:172–210.

Clark, Sheldon. 1994. Variations in item content and presentation in the Survey of Doctorate Recipients, 1973–1991. National Science Foundation Working Paper, Arlington, VA.

Cole, Jonathan R., and Harriet Zuckerman. 1987. Marriage, motherhood, and research performance in science. Scientific American 255:119–25.

Committee on Gender Differences in the Careers of Science, Engineering, and Mathematics Faculty; Committee on Women in Science, Engineering, and Medicine; and Committee on National Statistics. 2009. Gender differences at critical transitions in the careers of science, engineering, and mathematics faculty. Washington, DC: National Academies Press.

Committee on Maximizing the Potential of Women in Academic Science and Engineering. 2007. Beyond bias and barriers: Fulfilling the potential of women in academic science and engineering. Washington, DC: National Academies Press.

Committee on Policy Implications of International Graduate Students and Postdoctoral Scholars in the United States, Committee on Science, Engineering, and Public Policy, Board on Higher Education and Workforce. 2005. Policy implications of international graduate students and postdoctoral scholars in the United States. Washington, DC: National Academies Press.

Committee on Prospering in the Global Economy of the 21st Century. 2007. Rising above the gathering storm: Energizing and employing America for a brighter future. Washington, DC: National Academies Press.

Congressional Commission on the Advancement of Women and Minorities in Science, Engineering and Technology Development. 2000. Land of plenty: Diversity as America's competitive edge in science, engineering and technology. Washington, DC: National Science Foundation.

Cunningham, F. Gary, Kenneth Leveno, Steven Bloom, John Hauth, Dwight Rouse, and Catherine Spong. 2009. Williams obstetrics. 23rd ed. New York, NY: McGraw-Hill Professional.

Davis, Geoff. 2005. Doctors without orders: Highlights of the Sigma Xi postdoc survey. American Scientist 93 (3 Suppl.)

Drago, Robert, Carol Colbeck, Kai Dawn Stauffer, Amy Pirretti, Kurt Burkum, Jennifer Fazioli, Gabriela Lazarro, and Tara Habasevich. 2004. Bias against caregiving: Faculty members rarely take advantage of family-friendly workplace policies. What are we so afraid of? *Academe* 91 (5): 22–25.

Frasch, Karie, Marc Goulden, and Mary Ann Mason. 2008a. Federal agency grants, contracts, and family accommodation policies and programs survey. Available from http://ucfamilyedge.berkeley.edu/Federal%20Agency%20Survey.

Frasch, Karie, Marc Goulden, and Mary Ann Mason. 2008b. University's family accommodations policies and programs for researchers survey. Available from http://ucfamilyedge.berkeley.edu/AAU%20Family%20Friendly%20Policies%20Survey.html.

Galama, Titus, and James Hosek. 2008. *U.S. competitiveness in science and technology*. Santa Monica, CA: RAND National Defense Research Institute.

Ginther, Donna K. 2001. Does science discriminate against women? Evidence from academia, 1973–97. Federal Reserve Bank of Atlanta Working Paper 2001-2, Atlanta, GA.

Goulden, Marc, Karie Frasch, and Mary Ann Mason. 2008. *Survey of University of California postdoctoral scholars on career and life issues*. Available from http://ucfamilyedge.berkeley.edu/UC%20Postdoctoral%20Survey.html.

Goulden, Marc, Karie Frasch, and Mary Ann Mason. 2009. *Staying competitive: Patching America's leaky pipeline in the sciences*. Berkeley, CA: Berkeley Center on Health, Economic, & Family Security and the Center for American Progress.

Goulden, Marc, and Mary Ann Mason. 2006. Survey of University of California doctoral students on career, family, and life plans. Available from http://ucfamilyedge.berkeley.edu/grad%20life%20survey.html.

Grant, Jonathan, and Lawrence Low. 1997. *Women and peer review: An audit of the Wellcome Trust's decision making on grants*. London: Wellcome Trust.

Hill, Derek, Alan I. Rapoport, Rolf F. Lehming, and Robert K. Bell. 2007. *Changing U.S. output of scientific articles: 1988–2003*. Arlington, VA: National Science Foundation.

Hosek, Susan D., Amy G. Cox, Bonnie Ghosh-Dastidar, Aaron Kofner, Nishal Ramphal, Jon Scott, and Sandra H. Berr. 2005. Gender differences in major federal external grant programs. In *Technical report of the RAND infrastructure, safety, and environment*. Santa Monica, CA: RAND Corporation.

Jackson, Shirley Ann. 2003. *Envisioning a 21st century science and engineering workforce for the United States*. Washington, DC: National Academies Press.

Jacobs, Janis. 2005. Twenty-five years of research on gender and ethnic differences in math and science career choices: What have we learned? *New Directions for Child and Adolescent Development* 11:85–94.

Jacobs, Jerry A. 1996. Gender inequality and higher education. *Annual Review of Sociology* 22:153–85.

Jaschik, Scott. 18 February 2005. What Larry Summers said. *Inside Higher Education*. Available from www.insidehighered.com/news/2005/02/18/summers2_18.

Kazmierczak, Mathew, Josh James, and William Archey. 2005. *Losing the competitive advantage? The challenge for science and technology in the United States*. Washington, DC: American Electronics Association.

Kazmierczak, Mathew, Josh James, and William Archey. 2007. *We are still losing the competitive advantage: Now is the time to act*. Washington, DC: American Electronics Association.

Lane, Neal. 2008. U.S. science and technology: An uncoordinated system that seems to work. *Technology in Society* 30:248–63.

Long, J. Scott. 2001. *From scarcity to visibility: Gender differences in the careers of doctoral scientists and engineers*. Washington, DC: National Academies Press and National Research Council.

Long, J. Scott, Paul D. Allison, and Robert McGinnis. 1993. Rank advancement in academic careers: Sex differences and the effects of productivity. *American Sociological Review* 58:703–22.

Lubinski, David, and Camilla Persson Benbow. 2006. Study of mathematically precocious youth after 35 years: Uncovering antecedents for the development of math-science expertise. *Perspectives on Psychological Science* 1:316–45.

Martinez, Elisabeth D., Jeannine Botos, Kathleen M. Dohoney, Theresa M. Geiman, Sarah S. Kolla, Ana Olivera, Yi Qiu, Geetha Vani Rayasam, Diana A. Stavreva, and Orna Cohen-Fi. 2007. Falling off the academic bandwagon: Women are more likely to quit at the postdoc to principal investigator transition. *EMBO Reports* 8:977–81.

Mason, Mary Ann, and Marc Goulden. 2002. Do babies matter? The effect of family formation on the lifelong careers of academic men and women. *Academe* 88:21–27.

Mason, Mary Ann, and Marc Goulden. 2004a. Do babies matter (part II)? Closing the baby gap. *Academe* 90:3–7.

Mason, Mary Ann, and Marc Goulden. 2004b. Marriage and baby blues: Redefining gender equity in the academy. *The Annals of the American Academy of Political and Social Science* 596:86–103.

Mason, Mary Ann, Marc Goulden, and Karie Frasch. 2009. Why graduate students reject the fast track: A study of thousands of doctoral students shows that they want balanced lives. *Academe* 95:11–16.

Mason, Mary Ann, Angelica Stacy, and Marc Goulden. 2002. University of California faculty work and family survey. Available from http://ucfamilyedge.berkeley.edu/workfamily.htm.

Mason, Mary Ann, Angelica Stacy, Marc Goulden, Carol Hoffman, and Karie Frasch. 2005. *University of California faculty family friendly edge: An initiative for tenure-track faculty at the University of California*. Available from ucfamilyedge.berkeley.edu/ucfamilyedge.pdf.

Massachusetts Institute of Technology. 1999. *A study on the status of women faculty in science at MIT*. Available from web.mit.edu/fnl/women/women.pdf.

National Science Board. 2010. *Science and engineering indicators 2010*. Arlington, VA: National Science Foundation.

National Science Foundation (NSF). 12 April 1995. Changes to the Survey of Doctorate Recipients in 1991 and 1993: Implications for data users. Paper presented at the National Science Foundation, Arlington, VA.

National Science Foundation (NSF). 15 April 2008a. National Science Foundation announces graduate research fellows for 2008. Press release 08-062. Available from www.nsf.gov/news/news_summ.jsp?cntn_id=111452.

National Science Foundation (NSF). 2008b. *Survey of earned doctorates*. Arlington, VA: NSF.

National Science Foundation (NSF). 2009. *FY 2008 annual performance report*. Available from www.nsf.gov/pubs/2009/nsf0922/fy2008_annual_performance_report.pdf.

National Science Foundation (NSF). 2010. *Survey of doctorate recipients*. Arlington, VA: NSF.

Nelson, Donna. 2007. *National analysis of diversity in science & engineering faculties at research universities*. Available from http://chem.ou.edu/~djn/diversity/briefings/Diversity%20Report%20Final.pdf.

NIH Office of Extramural Research. 2008a. *Average age of principal investigators*. Bethesda, MD: National Institutes of Health.

NIH Office of Extramural Research. 2008b. *Women in research: The involvement of women in career development, Ruth L. Kirschstein NRSA training and fellowship programs, and NIH extramural research*. Bethesda, MD: National Institutes of Health.

Office of Management and Budget. 8 August 2000. *Cost principles for educational institutions*. OMB Circular A-21. Washington, DC: Office of Management and Budget.

Perna, Laura W. 2001. The relationship between family responsibilities and employment status among college and university faculty. *Journal of Higher Education* 72:584–611.

Rosenbloom, Joshua, Ronald A. Ash, Brandon Dupont, and LeAnne Coder. 2008. Why are there so few women in information technology? Assessing the role of personality in career choices. *Journal of Economic Psychology* 29 (4): 543–54.

Schaffer, Walter T. 2008. *Women in biomedical research*. Bethesda, MD: National Institutes of Health.

U.S. Census Bureau. 2008. *Educational attainment in the United States: 2008*. Available from www.census.gov/population/www/socdemo/education/cps2008.html.

Valian, Virginia. 1998. *Why so slow? The advancement of women*. Cambridge, MA: MIT Press.

Van Anders, Sari. 2004. Why the academic pipeline leaks: Fewer men than women perceive barriers to becoming professors. *Sex Roles* 51:511–21.

Ward, Kelly, and Lisa Wolf-Wendel. 2004. Academic motherhood: Managing complex roles in research universities. *Review of Higher Education* 27 (2): 233–57.

Williams, Joan. 2000. *Unbending gender: Why family and work conflict and what to do about it*. Oxford: Oxford University Press.

Williams, Joan. 2004. Hitting the maternal wall. *Academe* 90:8–12.

Wolfinger, Nicholas, Mary Ann Mason, and Marc Goulden. 2008. Problems in the pipeline: Gender, marriage, and fertility in the ivory tower. *Journal of Higher Education* 79 (4): 388–405.

Zedeck, Sheldon, Angelica Stacy, and Marc Goulden. 2009. *Survey of University of California, Berkeley faculty on workplace climate and career/life issues*. Available from http://ucfamilyedge.berkeley.edu/UCB%20Faculty%20Climate%20Survey.html.

Military Families: Extreme Work and Extreme "Work-Family"

By
SHELLEY MacDERMID
WADSWORTH
and
KENONA SOUTHWELL

While the U.S. military might at first glance appear to be a model of rigidity rather than flexibility, there are strong incentives to address the work-family concerns of service members and their families. From a work-family perspective, military service generates substantial structural, energy, psychological, and behavioral tensions with family life. Although the U.S. military had already implemented extensive programs, policies, and practices to support families prior to the current conflicts, the wars and demographic changes have spurred the development of innovative new models, some far outside previous boundaries of military workforce flexibility. Future challenges include continuing to adapt as military conflicts and missions evolve, defining the ideal balance between military support and family self-sufficiency, sustaining excellent leadership throughout the military around work-family issues, and caring for the millions of individuals whose lives have been changed by their own or a loved one's military service during the past decade.

Keywords: work-family balance; military; workplace flexibility; workplace policies; deployment; trauma; programs

Shelley MacDermid Wadsworth is a professor in the Department of Human Development and Family Studies at Purdue University, where she also directs the Military Family Research Institute and the Center for Families.

Kenona Southwell is a PhD student in the Department of Human Development and Family Studies at Purdue University. She is also a graduate research assistant at the Military Family Research Institute. Her research focuses on the relationship between work and family life.

NOTE: Preparation of this article was supported by funding from the Lilly Endowment (no. 300906) and the Alfred P. Sloan Foundation to the first author. We are grateful to the faculty partners, staff, and students at the Military Family Research Institute at Purdue University for their support and assistance.

DOI: 10.1177/0002716211416445

Specialist Alexis Hutchinson, a 21-year-old Army cook and single parent, was days from deploying to Afghanistan last fall when her mother backed out of an agreement to take care of her 10-month-old son for the duration of her one-year tour. Specialist Hutchinson's mother, Angelique Hughes, had a child of her own at home and was also caring for a sick sister while running a day care center from her home in Oakland, California. Feeling overwhelmed, Ms. Hughes took the boy back to Savannah, Georgia, where Specialist Hutchinson was based and begged her to find someone else. That is when Specialist Hutchinson did what might seem natural to a parent but to the Army was a serious offense: she stayed home with her child and missed her flight to Afghanistan. She was arrested and later charged with offenses that could have led to a court-martial and jail time. Specialist Hutchinson received an other-than-honorable discharge, ending an impasse that had surprised many legal experts and spurred lively debate in military circles. . . . The legal wrangling over Specialist Hutchinson's case stirred much discussion on blogs, with sympathizers wondering why the Army would prosecute a parent struggling with childcare problems and critics questioning the soldier's motives. Ms. Hughes has heard some of that criticism firsthand. "People have said to me, 'She signed this contract. She's supposed to go. That's her first priority,'" Mrs. Hughes said. "My response is: 'I don't think so. This is her child. This is her family. This is her priority. The military is a job.'" (Dao 2010)

The case of Alexis Hutchinson, summarized above by a *New York Times* journalist, brings painful tensions among work, family, and gender into sharp relief. The reactions below demonstrate that her situation is not only complex but also emotionally evocative. The first, by a conservative blogger, disparages Ms. Hutchinson for being irresponsible and the Army for being too accommodating. It targets her gender, ignoring the single fathers in the military whose children are presumably deprived of their mothers (using the writer's logic):

Statistics show that a large number of female soldiers in the military are, indeed, single mothers, likely with no father figure in their kids' lives. That's bad enough. What happens if they die? What happens if they refuse to go when called up to go to war, using their kids as an excuse? That's what's happening in Hutchinson's case. Her story shows how much our military is hampered by and bends over backwards for single mothers in its ranks. It's absurd. It's time to ban single mothers—and perhaps any mothers of kids younger than their teens—from the military. It clearly exacts more costs and bureaucratic BS than it's worth. And it harms the kids even more than they're already harmed without having a father in their lives. (Schlussel 2009)

The next response, which appeared on the progressive Web site Truthout, reported by Jamail (2010), focuses on the gap between the diversity of modern families and the mind-sets of military leaders who are perceived as closed-minded and unyielding:

Her situation shows the Army is not really friendly to families, Sussman [Hutchinson's attorney] told Truthout. "The lives of military families are very difficult and they often face a command that isn't understanding or empathetic towards the situation of raising a child in that environment." (Jamail 2010)

This conflict between the family responsibilities of an individual service member and military policies throws into sharp relief some of the special dilemmas related to personal life and military service. The purpose of this article is to consider workplace flexibility from a military perspective. We begin by describing military families, all of whom are working families, and the challenges they experience in relation to war. We then consider the tensions between military work and the personal lives of members, some of which are similar to those experienced by civilian workers, but some of which are unique. Finally, we describe responses by the Department of Defense (the DoD) and others to try to provide greater flexibility and support to military families and offer some observations about their likely work-family challenges in the future.

Every Military Family Is a Working Family

There are nearly 1.4 million service members on active duty in the Army, Navy, Air Force, and Marine Corps (Deputy Under Secretary of Defense, Military Community and Family Policy [DUSD] 2010). The Reserve component, which includes the National Guard and several categories of Reserves (e.g., the Individual Ready Reserve and the Selected Reserve), includes an additional 539,775 members (Institute of Medicine [IOM] 2010). Women compose 14.3 percent of the active-duty and 17.8 percent of the Selected Reserve populations (DUSD 2010). About one-third of service members (36 percent active duty, 30 percent of Selected Reserve) are members of ethnic minority groups (DUSD 2010). Regardless of active or reserve status, more than 90 percent of enlisted members have high school diplomas, while more than 85 percent of officers have bachelor's degrees; these rates are much higher than those in the civilian workforce (DUSD 2010; MacDermid Wadsworth 2010). More than half (52.3 percent) of active duty enlisted personnel and 39.4 percent of Selected Reserve enlisted members are 25 or younger. In contrast, 44.4 percent of active-duty and 72.1 percent of Selected Reserve officers are 36 or older, compared to 50.9 percent in the U.S. population. More than half of all military members have family responsibilities for spouses, children, or other dependents (DUSD 2010). New entrants to the military come from all social classes, with underrepresentations of individuals at household median income levels below $34,000 and above $65,000 (Office of the Under Secretary of Defense for Personnel and Readiness 2007).

In total, military personnel report about 1.1 million spouses and 1.9 million children; thus, there are considerably more family members than service members, especially if parents and unmarried partners were to be considered (DUSD 2010). The largest group of children of service members on active duty are preschool-aged (i.e., 41.5 percent are younger than 5), whereas the largest group of children of service members in the Selected Reserve are school-aged (i.e., 45.3 percent are ages 6 to 14 [DUSD 2010]).

Among married personnel, 12.1 percent of active-duty and 5.4 percent of Selected Reserve members are married to other service members. Slightly more than one in twenty service members on active duty (5.3 percent) and slightly less than one in ten service members in the Selected Reserve (8.7 percent) are single parents, compared to almost one in five (17.1 percent) of the households in the U.S. population. The circumstances of women in the military are distinct from those of men in several ways. Women are much more likely to be in dual-military marriages: almost one in two of the married women on active duty (48.4 percent) and one in four in the Selected Reserve (23 percent) are married to other service members, compared to only 7.2 percent and 2.6 percent of men, respectively (DUSD 2010). The marriages of female service members are about twice as likely to end in divorce (Karney and Crown 2007); women have a greater probability of being single parents, although the number of single fathers is about double that of single mothers (DUSD 2010).

War Poses Unique Work-Family Challenges for Military Families

As of April 2009, 1.9 million service members had completed three million deployments of 30 days or longer to Iraq or Afghanistan since September 2001. The current conflicts have placed heavier demands on military forces than seen in recent history: among current service members, 40 percent have been deployed more than once; and although policies specify goals for "dwell time"—the time between deployments—of two and five years for active and Reserve component members, respectively, actual dwell time over the past decade has averaged less than 600 days for both groups (IOM 2010). There has been extensive use of "individual augmentees," or service members drawn from units in other states, components, or even branches, to fill empty slots. Thus, members of the Navy might be deployed in small groups from all over the world to serve in an Army unit deploying from Kansas, leaving families behind and potentially being isolated because no one around them is experiencing the same deployment.

Deployments occur for many reasons and each is unique. Nevertheless, every deployment has certain operational stages to which families must respond. Prior to deployment, families must prepare for someone to assume full financial and logistical responsibility for the household—including legal preparation for this situation to be permanent in the event of the death or incapacitation of the service member (Castaneda et al. 2008). Single service members may need to prepare to become essentially homeless during deployment, losing leases on apartments and having to put belongings in storage. If there are children, the at-home parent may need to alter arrangements for employment and childcare. In Reserve component families, service members may lose access to their employer's health insurance plan while activated, requiring the family to find new medical providers. The service member's income will change, requiring additional planning. And of course, everyone in the family must prepare for the emotions that accompany the impending separation (Castaneda et al. 2008).

Based on data from prior wars, exposure to combat is the aspect of deployment with the most consistently negative later impact on personal and family life—both the marriages and the lives of veterans exposed to combat end sooner than those of veterans not exposed (MacLean and Elder 2007). According to the Institute of Medicine (2008), there is an association between deployment to a war zone during the first Gulf War and subsequent psychiatric disorders including post-traumatic stress disorder (PTSD) and depression, alcohol abuse, accidental death, and suicide in the early years after deployment, as well as marital and family conflict. These sequelae are long-lasting: needs for care typically peak several decades after a given conflict—47 years after World War I, 33 years after World War II, and still rising for Vietnam veterans (IOM 2010). Veterans who experience symptoms of combat stress are at even higher risk for negative outcomes, including increased likelihood of aggressive behavior, disrupted relationships with spouses and children, difficulties finding and maintaining employment, elevated risk of substance abuse, and other factors (MacDermid Wadsworth 2010).

As of November 2009, 5,286 U.S. military members had been killed and 36,021 seriously wounded in the conflicts in Iraq and Afghanistan (IOM 2010). The likelihood of survival is much higher during the current conflicts than in the past, which has increased the number of service members returning from deployment with wounds or injuries that will alter the course of their—and their families'—lives (IOM 2010). An estimated 10 to 20 percent of Army soldiers and Marines have experienced concussions, which are associated with higher rates of PTSD, sleep disruptions, and persistent severe headaches (Ruff, Ruff, and Wang 2008). As more service members have survived their physical injuries, concerns about psychological injuries have intensified: based on data gathered in Iraq and Afghanistan from service members during deployment, about 27 percent of those who had been deployed three or four times had received diagnoses of depression, anxiety, or acute stress, compared with 12 percent of those deployed once (Mental Health Advisory Team V 2008). Suicide rates, which were lower in the military than among civilians of comparable age and gender in 2003, are now as much as double those among civilians, with relationship issues often implicated. Diagnoses of alcoholism and alcohol abuse also have almost doubled since 2003 (IOM 2010).

Not surprisingly, deployments have effects beyond service members. Depending on the nature of the deployment, ambiguity can be particularly stressful for family members. For example, a qualitative longitudinal study found that service members' spouses, parents, siblings, and others were more likely to worry about their safety when they knew little about members' locations or duties (Faber et al. 2008). Spouses report finding it stressful to perform all of the adult duties in the family by themselves. For example, in one study of 346 spouses, the geographical separation caused by deployment was negatively related to psychological well-being, physical well-being, and marital satisfaction (Burrell et al. 2006). Spouses of service members with symptoms of PTSD are themselves more likely to experience elevated symptoms of depression and PTSD (Renshaw, Rodrigues, and Jones 2008).

Although the reunion period is very welcome for most families, it also can be challenging, as families once again reorganize to accommodate a change in structure. Domestic divisions of labor, standards and rules for children, and patterns of authority all must be renegotiated (Faber et al. 2008; Hosek, Kavanaugh, and Miller 2006). Despite these challenges, rates of divorce and unemployment are so far not substantially higher among Operation Iraqi Freedom and Operation Enduring Freedom (OIF/OEF) veterans than among their civilian counterparts (Karney and Crown 2007; U.S. Bureau of Labor Statistics 2010). The conclusion about marital stability is preliminary, however, because the data focus only on military couples who married after 2001, following them through 2005. The reintegration stage can be especially difficult for veterans returning with combat-related disabilities (Ahrens 2009). In a random sample in 2007 of 1,730 OEF and OIF active component, Reserve component, and retired veterans, between 15 and 37 percent reported having a family member or friend who had relocated or left a job to provide care for a veteran (IOM 2010).

Deployment also affects children. Multiple studies have shown that compromised mental health among caregivers in relation to deployment is associated with lower levels of child well-being (e.g., Chandra et al. 2010). According to both parents' and teachers' ratings about children attending a military child development center, preschool children's behavioral responses (such as depression and aggression) to their parent's deployment appear to vary according to age. Children between the ages of three and five appear to be especially vulnerable to behavioral problems, while children age seven and older, especially girls and children whose parents have longer deployment periods, may experience more difficulty at home, school, and with peers (Chandra et al. 2010). Regrettably, rates of child maltreatment appear to rise in association with deployment and reunion, at least according to rates observed in Texas in concert with rates of departures and returns of service members from that state (Rentz et al. 2006).

Understanding Military Families through a Work-Family Lens

When considering flexible work arrangements, the U.S. military does not usually spring to mind. The military is a male-predominated and -dominated organization (DUSD 2010) with an overt and rigid hierarchical structure of ranks and privileges that emphasizes "command and control." Its members must legally commit to several years of service, and by law can be prevented from leaving even when their terms of service are complete. They can be recalled several, sometimes many, years beyond their original term of service (U.S. Army Human Resources Command n.d.). Service members face rigorous standards for personal behavior to maintain their occupation and their security clearances, including submitting to random drug tests; meeting requirements for weight and skill level; and avoiding questionable behavior related to finances, sexual behavior, personal conduct, and use of alcohol and drugs (Cohen 2000). Failure to satisfy these expectations can lead to military disciplinary action.

In addition to these internal restrictions, the activities of the military are constrained by many external stakeholders. For example, Congress not only oversees but is actively involved in structuring the DoD budget, regulating matters such as which bases are closed, whether aircraft are ordered, how many high-ranking officers there will be, and how service members will be compensated. Every state passes laws that affect service members and their families, such as rules regarding residency and taxation. And as commander-in-chief, the president can change the assignments of thousands of service members with the stroke of a pen.

For all these reasons, the U.S. military can be seen as rigid rather than flexible. But there are also counterbalancing factors. First, for almost 40 years the military has been composed entirely of volunteers, requiring the DoD to constantly adapt its policies, programs, and practices to compete successfully with private employers for workers who meet its standards, despite the difficult and dangerous work it requires. The percentage of the population age 17 to 24 qualified to join the military has fallen to 25 percent, increasing the competition (Gilroy 2009). And as diversity in the population grows, the diversity of service members also grows, putting pressure on the military to be more accommodating.

Second, there are strong incentives to retain members because training and therefore replacement costs are very high given the military's secret and specialized technologies. Retention is also very important because virtually all military members are hired at entry-level positions and thus all promotions are obtained from within. This means that the person who will be the chairman of the Joint Chiefs 20 years from now is already serving and must be prepared for that leadership opportunity when it arrives.

Third, the military must constantly find ways to inspire its members to contribute discretionary effort. Every medal that is given for valor documents the effort of a service member to complete his or her mission despite odds many would consider insurmountable. In the heat of battle, the confusion of natural disasters, or the ambiguity of urban warfare, service members must choose over and over again to engage in danger—sometimes with tragic results.

Finally, the military is a 24/7 global organization that must always be ready to mobilize with little or no advance notice, usually into situations that are highly unpredictable and require flexible and rapid responses. For example, within three weeks of the 9/11 terrorist attacks, OEF was launched in Afghanistan, and within 100 days, the military destroyed eleven terrorist training camps and thirty-nine Taliban command and control sites (Bush 2001).

Thus, despite the barriers that make it difficult for the military to offer flexibility to its members, there are powerful incentives to recruit and retain the best possible workers, to engage them in contributing high levels of discretionary effort, and to embrace their diversity. Because the family and the military are "greedy institutions," however, both requiring substantial amounts of time, commitment, and loyalty, this is a daunting challenge (Segal 1986).

In this section, we examine tensions related to military life that might benefit from greater flexibility in work arrangements. There is of course a large and well-developed literature regarding the connections between work and nonwork life among workers in the civilian sector. These constructs and mechanisms have well-established implications for important outcomes such as psychological well-being, physical symptoms, quality of sleep, substance use, and the quality of relationships with spouses and children (Adams, Jex, and Cunningham 2006). Although there is no evidence that these fundamental processes operate differently in military populations, and military jobs are not the only jobs that expose workers to danger, family separation, or heavy work demands, military jobs are unusual in the degree to which they require all of these for prolonged periods, and they have substantial implications for the welfare of the country. Therefore, it is important to consider the specific work-family circumstances of military families and what strategies might best support their abilities to continue their military service without having to forgo family life and reduce feelings of overload and strain even when job demands are extreme. We focus primarily on four types of tensions implicated in the work-family interface: time-based or structural, strain- or energy-based, psychological, and behavior-based (van Steenbergen et al. 2008). We recognize that the following summary cannot possibly do justice to the enormous range of military work assignments and environments.

Tensions related to the structure of work and family

These tensions pertain to how much, when, and where work occurs. Perhaps the most notable feature of military service is that members can be charged with a crime if they try to leave the military before their service obligation has expired. Theirs is a 24/7 obligation—service members must always be ready to be called to duty with no advance notice and stay until the job is done, regardless of location. This occurs, of course, with deployments, but it also can occur whenever a supervisor decides that any job is not yet complete—with no possibility of overtime pay. Common features of military life include repeated relocations, some overseas, and frequent separations because of training, temporary duty assignments, or deployment (Drummet, Coleman, and Cable 2003). Deployments related to war are only one of many types of deployments that occur every day for disaster relief, humanitarian aid, border patrol, and training (DoD 2009a). Sometimes these separations occur with little advance notice, little information available to family members, and sparse communication while away.

Military service also affects where active-duty families live, in terms of both where around the world they are assigned as a "home base" and where they live in that local area. Most military families live and most military children attend school in civilian communities (DoD Education Activity 2009). The mobility of military families and the remote or overseas locations of many installations can make it difficult for spouses to complete educational degrees, transfer licenses and certifications, maintain employment, or pursue careers. As a result, military spouses are less likely than their civilian counterparts to work full time, and, on average, they work fewer hours and fewer days in the year (Hosek et al. 2002; Little and Hisnanick 2007). In 2000, military wives earned 50 percent less than civilian wives, while military husbands earned 30 percent less than civilian husbands (Little and Hisnanick 2007).

Mobility also can impede children's education by interrupting involvement in sports teams or requiring extra courses to satisfy academic requirements unique to each new state. The Military Child Education Coalition has tackled this problem, and so far thirty-five states have signed an interstate compact to ease the transitions of military children (USA4 Military Families 2010).

Tensions related to capacity and energy

Since the current conflicts began in 2001, deployments have reached levels not seen since World War II. War increases workloads throughout the military (not only among deployed service members) because it takes enormous effort and resources to support service members during deployment with food, vehicles and fuel, weapons, medical services, housing, and the necessities of daily life (IOM 2010). During deployment, service members may be exposed to harsh physical conditions (e.g., heat, cold, rain, mud, and the resulting sleep disruptions); toxins in the form of biological or chemical weapons, burn pits, or other environmental challenges; a variety of diseases transmitted through physical contact, air, water, or insects; or injury from weapons (McCarroll et al. 2005).

Family members also experience increased workloads associated with deployment. The continuous or intermittent absence of the service member due to overseas deployment or extended work hours at home can require other family members to take on new responsibilities for caregiving, household maintenance, emotional support, or other matters (Castaneda and Harrell 2008). Family members may feel that they are under extra military scrutiny to ensure that they do nothing to disrupt the service member's readiness and performance.

Psychological and emotional tensions

The tight interconnections between personal and professional life in the military, as well as the heavy workloads and serious consequences of errors, can easily produce the combination of high-demand and low-control work environments that Kelly et al. (2008) indicated in the production of work-family conflict. When lengthy or risky deployments occur, additional psychological tensions may come into play, including worry and anxiety about separated family members, feelings of ambiguity about commitment to the relationships in the family, anger at the military or others, and feelings of hopelessness or boredom. These stressors are thought to contribute to problems with substance abuse or other addictive behavior, risk-taking, and promiscuity (McCarroll et al. 2005).

Tensions related to behavior, moral conflicts, and injuries

Tensions in this category include not only incompatible behavior but also moral conflicts and injuries that affect personal life. During many types of deployments, service members are at risk of being exposed to traumatic experiences including being the targets or perpetrators of violence, seeing or handling dead bodies, explosions, and other disturbing experiences. In addition, service members and their families may feel ambivalent about their assignment or find their own views out of step with those of friends and neighbors, political leaders, or the commander-in-chief (McCarroll et al. 2005). Military life also may impose codes of conduct for family members, especially when living in military housing, using military support services, or when the service member occupies a leadership position (Segal 1986).

Although our focus in this section has been on tensions between military and personal life, military families also report significant positive effects from military service (Schok et al. 2008). These include increased earnings from hazardous duty pay, personal growth from surmounting difficult challenges, increased appreciation of personal relationships, and a sense of purpose from performing an important mission for the country (Newby et al. 2005). In the next section, we discuss organizational responses aimed at supporting military families.

Military Policies, Programs, and Practices Related to Work-Family Relationships

The relationship between the U.S. military and the families of service members has been officially recognized for centuries, even though it was 1942 before service members were permitted to enlist or reenlist during peacetime if they had wives or children (Albano 1994). Albano (1994) argues that six trends characterize the historical evolution of military policies and programs related to families:

1. from neglect to a partnership philosophy;
2. from informal to formal support systems;
3. from categorical to universal support;
4. from local, private funding to federal funding and guidance;
5. from in-kind benefits to monetary allowances to a mixed benefits system; and
6. from an ad hoc, reactive, piecemeal approach to a proactive, planned approach to program development and a comprehensive system of services (pp. 294–98).

The tradition of support for disabled soldiers extends back to Plymouth Colony, and in 1865, Abraham Lincoln included a line in his second inaugural address that is now the mission of the Veterans Administration: "To care for him who shall have borne the battle and for his widow and his orphan" (U.S. Department of Veterans Affairs n.d.-a). In 1917, Congress passed legislation creating the first system of "family allotments" that included financial benefits and allowances, and by 1942 additional policies addressed family housing, education of children, and family insurance in the case of death or dismemberment of the service member (Albano 1994).

Since the advent of the all-volunteer force in 1973 and the subsequent growth of the proportion of service members with spouses or children, the array of services and programs that address the work-family dynamic has expanded to rival or exceed that of many large employers in the civilian sector. Today, military leaders routinely assert that the ability of service members to do their jobs depends heavily upon their families, as in a recent speech by Chairman of the Joint Chiefs Admiral Michael Mullen (2009):

> Our readiness to be able to carry out our mission as United States military is directly impacted, fully integrated, by how our families are taken care of, paid attention to, and that is a fundamental readiness issue. . . . And there's a real basic principle here for all of us in the military—been that way a long time. If it's not going well at home, it's not going well wherever I am. I cannot focus; I can't stay focused on what's going on.

Today, the U.S. military offers an array of policies, practices, and programs that include not only traditional benefits, such as pensions and health care, but also modern benefits, such as subsidized childcare. According to the Congressional Budget Office, when basic pay, cash allowances, and tax breaks are included, military compensation has exceeded the compensation of civilians in comparable jobs since about 2001 (Murray 2010). Examples of military benefits include:

- **Basic benefits:** health care for service member and family members, allowances for housing and cost of living and (when applicable) hazardous duty and subsistence, defined benefit retirement plan, and coverage for job-related relocations.
- **Care for children:** subsidized care for children and a large system of child development centers and family childcare homes, youth programs such as 4-H on military installations, DoD schools in remote areas and overseas, and support for children with special needs including consideration in parents' work assignments.
- **Family functioning:** family support services including marital and family therapy, parenting classes and new parent support, programs for prevention and treatment of domestic violence and substance use, programs for spousal employment and education, and transition assistance and tuition support.
- **Deployment cycle support:** training before, during, and after deployment; family support groups; and military liaisons assigned to address family concerns (IOM 2010).

Moving from general benefits to those focused specifically on workplace flexibility, we next examine military work according to the flexibility taxonomy developed by Workplace Flexibility 2010 (Georgetown University Law Center 2009). We were unable to locate published or unpublished data documenting service members' perceptions of access to each type of flexibility, so we rely here on review of policies and assessments by informants with experience as administrators of military personnel policies.

The first category of flexibility defined by Workplace Flexibility 2010 pertains to how much, when, and where work is done. Alternative work schedule programs have been implemented in the DoD, but most apply only to civilian employees. There are exceptions, however. For example, the Coast Guard alternative work schedules program permits military members to work 80 hours in eight- or nine-day compressed workweek schedules or flexible schedules with core hours (U.S. Coast Guard Commandant 2009). All of these programs are based on full-time work. In terms of military members' ability to choose to work some or all of the time at a different location, such as at home, the DoD almost a decade ago authorized telework programs for both civilian employees and military members to carry out assigned official duties including training (see, e.g., DoD Instruction 1035.1 [DoD 2010]). In response, the Air Force established guidelines for reserve personnel to complete training remotely (see Air Force Instruction 36-2254 [Department of the Air Force 2010]). Service members' access to control over how much, when, and where work is done appears to be similar to that of civilians: while there are examples of significant flexibility, access overall is limited, tends to favor officers, and command approval is required for every absence. Regardless of policies, there are also many examples of informal flexibility practices in many jobs.

The second category of flexibility defined by Workplace Flexibility 2010 is time off from work in either short (e.g., unexpected illness), episodic (e.g., for repeated medical treatments or regular volunteer work), or longer increments (e.g., for the birth of a child). Military members compare favorably to civilians in this category, accruing 2.5 days of paid leave per month to use for family emergencies, national holidays, religious observances, adjusting to moves, and resting after difficult work tasks. They also have access to several additional types of leave that are not "charged" against their regular paid leave, including "special leave" that accrues separately as a function of deployment to hazardous areas; leaves for morale or rest and recuperation; for convalescence, maternity, paternity, or adoption; and emergency unpaid leave. Short periods of "special liberty" may be given under special circumstances such as a reward for exceptional performance. Finally, permission may be given for administrative absences to participate in professional development, retirement preparation programs, or other special events (see DoD Instruction 1327.06 [DoD 2009b]).

The third category of flexibility defined by Workplace Flexibility 2010 is career flexibility, including employee control over when to leave his or her career permanently or intermittently and when to enter or reenter. In the military, service members may leave their military careers only when terms of enlistment or service obligations are fulfilled. Substantial incentives are offered to some service members to reenlist, and if a member stays in long enough to formally retire, there is a public ceremony, often a service medal, and a substantial retirement benefit. Some service members return to active duty, but these are isolated examples.

The policies, programs, and practices that affect military service members and their families do not reside only in the DoD. Over half of military spouses and an unknown percentage of parents of service members are employed (DUSD 2010). In addition, military members who serve in the Reserve component must leave and return to employment in the civilian sector as they complete each cycle of deployment. Service members receive some assistance from the Uniformed Services Employment and Reemployment Rights Act (USERRA), which protects their rights to employment, reemployment, retention, promotion, and other benefits (Veterans' Employment and Training Service n.d.). Employer Support of the Guard and Reserve, a DoD organization, formally recognizes especially supportive civilian employers for practices such as maintaining contact with employees while they are performing military service, publicly acknowledging their contributions, publishing policies for leave and military mobilization, providing pay differential or "top-up pay" during military training and mobilization, continuing insurance and financial benefits during mobilizations, and assigning a company sponsor to Guard and Reserve family members during deployments (Employer Support of the Guard and Reserve n.d.).

Responses to Military Families' Work-Family Challenges since 9/11

As the demands of the wars in Afghanistan and later Iraq evolved, the work-family challenges of service members and their families also changed, and in response new programs and policies began to emerge in the DoD and the military branches. As it became clear that the wars would impact hundreds of thousands of families, the DoD devoted more resources to assisting families who were not within easy reach of installation-based services and facilities. In 2002, a technology-based employee assistance program called Military OneSource was created, giving service members and their families continuous global access by Internet or telephone to counselors who could locate resources, make referrals, or provide other assistance in over 100 languages (Marine Corps News Room 2005). OneSource was eventually expanded to include multiple sessions of free nonmedical counseling for service members and their families.

The extensive deployments of Reserve component forces made it clear that the support infrastructure, designed originally for active component families, contained significant gaps. The Joint Family Support Assistance Program was created in 2007 to provide comprehensive state-based deployment cycle support to Reserve component families. Military family life consultants—counselors who could provide support, reassurance, and very short-term counseling to families (Managed Health Network n.d.)—were assigned to each state, as were resources for information and referral, financial assistance, child care assistance, outreach by military food and retail stores, and recreational programs (Military Community and Family Policy 2010). In 2008, the DoD Yellow Ribbon Reintegration Program was developed to provide programming to Reserve component members and their families throughout the deployment cycle. Now, instead of being prohibited from being called to duty for 90 days following their return from deployment, Reserve component members are required to gather at their usual 30-day intervals, not to train for deployment, but instead to work on returning and reintegrating to their families and civilian life. Some programming is also available to family members, who receive some financial support for travel costs (Yellow Ribbon Program n.d.).

Educational benefits have also figured prominently in "family-friendly" benefits in the post-9/11 era. Perhaps the best known of these is the 2009 "Post-9/11 GI Bill," the most comprehensive veterans' education bill passed to date. Under this program, members of both the active and Reserve components who have served since September 10, 2001, can receive up to 36 months of tuition, fees, and funds for living expenses and supplies, regardless of whether they are still serving in the military. A popular innovation is the plan for qualified career service members to be able to transfer some unused benefits to family members (U.S. Department of Veterans Affairs n.d.-b). For members still completing their service, tuition assistance is also available from the DoD; approximately 45,000 degrees were completed in 2009. Officers are required to extend their years of service in exchange for receiving tuition assistance (Defense Activity for Non-traditional Education Support n.d.). In 2009, a tuition assistance program was also created for military spouses. So popular that it ran out of money, MyCAA (Military Spouse Career Advancement Accounts) was abruptly suspended in early 2010, generating considerable negative attention. Recently reinstated, the program now offers more constrained benefits than before, limiting participation to spouses of service members at junior enlisted or officer pay grades and in the active component or on activated status if in the Reserve component. It has limited the total benefit to $4,000 and limited degrees to associate's, licenses, and certificates, excluding bachelor's or advanced degrees (Schogol 2010).

Several cabinet departments have also implemented new policies to support military families during the war. Most visibly related to workplace flexibility are significant expansions in the Family and Medical Leave Act in 2008, which created new provisions for job-protected leave for the family of military members to allow them to care for injured service members, and also "qualifying exigencies" that allow time away from work to participate in activities related to deployment, such as farewell ceremonies and reintegration training. The new rules also allow coverage for family members not routinely included in military definitions of "family," such as parents of adult children (U.S. Department of Labor n.d.). State governments also have passed statutes targeting support for military families. For example, many states permit unemployment compensation to be paid to spouses of military personnel under certain circumstances, such as when a change in the military member's duty location causes a spouse to leave his/her job (National Conference of State Legislatures 2010; Sloan Work and Family Research Network 2008).

Perhaps the most visible military effort to systematically respond to workforce needs from a business perspective is the Navy's "Task Force Life/Work," launched in 2007 in response to a 10-year slide in representation of women among Navy officers and shifting attitudes and growing diversity of newer Navy personnel (Navy Personnel Command n.d.).

During an information-gathering effort to learn about the concerns of service members, Navy leaders learned that junior officers were leaving not because they disliked their military jobs but because of conflict between personal and professional goals. The loss of these junior officers was especially costly because of the lack of midcareer hiring in the military. Service members also reported lack of control and predictability as factors in increasing their thoughts of leaving. Heavy workloads, unpredictable moves and deployments, and lack of control over work schedules were described as interfering with service members' ability to maximize productivity by scheduling work time to avoid heavy commutes, pursue educational goals, or arrange childcare coverage. Data also showed that Navy women were about twice as likely as civilian women and Navy men to be childless (Barrett 2010).

Based on this information, the Navy selected three priorities for work-family policy efforts: Parenting Is a Priority, Flexibility Is the Key, and Demand for Balance (Covell 2010). These priorities have now been translated into numerous policy changes that are already implemented or under consideration:

- **Supporting parenting:** (1) one-year operational deferments for new mothers, extended from four months; (2) phased return from maternity; (3) paternity leave of 10 days; (4) coverage for in vitro fertilization treatment; and (5) 21 days' leave for adoptive parents (Covell 2010).
- **Supporting flexibility:** (1) a career intermission pilot program that allows sailors to move to the Reserve component for three years while maintaining benefits and promotion eligibility, in exchange for extending their service obligation (Covell 2010); (2) telework programs that permit eligible military and civilian personnel to work from remote locations, some full time and at large distances from their "parent command"; and (3) a "menu of options" that allows service members to choose monetary bonuses, geographic stability, jobs of choice, and other options that cater to individual and family needs while still satisfying all mission requirements (Barrett 2010; Covell 2010).
- **Supporting balance:** (1) part-time work for part-time pay; (2) two-year deferment for new reservists for individual augmentee assignments; and (3) compressed work week schedules (Covell 2010).

Since the task force was created to address these issues, the representation of women in both officer and enlisted ranks has risen to historic highs, and the representation of enlisted women in technical areas has risen from 42 to 51 percent (Covell 2010). Women are especially likely to report that the career intermission and operational deferment policies motivate them to stay in the Navy (Covell 2010). These and other efforts by the Navy to increase workplace flexibility have been recognized with numerous national awards in the past two years (Barrett 2010; Covell 2010).

Work-Family Challenges for Military Families in the Future

Given the extensive array of policies and programs available in the military, and the creative innovations being conceived to respond to the needs of increasingly diverse service members, why did Specialist Hutchinson end up in such a difficult situation? Of course she could have chosen not to enter the military, but civilian jobs with health care coverage, pensions, and subsidized childcare are not readily available to young workers with high school educations and limited work experience. Specialist Hutchinson joined the military well after 2001, when it was obvious that deployment would be very likely. Although she was required to make a family care plan and did so, it ultimately proved unworkable. In the end, the military expected her to have made adequate arrangements for her child and to deploy with her unit. How can young women like Specialist Hutchinson pursue their goals of having and raising children—who, like 40 percent of all children in the United States, are born to single mothers—and yet also fulfill the demanding responsibilities they accept when they swear to "obey the orders of the President of the United States and the orders of the officers appointed over [them]" (U.S. Army n.d.)?

As the relationship between the military and the families of service members has evolved, there has been greater examination of the issue of how best to support families. One topic of debate is the potential tension between the role of individual families and the military organization. Military policy-makers and service providers worry that providing too many entitlements encourages military families to believe that they are not able or expected to take action on their own behalf, ultimately making them feel *dis*empowered and less able to cope—completely opposite the original intent. In 2002, the DoD altered its stance toward family programs in its New Social Compact: "The Services have also recognized that quality of life is determined both by what an organization does and by what an individual does for oneself in concert with that organization" (Deputy Assistant Secretary of Defense 2002, 11–12). In addition, the DoD emphasized that supportive programs and services are intended to support work outcomes: "These initiatives demonstrate the Services' recognition of the strategic value in addressing the nexus of work life and personal/family life, as it affects key organizational goals related to recruitment, retention, morale, and mission readiness" (DUSD 2004, 61). The debate between accommodations that support the mission by making it possible for families to do their jobs and those that interfere with the mission by encouraging families to rely too heavily on external support will continue and will be complicated by the need to continually offer new incentives to attract new workers in a competitive marketplace.

The tension between individual workers and organizations also plays out in relation to flexible work arrangements, where one of the thorniest challenges is who controls workers' time. The military needs to be nimble, able to quickly deploy service members whenever and wherever they are needed. But service members appear to be becoming less tolerant of having so little control over their time as well as becoming more diverse in terms of ethnicity, family structure, overt sexual orientation, and gender (Covell 2010). To continue to attract high-quality recruits, the military will need to keep looking for ways to accommodate their interests. Creative innovations such as those in the Navy boost members' control over their time at key periods, such as after the birth of a child, and are not entitlements but selective investments generating a return in the form of extensions of service obligations. Thus, for a relatively small investment, the organization secures a firm retention commitment from a highly trained worker. But because they are selective, these programs would be unlikely to help junior enlisted members like Specialist Hutchinson.

Despite the extensive array of programs and services and increasing flexibility, significant work-family challenges persist in the military. One such challenge receiving widespread attention at present is stigma, particularly in relation to mental health problems. Service members and their families often express reluctance to seek a variety of types of help for fear that the service member's performance record will be damaged in some way (DoD Task Force on Mental Health 2007). Another challenge is that the ever-changing array of programs and services offered by the DoD, individual service branches, states, and local communities can be overwhelming in its scope and complexity, requiring an extraordinarily efficient exchange of information to ensure that families find what they need. The constant entry, exit, and mobility of service members makes it even more difficult to ensure that every family has the information they need at the moment they need it—especially when some families cannot or will not acknowledge that help is needed.

Even when services are used, they may not be effective. Allen and Schockley (2009) raise questions about workplace flexibility, for example, citing studies showing that its effects are mixed at best. Evaluating the effectiveness of many programs and services in the military is very challenging, because of the difficulty in controlling external factors such as changes in command, deployments, and the mobility of service members.

As in civilian workplaces, frontline supervisors are often the lynchpins in service members' quality of life and access to flexibility (Castro, Thomas, and Adler 2006). Because access to most types of leave and flexibility programs requires supervisor approval, service members may be denied access either because they ask and are refused or because they are hesitant to ask. In addition, the pressure of the wars has stretched commanders, adding many urgent tasks and domains of responsibility. The "lost art of leadership in garrison" was blamed in a recent report examining the high rates of suicide in the Army, which concluded that the heavy workload, dynamic deployment schedule, and rapid turnover caused by the wars in Iraq and Afghanistan have weakened the awareness, vigilance, and effectiveness of frontline commanders. As a result, service members' high-risk behavior has risen and communication and clarity of roles and responsibilities have fallen, creating a climate where worrisome signs are not acted upon (U.S. Army 2010).

The U.S. military exists to serve our country, and its mission evolves constantly with geopolitical, technological, and financial events. Trends in China, Iraq,

Mexico, and wherever al Qaeda functions—as well as other parts of the world—require vigilance. Since the end of the cold war, the nature of military conflict has shifted toward nonconventional or asymmetrical conflicts characterized by terrorism, urban warfare, and insurgency. Just as the members of the "greatest generation" of World War II veterans and their counterparts from the conflict in Vietnam remain a visible part of our society, the wartime experiences of the veterans of Operations Iraqi Freedom and Enduring Freedom are likely to affect our society for decades to come. The Reserve component of the Armed Forces has now become an operational force, expecting to deploy at least every five years, imbuing the term "citizen soldier" with new meaning. In some cases, service members and their families will be strengthened by their experiences; other families might experience no obvious consequences now but might experience psychological or physical symptoms later in life. Both their military employers and civilian workplaces have the potential to be affected and the potential to be part of strategies that reduce or exacerbate the challenges. Given the "extreme work" these service members and their families volunteered to perform on behalf of our country, it is reasonable to consider the need for "extreme work-family" support in return. But it is also important to attend to what works, what is cost-effective, and what makes sense, because above all, we rely on the military to complete its mission.

References

Adams, Gary A., Steve Jex, and Christopher Cunningham. 2006. Work-family conflict among military personnel. In *Military life: The psychology of serving in peace and combat*, eds. Carl Castro, Amy Adler, and Thomas Britt, 169–92. Westport, CT: Praeger.

Ahrens, Frank. 11 November 2009. Unemployment among young veterans much higher than the national average. *Washington Post*. Available from http://voices.washingtonpost.com/economy-watch/2009/11/today_im_going_to_take.html

Albano, Sondra. 1994. Military recognition of family concerns: Revolutionary War to 1993. *Armed Forces and Society* 20:283–302.

Allen, Tammy D., and Kristen Schockley. 2009. Flexible work arrangements: Help or hype? In *Handbook of families and work: Interdisciplinary perspectives*, eds. Russell Crane and Jeffrey Hill, 265–86. Lanham, MD: University Press of America.

Barrett, Ken. 2010. *Task force life/work*. Available from www.npc.navy.mil/NR/rdonlyres/9FD53936-1CA7-4181-AAC2-2788C436A22C/0/TFLWBRIEF.ppt.

Burrell, Lolita M., Gary Adams, Doris Durand, and Carl Castro. 2006. The impact of military lifestyle demands on well-being, army, and family outcomes. *Armed Forces and Society* 33 (1): 43–58.

Bush, George W. 2001. *The global war on terrorism: The first 100 days*. Washington, DC: The Coalition Information Centers.

Castaneda, Laura W., and Margaret Harrell. 2008. Military spouse employment: A grounded theory approach to experiences and perceptions. *Armed Forces and Society* 34:389–412.

Castaneda, Laura W., Margaret C. Harrell, Danielle M. Varda, Kimberly Curry Hall, Megan K. Beckett, and Stefanie Stern. 2008. *Deployment experiences of Guard and Reserve families: Implications for support and retention*. Santa Monica, CA: Rand National Defense Research Institute.

Castro, Carl A., Jeffrey Thomas, and Amy Adler. 2006. Toward a liberal theory of military leadership. In *Military life: The psychology of serving in peace and combat: Operational stress*, vol. 2, eds. Amy Adler, Carl Castro, and Thomas Britt, 192–212. Westport, CT: Praeger.

Chandra, Anita, Sandraluz Lara-Cinisomo, Lisa H. Jaycox, Terri Tanielian, Rachel M. Burns, Teague Ruder, and Bing Han. 2010. Children on the homefront: The experience of children from military families. *Pediatrics* 125 (1): 16–25.

Cohen, Sheldon I. 2000. *Security clearances and the protection of national security information: Law and procedures*. Monterey, CA: Defense Personnel Security Research Center. Available from www.dtic .mil/cgi-bin/GetTRDoc?AD=ADA388100&Location=U2&doc=GetTRDoc.pdf.

Covell, Cynthia. 31 August 2010. *Today's women and tomorrow's Navy organization*. Presentation to 4-Star Spouses, Washington, DC.

Dao, James. 12 February 2010. Single mother is spared court-martial. *New York Times*. Available from www.nytimes.com (accessed 9 September 2010).

Defense Activity for Non-traditional Education Support. n.d. *Desktop reference for education benefits*. Available from www.dantes.doded.mil/Dantes_web/EdBenefits/educationbenefits.asp (accessed September 2010).

Department of the Air Force. 26 May 2010. *Instruction 36-2254: Reserve personnel participation*. San Antonio, TX: Department of the Air Force.

Department of Defense (DoD). 2009a. *Department of Defense dictionary of military and associated terms*. Available from www.dtic.mil/doctrine/dod_dictionary/ (accessed 6 February 2009).

Department of Defense (DoD). 16 June 2009b. *Instruction 1327.06: Leave and liberty policy and procedures*. Alexandria, VA: DoD.

Department of Defense (DoD) Education Activity. 2009. *About DoDEA*. Available from www.dodea.edu/ home/about.cfm?cld=facts (accessed 21 February 2009).

Department of Defense (DoD). 21 October 2010. *Instruction 1035.1: Telework policy*. Alexandria, VA: DoD.

Department of Defense (DoD) Task Force on Mental Health. 2007. *An achievable vision: Report of the Department of Defense Task Force on Mental Health*. Falls Church, VA: Defense Health Board.

Deputy Assistant Secretary of Defense. 2002. *A new social compact: A reciprocal partnership between the Department of Defense, service members and their families*. Alexandria, VA: DoD. Available from http://cs.mhf.dod.mil/content/dav/mhf/QOL-Library/PDF/MHF/QOL%20Resources/ Reports/A%20New%20Social%20Compact.pdf (accessed 23 September 2010).

Deputy Under Secretary of Defense, Military Community and Family Policy (DUSD). 2004. *Report of the 1st quadrennial quality of life review: "Families also serve."* Washington, DC: DoD. Available from www.militaryhomefront.dod.mil/12038/MHF/pdf/QQLR.pdf (accessed 16 June 2011).

Deputy Under Secretary of Defense, Military Community and Family Policy (DUSD). 2010. *Profile of the military community: DoD 2008 demographics*. Alexandria, VA: ICF International.

Drummet, Amy R., Marilyn Coleman, and Susan Cable. 2003. Military families under stress: Implications for family life education. *Family Relations* 52:279–87.

Employer Support of the Guard and Reserve. n.d. *Above and beyond award*. Available from http://esgr .org/site/Programs/AboveandBeyondAward.aspx.

Faber, Anthony J., Elaine Willerton, Shelley R. Clymer, Shelley M. MacDermid, and Howard M. Weiss. 2008. Ambiguous absence, ambiguous presence: A qualitative study of military reserve families in wartime. *Journal of Family Psychology* 22:222–30.

Georgetown University Law Center. 2009. *Public policy platform on flexible work arrangements*. Workplace Flexibility 2010. Washington, DC: Georgetown University Law Center.

Gilroy, Curtis. 3 March 2009. *Recruiting, retention and end strength overview*. Statement prepared for Personnel and Readiness before the House Armed Services Subcommittee. Available from www.gpo .gov/fdsys/pkg/CHRG-111hhrg50088/pdf/CHRG-111hhrg50088.pdf.

Hosek, James, Beth Asch, C. Christine Fair, Craig Martin, and Michael Mattock. 2002. *Married to the military: The employment and earnings of military wives compared with those of civilian wives*. Santa Monica, CA: RAND National Defense Research Institute.

Hosek, James, Jennifer Kavanaugh, and Laura Miller. 2006. *How deployments affect service members*. Santa Monica, CA: RAND National Defense Research Institute.

Institute of Medicine (IOM). 2008. *Gulf War and health*, vol. 6. Washington, DC: National Academies Press.

Institute of Medicine (IOM). 2010. *Returning home from Iraq and Afghanistan: Preliminary assessment of the readjustment needs of veterans, service members, and their families*. Washington DC: National Academies Press.

Jamail, Dahr. 15 February 2010. Army to discharge single mom rather than court-martial her. *San Francisco Bay View*.

Karney, Benjamin R., and John Crown. 2007. *Families under stress: An assessment of data, theory and research on marriage and divorce in the military*. Santa Monica, CA: RAND National Defense Research Institute.

Kelly, Erin L., Ellen Ernst Kossek, Leslie B. Hammer, Mary Durham, Jeremy Bray, Kelly Chermack, Lauren A. Murphy, and Dan Kaskubar. 2008. Getting there from here: Research on the effects of work-family initiatives on work-family conflict and business outcomes. *Academy of Management Annals* 2:305–49.

Little, Roger D., and John Hisnanick. 2007. The earnings of tied-migrant military husbands. *Armed Forces and Society* 33:547–70.

MacDermid Wadsworth, Shelley M. 2010. Family risk and resilience in the context of war and terrorism. *Journal of Marriage and Family* 72:537–56.

MacLean, Alair, and Glen Elder. 2007. Military service in the life course. *Annual Review of Sociology* 33:175–96.

Managed Health Network. n.d. *Military and family life consultant program summary*. Available from www.mhngs.com/app/resourcesfor/MFLC_Brochure.pdf.

Marine Corps News Room. 22 September 2005. New military OneSource feature available online. Available from www.marine-corps-news.com/2005/09/new_military_onesource_feature.htm.

McCarroll, James E., Kenneth Hoffman, Thomas Grieger, and Harry Holloway. 2005. Psychological aspects of deployment and reunion. In *Military preventive medicine: Mobilization and deployment*, vol. 2, ed. Patrick Kelley, 1395–1424. Falls Church, VA: Office of the Surgeon General of the Army.

Mental Health Advisory Team V. 2008. *Operation Iraqi Freedom 06-08*. Washington, DC: Office of the Surgeon, Multinational Force-Iraq and Office of the Surgeon General, U.S. Army Medical Command.

Military Community and Family Policy. 2010. *Joint family support assistance program*. Available from http://cs.mhf.dod.mil/content/dav/mhf/QOL-Library/Project%20Documents/MilitaryHOMEFRONT/Service%20Providers/JFSAP/Joint_Family_Support_Assistance_Program__Fact_Sheet.pdf.

Mullen, Michael. 9 December 2009. *Total force health for the 21st century*. Speech at the Uniformed Services University of Health Sciences. Bethesda, MD. Available from www.jcs.mil/speech.aspx?ID=1288.

Murray, Carla T. 2010. *Evaluating military compensation*. Testimony before the U.S. Senate Subcommittee on Personnel of the Armed Services Committee, Washington, DC. Available from www.cbo.gov/ftpdocs/114xx/doc11463/04-28-MilitaryPay.pdf.

National Conference of State Legislatures. 2010. *Unemployment compensation for military spouses*. Available from www.ncsl.org/?TabId=13331.

Navy Personnel Command. n.d. *Task force life/work*. Available from www.npc.navy.mil/CommandSupport/TaskForceLifeWork/

Newby, John H., James E. McCarroll, R. J. Ursano, Zizhong Fan, Jun Shigemura, and Yvonne Tucker-Harris. 2005. Positive and negative consequences of a military deployment. *Military Medicine* 170:815–19.

Office of the Under Secretary of Defense for Personnel and Readiness. 2007. *Population representation in the military services*. Available from http://prhome.defense.gov/MPP/ACCESSION%20POLICY/PopRep2007/download/download.html.

Renshaw, Keith D., Camila Rodrigues, and David Jones. 2008. Psychological symptoms and marital satisfaction in spouses of Operation Iraqi Freedom veterans: Relationships with spouses' perceptions of veterans' experiences and symptoms. *Journal of Family Psychology* 3:586–94.

Rentz, Danielle E., Sandra L. Martin, Deborah A. Gibbs, Monique Clinton-Sherrod, Jennifer Hardison, and Stephen W. Marshall. 2006. Family violence in the military: A review of the literature. *Trauma, Violence, and Abuse* 7:93–108.

Ruff, Robert L., Suzanne Ruff, and Xiao-Feng Wang. 2008. Headaches among Operation Iraqi Freedom/Operation Enduring Freedom veterans with mild traumatic brain injury associated with exposure to explosions. *Journal of Rehabilitation Research & Development* 45:941–52.

Schlussel, Debbie. 2009. *Ban single moms from the U.S. military*. Available from www.debbieschlussel.com/12220/ban-single-moms-from-the-military/.

Schogol, Jeff. 5 August 2010. MyCAA cutbacks leave disillusioned spouses searching for tuition money. *Stars and Stripes*. Available from www.stripes.com/news/mycaa-cutbacks-leave-disillusioned-spouses-searching-for-tuition-money-1.113518.

Schok, Michaela L., Rolf Kleber, Martin Elands, and Jos Weerts. 2008. Meaning as a mission: A review of empirical studies on appraisals of war and peacekeeping experiences. *Clinical Psychology Review* 28:357–65.

Segal, Mady W. 1986. The military and the family as greedy institutions. *Armed Forces and Society* 13:9–38.

Sloan Work and Family Research Network. 2008. State policymakers: Supporting military families with children. *Policy Briefing Series, Issue 15*. Available from http://wfnetwork.bc.edu/pdfs/policy_makers15.pdf.

U.S. Army. 2010. *Health promotion, risk reduction, suicide prevention*. Available from http://usarmy.vo .llnwd.net/e1/HPRRSP/HP-RR-SPReport2010_v00.pdf.

U.S. Army. n.d. *Oaths of enlistment and oaths of office*. Available from www.history.army.mil/faq/oaths.htm.

U.S. Army Human Resources Command. n.d. Individual ready reserve FAQ. Available from www.hrc .army.mil/site/media/factsheets/irr.htm.

U.S. Bureau of Labor Statistics. 2010. *Economic news release: Employment situation of veterans summary*. Available from www.bls.gov/news.release/vet.nr0.htm.

U.S. Coast Guard Commandant. 2009. *Alternative work schedules for Coast Guard civilian and military members*. Commandant Instruction 5330.10. Available from www.uscg.mil/directives/ci/5000-5999/ CI_5330_10.pdf.

U.S. Department of Labor. n.d. Military family leave provisions of the Family and Medical Leave Act: Frequently asked questions and answers. Available from www.dol.gov/whd/fmla/finalrule/MilitaryFAQs.pdf.

U.S. Department of Veterans Affairs. n.d.-a. About VA and VA history. Available from www4.va.gov/ about_va/.

U.S. Department of Veterans Affairs. n.d.-b. Welcome to the GI Bill website. Available from www.gibill .va.gov.

USA4 Military Families. 2010. *Department of Defense and states, partnering to support military families*. Available from www.usa4militaryfamilies.dod.mil/.

van Steenbergen, Elianne F., Naomi Ellemers, Alexander Haslam, and Femke Urlings. 2008. There is nothing either good or bad but thinking makes it so: Informational support and cognitive appraisal of the work-family interface. *Journal of Occupational and Organizational Psychology* 81:349–67.

Veterans' Employment and Training Service. n.d. *Job rights for veterans and Reserve component members*. VETS USERRA Fact Sheet 3. Washington, DC: U.S. Department of Labor. Available from www.dol .gov/vets/programs/userra/userra_fs.htm.

Yellow Ribbon Program. n.d. Yellow Ribbon Program Welcome. Available from www.dodyrrp.mil.

0. STATEMENT OF OWNERSHIP, MANAGEMENT, AND CIRCULATION
    P.S. Form 3526 Facsimile

1. TITLE: ANNALS OF THE AMERICAN ACADEMY OF POLITICAL AND SOCIAL SCIENCE, THE
2. USPS PUB. #: 026-060

3. DATE OF FILING: OCTOBER 1, 2011

4. FREQUENCY OF ISSUE: Bi-monthly
5. NO. OF ISSUES ANNUALLY: 6
6. ANNUAL SUBSCRIPTION PRICE: Institution $772.00
                                                           Individual $103.00

7. PUBLISHER ADDRESS: 2455 Teller Road, Thousand Oaks, CA 91320
    CONTACT PERSON: Emily Koberling, Sr. Circulation Manager
    TELEPHONE: (805) 499-0721

8. HEADQUARTERS ADDRESS: 2455 Teller Road, Thousand Oaks, CA 91320

9. PUBLISHER: SAGE Publications Inc., 2455 Teller Road, Thousand Oaks, CA 91320
    EDITOR:
    Dr. Phyllis Kaniss, University of Pennsylvania, Fells Institute of Goverment, 3814 Walnut St., Philadelphia, PA 19104

10. OWNER: The American Academy of Political and Social Science, 3814 Walnut St.
    Philadelphia, PA 19104-6197

11. KNOWN BONDHOLDERS, ETC.
    None

12. NONPROFIT PURPOSE, FUNCTION, STATUS:
    Has Not Changed During Preceding 12 Months

13. PUBLICATION NAME: ANNALS OF THE AMERICAN ACADEMY OF POLITICAL AND SOCIAL SCIENCE, THE

14. ISSUE DATE FOR CIRCULATION DATA BELOW: July 2011

15. EXTENT & NATURE OF CIRCULATION:

		AVG. NO. COPIES EACH ISSUE DURING PRECEDING 12 MONTHS	ACT. NO. COPIES OF SINGLE ISSUE PUB. NEAREST TO FILING DATE
A.	TOTAL NO. COPIES	1124	1047
B.	PAID CIRCULATION		
	1. PAID/REQUESTED OUTSIDE-CO, ETC	536	588
	2. PAID IN-COUNTY SUBSCRIPTIONS	0	0
	3. SALES THROUGH DEALERS, ETC.	7	5
	4. OTHER CLASSES MAILED USPS	0	0
C.	TOTAL PAID CIRCULATION	543	593
D.	FREE DISTRIBUTION BY MAIL		
	1. OUTSIDE-COUNTY AS ON 3541	72	93
	2. IN-COUNTY AS STATED ON 3541	0	0
	3. OTHER CLASSES MAILED USPS	0	0
E.	FREE DISTRIBUTION OTHER	0	0
F.	TOTAL FREE DISTRIBUTION	72	93
G.	TOTAL DISTRIBUTION	615	686
H.	COPIES NOT DISTRIBUTED		
	1. OFFICE USE, ETC.	509	361
	2. RETURN FROM NEWS AGENTS	0	0
I.	TOTAL	1124	1047
	PERCENT PAID CIRCULATION	88%	86%

16. THIS STATEMENT OF OWNERSHIP WILL BE PRINTED IN THE NOVEMBER 2011 ISSUE OF THIS PUBLICATION.

17. I CERTIFY THAT ALL INFORMATION FURNISHED ON THIS FORM IS TRUE AND COMPLETE.
    I UNDERSTAND THAT ANYONE WHO FURNISHES FALSE OR MISLEADING INFORMATION ON
    THIS FORM OR WHO OMITS MATERIAL OR INFORMATION REQUESTED ON THE FORM MAY
    BE SUBJECT TO CRIMINAL SANCTIONS (INCLUDING FINES AND IMPRISONMENT) AND/OR
    CIVIL SANCTIONS (INCLUDING MULTIPLE DAMAGES AND CIVIL PENALTIES).

Emily Koberling

Emily Koberling   Date: 08/06/2011
Sr. Circulation Manager
SAGE Publications, Inc.